Localised or Localising Democracy

Gender and the Politics of Decentralisation in Contemporary Uganda

Josephine Ahikire

FOUNTAIN PUBLISHERS
Kampala

Fountain Publishers
P.O. Box 488
Kampala, Uganda
E-mail:fountain@starcom.co.ug
Website:www.fountainpublishers.co.ug

Distributed in Europe, North America and Australia by African
Books Collective Ltd (ABC), Unit 13, Kings Meadow, Ferry Hinksey
Road, Oxford OX2 0DP, United Kingdom.
Tel: 44(0) 1865-726686, Fax:44(0)1865-793298.
E-mail: orders@africanbookscollective.com
abc@africanbookscollective.com
Website: www.africanbookscollective.com

ISBN 978-9970-02-6913

Publication of this book was facilitated by a grant from Ford
Foundation.

Ahikire Josephine
Localised or localising democracy: Gender and politics of decentralisation in
contemporary Uganda/Josephine Ahikire. - Kampala: Fountain Publishers,
@2007 x viii; 215p.
ISBN 978-9970-02-6913
Has an appendix and index.- (1) Democracy (2) Decentralisation (3) Title

Dedication

To my beloved children
Fiona, Bridget, Apolinari and Grace
who tragically lost their lives in an accident
on 30 January 2007.

Contents

Dedication   iii
Acronyms & Abbreviations   vi
Acknowledgements   viii
Preface   ix

1. **Historical Background**   1
   Women as a Political Constituency in Uganda   3
   On to Decentralisation   16

2. **Framing the Debate: Some Useful Conceptual Considerations**
   on Gender and Decentralisation   23
   On Presence   30
   The Private/Public   39
   Presence and Deliberation: The Gendered Exercise of
   Citizenship   44

3. **The Local Government System in Uganda: Mapping out**
   Structures and their Gender Dimensions   48
   The Framework   49
   The Local Government (District/LC5)   52
   The Gendered Dual Mode: The Inclusive Patronage
   and the Exclusive Technocratic Modes   60
   Women, Patronage and the Legacy of Mobilisation
   in Local Government   71

4. **From Exclusion to Directed Inclusion: Women and the**
   Question of Quotas in Uganda   78
   Tracing the Inclusion Debate in the Constituent Assembly   79
   The Policy of One-third Women Representation:
   Peculiarities of Uganda's Quota System   86
   Translating Directed Inclusion into Electoral Mechanisms   90
   Quotas: Comparing Uganda with India and South Africa   97

5. **Of Local Democracy and Grassroots Tyranny: Gender and
    Local Council (LC) Elections**   **106**
    Gendered Mandates: Money, Morality and Marriage in
    the Local Sphere   109
    LC5 (Councillor) Campaigns in Mukono District: The Case of
    Nenyodde, Nakanyonyi Parish, Nabbale Sub-county   114
    On Marriage and Belonging   121
    The Local and the Unbending Patriarchal Power   128
    Chairperson and 'Chairman'   131
    The Sub-County (LC3) Chairperson   135
    The Village (LC1) Chairperson   139

6. **Women in Local Councils and the Politics of Presence**   **145**
    Decentralisation, Deliberation and Decision-Making   146
    Beyond Deliberation: Gender, Community Politics and the
    Question of Interest Representation   161
    Womanhood, Leadership and Political Legitimacy   170

7. **Envisioning Gender Inclusive Local Democracy
    in Uganda: A Conclusion**   **175**

Appendix 1: National Resistance Movement   185

Appendix 2: Typology of Decentralisation   186

Appendix 3: The Structure of Local Councils   187

References   **188**

Index   **219**

Acronymns & Abbreviations

ACFODE	Action for Development
ANC	African National Congress
CA	Constituent Assembly
CAO	Chief Administrative Officer
CBO	Community-based Organisations
DSC	District Service Commission
DWGS	Department of Women and Gender Studies
EC	Electoral Commission
FIDA-U	Uganda Women Lawyers' Association
FOWODE	Forum for Women in Democracy
GAD	Gender and Development
GIC	Gender Information Centre
IGG	Inspector General of Government
LC	Local Council
LEGCO	Legislative Council
LGA	Local Governments Act
NADIPU	National Union of People with Disabilities
NAOWU	National Association of Women's Organisations in Uganda
NCW	National Council of Women
NEMGROUP	NGO Election Monitoring Group
NGO	Non-governmental Organisation
NRA	National Resistance Army
NRC	National Resistance Council
NRM	National Resistance Movement
PPA	Priority Programme Areas
PR	Proportional Representation
PWDs	People with Disabilities
RC	Resistance Council
RDC	Resident District Commissioner
SFG	School Facilitation Grant

UDN	Uganda Debt Network
UPC	Uganda People's Congress
UWONET	Uganda Women's Network
WCs	Women Councils
WID	Women in Development
WORK	Women's Movement for the Return of Kaguta
YC	Youth Council

Acknowledgements

This book is an outcome of my Ph.D. work and in this regard my first appreciation goes to Makerere University for providing the requisite funding, and to my supervisor, Prof. Sheila Meintjes of the University of the Witwatersrand, Johannesburg, South Africa.

I also acknowledge the African Gender Institute (AGI) at the University of Cape Town, whose Associates Programme (2000) provided me with the opportunity to conduct the initial preparation for the much needed critical research questions. To my South African friends, Shamim Meer and Bobby Marie, without whose support my life as a student in Johannesburg would have been different, I say thanks.

I am indebted to all the women and men who participated in the research in one way or another. Specifically, I thank the women councillors in Mukono, Kanungu and Kabale districts for the invaluable information and time. I acknowledge with thanks a number of people who walked the field research journey with me. Christine Ampaire, your ingenious questions and inexhaustible energy cannot be forgotten. I thank Dereva, Jackson Turyasiima and Meneja Eunice Buteraba.

I acknowledge the input of the staff and researchers at the Centre for Basic Research (CBR). As member of CBR, I enjoyed enormous and rare benefits – from the intellectual terrain to resource materials. Gertrude Kizito and Mkontani Rugyendo, I thank you for the expeditious editorial input. To Charles, Justine, Gabriel and Anthony, I say bravo.

Last, but not least, I am grateful to my partner and companion, Patrick Tumwebaze, whose untiring support sails us through the thick and the thin of life.

J.A.
April 2007

Preface

Research for this book was conducted in three purposively selected districts, namely Mukono, Kabale and Kanungu.

Mukono is located in the central region of Uganda, east of Kampala, the capital city; and is one of the biggest districts, relatively well endowed with natural resources, which include Lake Victoria and soils suitable for coffee-growing and horticulture. Its proximity to the capital city and the several industries located within it, combine to make Mukono one of the richest districts (in terms of relative potential).

Kabale is located in south-western Uganda, and borders Rwanda. Kabale is a small district with a weaker resource base than Mukono. In the past, it thrived on cross-border trade and smuggling between Rwanda and Uganda that became entrenched during Amin's reign in the 1970s. However, this trade has lost impetus owing to political and economic changes in the region.

Kanungu, the third case, is a new district, created in 2001. It was formerly part of Rukungiri District in south-western Uganda. A large part of the district lies in the Western Rift Valley; and this topography, combined with a weak resource base and a feeling of remoteness from centres of national or district political activity, fired up its agitation for district status. But the single most significant reason for selecting Kanungu was because it was the only district out of the 56 districts in the country with a female district (Local Council) chairperson. The idea was to explore differences from and similarities with other districts and the extent to which Kanungu presented a rupture from or continuity with the past.

The depth of the research varied in the three districts. On the basis of the vicinity of Mukono District, the researcher was able to do consistent follow-up through frequent visits over the four-year period of this research. This enabled the research to capture deeper experiences. This, is in view of the fact that one-off research modes tend to uncover only superficial evidence, and, in the specific case of topics such as decentralisation, which are in vogue, interviews run the risk of 'fruit picking' already packaged answers. This approach ensured follow-up of critical issues in view of new evidence in the different life experiences of informants over time.

Kabale and Kanungu were visited during one two-week-long field trip to each district. Information from other districts was also gathered in the course of the research.

In some cases, information from other districts was obtained through interviews with visiting district officials at workshops and seminars. In particular, two short visits, during training workshops in districts[1] were used to gather key information on women's participation levels in Local Councils.

Various methods were employed to adequately study and understand the gendered nature of local-level politics. First, unstructured interviews with a variety of actors were used.[2] One method was to let people's experiences and their perceptions unfold through life histories. Here the aim was to capture female councillors' experiences and their own evaluation of what they had or had not done, and why.

The diary method was also used to capture women's self-evaluation. Ten of the women councillors in Mukono received diaries to document their experiences, particularly those related to council activities as they unfolded. The self-evaluation, negation and validation contained in the notes made by women themselves helped to capture and understand some of the intricate dynamics of local government. The researcher was nevertheless mindful of the dangers embedded within this method. In addition to a high risk of non-response, a person chose what to document and what not to document on the basis of selective memory or intentional selective reporting. Since this method was used in conjunction with other methods, these pitfalls were minimised. The data from these diaries were used to enhance that collected through other methods.

Interview discussions involved other key informants, such as the district leadership, officials in the Ministry of Local Government, the Electoral Commission, election monitors and leaders of women's organisations. The research also included interviews with key people who participated in the 1994 Constituent Assembly (CA) that debated the 1995 Constitution in which the principle of decentralisation is enshrined. These included former delegates who served on the committee that discussed the matter of local government. Insights from the discussions that took place in the committee and the CA at large were informative as far as the construction of gender in the polity was concerned.

Furthermore, open and unstructured group discussions were used to engage people in a discursive manner. Group discussions were organised in the three districts visited. Discussions with councillors, both men and women, in groups, proved valuable. Other group discussions included ordinary people. In most of the cases, these were members of local community-based organisations (CBOs). This was done purely for pragmatic reasons, because members of a group could be mobilised easily. It turned out that discussion with a group of people with specific shared interests often elicited uncensored views.

It is often argued that women tend to be silenced when they are required to talk in the presence of men. Hence, emphasis in current research has been on women-only groups or individual interviews. Having moved from androcentric approaches that regarded only men as 'knowers' (Obbo, 1997), there is an assumption that one should strive to derive 'pure information from women' — that which is collected without the interruption of men. Mixed groups were only organised as control samples.

Emerging evidence, on the other hand, seems to suggest that mixed groups create real-life situations and researchers should be able to adequately deal with the outcomes, such as silence and exclusion. As the research proceeded the researcher realised that the notion of women's silence is not as absolute as is often portrayed. Women engaged as intensely in discussions as men did. This experience revealed that women's silence depends largely on the issues at hand and the manner in which the discussions are handled. In this particular research, mixed group discussions had the additional value of naturally uncovering critical points of difference and contestation in local situations.

However, cognisance was taken of the fact that group discussions could yield superficial information, since contributions in a group may well be influenced by the people present. Groups were therefore used in specific cases, where the matters for discussion did not have significant explosive potential (politically).

The other major method used by the research was direct observation of participation in council meetings in Mukono District. Five council meetings (four at the district and one at sub-county level) and two workshops (one for the youth and the other for women). District and sub-county council meetings were very informative and the researcher was able to observe the manner in which council business was conducted, observing both the inclusion and exclusionary mechanisms in these spaces. Particular points of observation focused on the issues to which women contributed, the mode of presentation and the manner in which the speaker and the general council treated or   received women's contributions in practice. This form of participant observation, albeit limited, presented an opportunity to capture some fascinating gendered subtexts.

Documentary research was also carried out. District and sub-county records were studied and minutes of meetings and budgetary records consulted. Government publications and laws pertaining to local government were studied to understand the scope of local government powers. The *Hansard* (the parliamentary debate record) was studied, particularly with regard to discussions about local government and quotas for women.

Newspapers, both local and international, were consulted. Newspapers constitute an important social space for signalling change and for recording what is considered crucial and newsworthy at any point in time, thereby, as in this case, informing the collective identity of males and females in public politics.

In Mukono District, nomination functions and campaign meetings were attended, enabling the researcher to observe actual campaigns and voting, as well as intricacies of community politics in the selection of those who ultimately govern. The campaign period (October 2001-

February 2002) was very informative in that significant gender icons in the crafting of community mandates were made visible. For example, campaigns demonstrated clearly how men and women were located within the electoral space, with women relegated to the margins and in need of justification. It was interesting to observe those who stood for re-election and the issues at stake in their re-election, as well as the gendered nature of old and new mandates. Here, too, participant observation proved valuable.

The research was justified on two levels, one empirical and the other theoretical, or broadly, methodological. At the empirical level, the numerical increase of women in local government from less than five per cent to a minimum of 30 per cent was unprecedented in the history of Uganda. Questions about women's presence in governance structures have tended to centre on whether or not it matters that women are present (Goetz, 1998; Meintjes & Simons, 2002; Mbatha, 2003). This study sought to broaden the debate, by studying actual processes on the ground, explicating the experiences and institutional contexts. The debate about whether it matters for women to be in structures governing society is reframed to take into account concerns about gender equality and the transformation of political space.

On the theoretical level, methodological concerns are linked to gender and politics. Most studies of gender politics have been concerned with micro realities and the relations of individual men and women, and in this undertaking, the household and conjugal relations have been central to the questions posed. National politics and the way broad state policy affects women have also been studied. There exists a lacuna in the treatment of gender politics at intermediate levels. The 'in-between' arena of social representation and legitimacy, what is termed 'community politics', has tended to be neglected.[3] Waylen makes this point in relation to gender and politics in the Third World, highlighting the fact that studies have been either macro or micro, with little in between (1996a:16). Uganda presents a glaring example of this lacuna. There is a need to understand how the in-between dynamics of gender at community level plays a role in the construction of citizenship and local democracy in Uganda in particular and Africa in general.

Research questions fell broadly within the field of local government, which has largely been the domain of mainstream political science. Political science as a discipline has been largely resistant to taking on feminist concerns (Hassim, 1998). This resistance is not merely due to gender bias but also relates to the very conception of the political. Gibbon, for instance, argues that, although social science recognises the fact that a proper grasp of national politics requires that the study of 'high' and central state politics be complemented by that of local-level politics, practice has tended to trail behind the acknowledgement of this principle (1994:11). The focus on big players in the polity and a preoccupation with structures and their performance and efficiency often means that the power dynamics and what people — men and women — bring to political processes remain unexplored. This book therefore hopes to make a contribution to a gendered understanding of local-level politics in Uganda.

The study proceeded with a methodological orientation that aimed at validating gender experiences and bringing them to bear on key political processes at local government level. The research proceeded from a complex'feminist viewpoint that 'conceptualises women as knowers' and gives them a subject as opposed to an object status in the research process, and thus validating the voice of the researched (Harding, 1987). But voice is not an unproblematic issue. There are questions about the extent to which claims of giving voice to research subjects are real. The issue raised by a number of critics is whether or not the pretext of giving voice carries with it a danger of recreating inequalities in knowledge production thereby 'masking deeper and more dangerous forms of exploitation' (Stacey in Tripp, 2000:xxii). In engaging with these questions, Tripp (2000) suggests that, while such caution is legitimate, it may also lead to paralysis and a cynical questioning of the utility and purpose of the whole research enterprise.

However, the way out of this impasse is not to abandon the whole idea, because it is key to feminist research, but to acknowledge the fact that the research product is filtered through the conceptual lens of the researcher. This is why the researcher cannot claim that women councillors, for example, talked through the researcher. The ways in which the researcher proceeded to interpret and reanalyse the women's experiences might well differ from 'the actual' women's voices. Indeed, even selecting realities to highlight or to ignore is dependent on one's positioning and inclination (Nielsen, 1990). This is not a limitation, as it forms the very basis of theory-building and the creation of new knowledge.

Aware of feminist debates on feminist empiricist versus feminist positions, the research sought to go beyond the dichotomisation of knowledge, as if it can only be presented as binary opposites. Empiricism places a heavy premium on science and claims of objectivity, while standpoint epistemology swings to the opposite side. Over-celebration of 'epistemic advantage' risks negating any intellectual project by positing, as it were, that 'it-takes-one-to-know-one' (Narayan, 1989:264). Walby presents a third type of epistemology, namely realism, with the view that there are deep social structures, the discovery of which is key to understanding gender relations (1990:19). Realism allows for the consideration of deep social structures, the contextual space of actors and the ways in which it defines social practice and interaction.

This exposes the famous trap in gender studies, especially in the African context that of victimology. It has tended to be an unwritten rule that, in dealing with gender questions, lamentations about women's suffering must be part and parcel, if not the sole concern, of research. Lamentations tend to create an identity of womanhood that is so objectified that it would seem that women are totally incapable of defining their destiny. Victimologies 'tend to create a false impression that women have only been victims, that women cannot be effective social agents on behalf of themselves or others' (Harding, 1987:5).

Christine Obbo's book, *African Women: Their Struggle for Economic Independence* (1980) was one of the earliest studies that treated Ugandan women as actors. Uncharacteristic of studies of women living in slums, Obbo's analysis brought out the ways in which migration to town, especially by single females, constituted a struggle for independence amidst social control mechanisms and stereotypes. Aili Tripp's (2000) analysis of women and politics in Uganda is another example of exploring women's agency and associational engagement. Needless to say, victimologies have tended to be more dominant in the study of women in Uganda and studies like Obbo's are few and far between.

The present analysis adopts a stance that recognises systems of domination while, at the same time, conceptualising women and men as social agents who have an impact on the systems in the way they conform to or contest and/or negotiate power relations. The research takes gender as a key analytical category, in a way that allows for consideration of the specificity of women's and men's experiences. Although most analyses have tended to dwell on individual relationships of men and women, women as a social group are indeed a heterogeneous category which, at certain junctures, might be subjected to systemic gender subordination that manifests itself in diverse ways.

Chapter One sets the context by outlining the broad overview of the Ugandan political landscape, focusing particularly on the 'post-war' (post-1986) period and the process through which women became a specific political constituency. Chapter Two seeks to frame the debate. By re-theorising feminist discourses on the political, the chapter provides the framework in which the question of gender, decentralisation and political space is examined. Consideration of the conceptual terrain is considered critical for understanding gender and the fact that a theory-building enterprise is necessary since gender studies is a relatively new field of study. Chapter Three deals with the institutional framework for decentralisation in Uganda, evaluating the potential democratic outcomes and deficits on a broad level.

Chapter Four tackles the mechanisms of the inclusion of women in local government structures and the unique features of the Ugandan political system. A comparison with India and South Africa, two other countries which have included a large number of women in local government leadership in recent times, is presented. This is done in order to have a clear view of what the Ugandan system has to offer.

Chapter Five then looks at local government elections and the ways in which the local is a much more contested terrain than is often realised. Periodical elections are seen as one of the key features of the decentralisation process in Uganda; and in this chapter, the actual experiences, the gender texts and sub-texts of this particular political process are examined. The specific positioning of female candidates is characterised and problematised.

Chapter Six proceeds to interrogate the politics of presence. In other words, once the electoral hurdle is over, questions around political legitimacy become paramount. Investigating the different experiences of participation, the chapter illuminates the various contestations and the ways in which gender identities are constructed and negotiated, and the impact it has on political space. The more or less contentious question of representation with regard to women's and gender interests is analysed. Representation has occupied feminist debate for quite some time. In revisiting representation, this book seeks to contribute to the debate, first of all by re-centring democracy and the whole question of democratic politics in the analysis of interests. Secondly, the question of interests in terms of the possibilities, potentialities and outcomes with reference to women councillors who have to carry the prescribed 'dual mandate', is reviewed critically. The dual mandate is understood as a construction of double expectations from women as councillors and as 'custodians' of women's and gender interests in local government functioning.

Chapter Seven, the conclusion, attempts to pull the threads together and to highlight salient issues of feminist theorisation of political space and local politics. It points to critical areas of action.

Notes

1. Gender Training and Skills Development for Decentralisation in Uganda carried out by the Department of Women and Gender Studies, Makerere University, 15-17 April 2001 and 18-20 December 2001.

2. Names of participants in this study are not revealed. In view of the high level of interaction at local level, it was decided to avoid situations that could compromise individuals. While the writer was presenting tentative findings to female councillors in Mukono District, some preferred to remain anonymous. Except for those indicated in the text for particular emphasis, no names are given.

3. The relationship between these three arenas is dynamic rather than static. There exists an interrelationship and there are significant ways in which the micro and the macro shape community politics.

1

Historical Background

Why and through what processes did women become a specific constituency in Uganda's politics? Article 32 (1) of the Constitution of the Republic of Uganda, 1995 provides for affirmative action in favour of marginalised groups. It states that the state shall take affirmative action in favour of groups marginalised on the basis of gender, age, disability or any other reason created by history, tradition or custom, for the purpose of redressing imbalances that exist against them. Article 33 (5) of the same Constitution provides: that 'Without prejudice to Article 32…women shall have the right to affirmative action for the purpose of redressing the imbalances created by history, tradition or custom.' Affirmative action, both at the national and local levels, which brought women to nearly 25 percent of parliament and a minimum of 30 percent of local government councillors, places Uganda well above the regional (sub-Saharan Africa) average of 14.3 percent, second only to South Africa (27 percent) and the Nordic countries (39.7 percent) (IPU 2001).

With specific reference to women's representation in local government, Article 180(1)(b) stipulates that one-third of the membership of each local government council shall be reserved for women. This position is followed through by the Local Governments Act (LGA) (1997), which provides specific mechanisms for women's inclusion. The increase in the number of women in local government took place in the specific context of decentralisation, which involved the transfer of administrative, fiscal and financial powers from the centre to the locally elected district and lower councils. The interface between decentralisation and an increase in the number of women at local government level opened a new area of the local political landscape, which calls for critical examination. This book traces women's increased numerical presence through the politics of mass struggle and mobilisation in the 1980s, and how this informed the nature and character of women's inclusion in local government structures. The major interest lies in discerning the impact of mobilisation politics on the gender terrain in political space. The point of specific reference is the Resistance Council (RC) system, and the nature of decentralisation in the contemporary period.

Decentralisation is generally regarded as a process that can guarantee the most developed forms of democracy, in that it tends to be more accountable, accessible, innovative and effective than centralised governance because of its closeness to the people (Montero, 2000). In other words, decentralisation is believed to increase the accountability of government by increasing its localisation. However, there are also contrary views that claim that decentralisation tends to re-arm local powers that serve particular interests of privileged rather than universal concerns (Slater, 1989).

Beyond the generalities, this analysis takes a gender perspective to decentralisation, and seeks to examine the politics of inclusion and the effect of the presence of women. The major thrust is to analyse the ways in which gender as an aspect of politics unfolded in an era of relatively visible and increased people's participation, and more particularly, in the context of a substantial numerical increase of women in local government. I investigate the extent to which the visibility and presence of women in decision-making structures translates into the transformation of political space and greater politicisation of inequalities in gender relations. Do women in fact participate more effectively in local-level politics, as has been generally argued? Does decentralisation necessarily enhance democracy at the local level? The analysis investigates the conception of local democracy, not as a unitary and unilinear phenomenon, but rather as a complex process that involves negotiation and renegotiation of identities. How do women, as members of previously excluded groups, fit into this equation? Taking the decentralisation process as a major watershed, the study seeks to create a concrete understanding of the local organisation of power in its gendered manifestations, hence deepening our understanding of, and further problematising, the notion of local democracy. Against this background, the book traces the process through which women constituted a specific political constituency, and how this nexus is positioned within Uganda's decentralisation process.

Women as a Political Constituency in Uganda

That the significant public presence of women is related directly to affirmative action policies instituted by the National Resistance Movement (NRM), a former guerrilla movement that seized state power in 1986, is well documented (Tamale, 1999; Tripp, 2000; Goetz, 2002; Kwesiga, 1995). Prior to 1986, women's participation in public politics was dismal, as manifested in 1980 when there was one woman in a legislature of 126 members (Tamale, 1999).

Right from the colonial period onwards, public politics as a distinct state-centred activity was constructed as a male domain, with women conversely constructed as 'the other' - occupiers of the private sphere. Whereas the entire Ugandan populace was disenfranchised in the early colonial period, once the concession to Africans was made, it had an ingrained gender bias. In the first nation-wide legislative council (LEGCO) elections of 1957, the property restrictions imposed on the franchise effectively excluded women both as candidates and as voters (Kanyeihamba, 1975). Women, in particular, were excluded from standing as candidates for the LEGCO and the exclusion was pursued actively, such that the few who attempted to stand as candidates were either discouraged or opposed aggressively. An example is that of Rebecca Mulira, one of the very first Ugandan women to attempt election to the LEGCO. Mulira, a prominent woman in Uganda's politics and one of the pioneers of the attempt to mobilise a semblance of a women's movement in Uganda, made a decision in 1962 to stand for the LEGCO. But she said:

> Men campaigned against us and we lost. They claimed that the Kabaka did not want women in politics. After that loss I realised that women had to fight to enter into decision-making ranks. When I was defeated, Kabaka Mutesa advised me to go to Mengo Municipal Council. I refused, saying that was too small for me...I

said that I wanted to be a Saza Chief. The Kabaka said that that was too big for me... (ACFODE, 1996:23).

Mulira was eventually nominated to the LEGCO, as was her husband. But this yielded yet another controversy, as she elucidates:

People said that a husband and a wife could not belong to the LEGCO so they got Florence Lubega to replace me although she did not. I contacted Sibra Visram. Her husband refused her but he eventually relented at my insistence... (ACFODE, 1996:23).

By independence in 1962, only five women had ever served on the LEGCO, three of them nominated by the colonial governor. But independence did not offer much to women either. This was partly because, as in most African countries, the nationalist project that led Uganda to independence had a narrow social base, more inclined to deracialisation of colonial privilege than democratisation (Mamdani, 1996). Contrary to the nationalism of the general strikes of the 1940s, the 1950s saw a take-over by the middle class that aimed at little more than inheriting colonial state power (Mamdani, 1983). This animated the class and gender character of politics that saw Uganda through to independence. Exclusion of women from national politics was compounded by the lack of a strong women's movement – a situation that Tamale describes as having been characterised by activities 'confined to a handful of prominent women' attending conferences and other similar fora (1999:14).

This situation was to change two decades after independence, when the NRM successfully led a mass struggle and captured state power in 1986. The takeover came in the wake of terrorism and civil strife unleashed on the Ugandan population by the post-independence regimes[1] The guerrilla movement was part of the larger crisis of the post-colonial state that plunged Uganda into civil war and military dictatorships (Karugire, 1980; Tukaheebwa, 1998). The guerrilla struggle had a de-centering effect on Uganda's politics, extended the social parameters of participation in public affairs and specifically increased women's political participation and public presence.

The origins of the civil war are normally traced to the 1980 elections (Tukaheebwa, 1998; Nuwagaba, 1991) when there were allegations of mass rigging on the part of the regime.[2] Museveni, one of the unsuccessful candidates in the elections, led the struggle that grew from a little under thirty men to become one of the few successful guerrilla struggles in Africa. Ddungu and Wabwire (1991), however, argue strongly that the fundamental causes of the armed resistance cannot be sought in a single instance of rigging an election. Rather, armed insurrection resulted from a gradual accumulation of contradictions and the level of development of social forces (1991:8). Broad causes of the armed insurrection in the 1980s can be traced to the crisis of the post-colonial state, manifested in military takeovers, state repression and economic crisis. Hence the civil war was caused by a constellation and accumulation of social frustration resulting from the exclusion and oppression of large numbers of the elite, and the suffering of ordinary people from economic exploitation and brigandage of the Amin and Obote II regimes, to a point where nothing good was expected of the government.

The NRM promised fundamental change in Uganda and focused its mobilisation on the rural peasantry and other marginalised social forces. If it was to expect popular support to counter and survive state oppression, the NRM had to broaden the parameters of popular participation (Ddungu & Wabwire, 1991). It was compelled to address the question of building state power with a difference in liberated zones under its command in order to marshal the support of the peasantry against the Obote II regime (Mamdani, 1996).

One of the major reforms was the introduction of the RC system. The RC system was first established in the war zones to enable people to choose leaders and to participate in decision-making in their communities. These councils served as governing bodies, by handling administrative matters and adjudicating disputes. Through affirmative action, women participated in the committees and thus began to play a role in decision-making at the local level. Each committee had to have at least one (mandatory) woman. Every village community was organised into a council and, in turn, elected a nine-person committee consisting of the chairperson, vice chairperson, secretary, secretary for women, secretary for youth, secretary for information, secretary for security, secretary for finance and secretary for mass mobilisation. As the NRM expanded the geographical area under its command, these people's committees expanded from village to parish and to sub-county level (Ddungu, 1994: 376).

After the NRM assumed power, the RC model of local government was formalised by the Resistance Councils and Committees Statute (1987). The hierarchical structure, therefore, connected every village to its district through the five tiers of elected councils (Kasfir, 2000). The apex was the National Resistance Council (NRC), which served as the national legislature until the promulgation of the 1995 Constitution, when it was replaced by Parliament.

The participatory nature of the politics engendered by this otherwise populist structure cannot be overemphasised. The elections and the deliberations at the different levels (especially the local level) brought about new energies unheard of in the history of Uganda. The NRM system in general, and the RCs in particular, brought about a change in political space, from one characterised by total male dominance to one in which an alternative, more participatory politics was made possible, at least in the quantitative sense. It meant greater numbers for women in public space. The one woman on the RC may have seemed a token but the aggregation of the different levels brought about a new level for women's visibility that changed the gender dynamics of politics, both locally and nationally. At a minimum, the introduction of the category 'woman' in the language of representation brought about by the politics of mobilisation introduced a continuing relevance of women's presence in politics in Uganda.

The participation of women in the war was part of a wider process of popular mobilisation in response to the repression and brutality of the time, coupled with the appeal of the NRM's vision and strategy (Byanyima, 1992; Ddungu & Wabwire, 1991). Women became heavily involved in the struggle, at different levels and for various reasons. Some were middle class women whose husbands had been imprisoned, tortured or killed by the Obote II regime. But there were also women members of the general peasantry in the war zones, who served as combatants, mobilisers, information seekers and food providers. As government troops inflicted vengeance on the entire population in the war zones for supporting the guerrilla resistance, more women found refuge in what came to be the only promise of a future (Byanyima, 1992:137). The phenomenon of 'female liberators' (Byanyima, 1992) was a turning point in Uganda's history. Much more importantly, the reforms instituted in its aftermath with regard to women's political participation, changed the general political landscape.

What is the relationship between women's role and place in the struggle and their gains in the aftermath? The women's question in revolutionary politics is a complex one. The outcome for women in any specific conflict is very much dependent on what kinds of appeal are invoked and how the gender question is addressed in the aftermath (Moghadam, 1991). Tamale observed that the NRM became the first post-colonial government in Uganda to take proactive measures to include women in formal politics and posed the question:

> How can we account for the drastic changes favouring women introduced by the NRM? Were the NRM males fundamentally different from the patriarchal 'old boys'? (1999:19).

The most popular answer, according to Tamale, is that Museveni's approach towards women's demands was opportunistic:

> What better way to show the international community that NRM is committed to democracy than to make women more visible in the arena of decision-making? What better way for a regime that had ascended to power behind the barrel of the gun to gain legitimacy and to place the hitherto 'sick man of Africa' back on the world map? At the home front it may be that Museveni realised the potential that can be reaped from gaining the favour of a constituency that not only constituted the larger half of the population but could also exert critical influence on men as their wives, sisters, and daughters. Indeed observers have used terms such as 'political expediency' and 'a gimmick' to epitomise NRM policies on women (Tamale, 1999:17-9).

Similarly, Goetz (2002) asserts that Museveni made quick political capital with urban women. Analysing the aftermath, Goetz (2002) observes that a small group of urban women's organisations mobilised to lobby Museveni soon after his seizure of state power. They demanded that women be appointed to leadership positions, on the basis of women's support for the NRM during the guerrilla war. These demands emanating from small elite lobbies and made to Museveni directly (ACFODE, 1995) were narrow, and focused exclusively on entry into political structures. Most of the demands made by women at that particular point were met with relative ease, exceeding what the women had asked for (Goetz, 2002). That these demands were met through the person of the president provides some evidence of opportunism and political expediency.

However, there is a need to avoid extreme voluntarism. Political outcomes cannot be understood purely on the basis of powerful actors and their predetermined agendas. For example, Razavi (2000), theorises about the question of gender and transition politics, and argues that there are moments when a state is more amenable to incursions than others. This resonates with Meintjes, Pillay and Turshen (2001), who wrote about the importance of timing in consolidating wartime gains for women and the political context of struggle and transformation or the lack of it.

The actual positioning of women and the gender question in the NRA guerrilla war has only been researched cursorily. Apart from an article by Byanyima (1992), an overview from an insider's viewpoint by a woman who participated directly in what is known as 'the bush war', little authoritative documentation and analysis exists. The general information found in a range of magazines and short articles nonetheless provides a general understanding of women's roles in the struggle.[3] According to Tidemand (1994b), the roles that Ugandan women played in the 1980s struggle did not approximate the ones in the Mau Mau of Kenya, or the struggles for independence in Zimbabwe or Eritrea. The NRM did not even have a specific agenda for the woman question.[4] How then did it happen that, in Uganda, the aftermath of the mass struggle benefited women's public role, especially with regard to their inclusion in the political structures, both at national and local levels?

In Africa, the mass struggles in Zimbabwe, Mozambique and Algeria mobilised women within their ambit. Samora Machel, the leader of FRELIMO in Mozambique, argued:

> The liberation of women is a fundamental necessity for the revolution, a guarantee for its continuity and a precondition for its victory (Urdang, 1995).

According to Urdang (1995), one reason for a guerrilla movement's commitment to involving women could be sheer need: every man, woman and child is called upon to participate in some way to overthrow repressive colonial regimes. However, this argument was framed in terms of the practical aspects of the struggle and tended to privilege the voluntarist aspects of mobilisation and involvement within guerrilla movements. Within such a conception, the political involvement of women and other social groups in such times of mass struggle were emptied of any social agency. In relation to women in particular, such a construction placed them outside the revolutionary project, thereby constructing them as the 'other' (Kannabiran, 1989).

Moghadam (1991) refers to the dangers of empiricism and analysing gender merely as a contingent factor within other systems of domination. She says that discourses about women and the family tend to signal the political, economic and cultural agenda of revolutionaries and new states, even in cases where these questions may cause trouble. In other words, women are not mobilised simply on the basis of need, but also because gender relations are constitutive of the way society is organised. Because of women's key roles in production and reproduction, they cannot be relegated to a secondary status in the struggle. In this way therefore, the sheer need of guerrilla movements to mobilise support can be reframed to underscore the fact that, by their nature, such movements tend to mobilise political efforts that offer alternative choices; and these processes of redefinition always tend to touch the core of existing systems of domination, gender being one of them.

The impact of conflict and mass struggle has an additional dimension. Apart from horrendous stories of killings, rape and destruction, there is the other side to the coin. Because conflict tends to undermine people's daily modes of existence, it also, more often than not, severs the threads of gender ideologies, albeit temporarily (Sorensen, 1999; Wells, 2001). Conflict often brings about discontinuities in gender roles as social experience shifts conventional relations. Referring to the Mau Mau rebellion against colonialism in Kenya, Presley (1992) observes that such rebel movements engendered transformation of ideas about women's place and politics. To Presley, the Mau Mau rebellion brought about a break with past custom, permitting, for instance, women to give and take oaths, making a case for the ways in which nationalism introduced significant shifts in gender roles. It is in these role changes, as war draws ordinary women and men into fighting, that opportunities emerge to forge new relationships and identities, including those of gender (Meintjes, 2001).

In Uganda, the turmoil of the post-independence era, and the guerrilla struggle in the 1980s in particular, not only undermined people's bases of existence but also altered several roles, such as the dominance of men in the cash economy and household headship. Women, for the first time in Ugandan history, joined men in the combat terrain and, though there was exclusivity, initially, in terms of what men and women combatants could do, the boundaries became increasingly fluid as women struggled to gain legitimacy in arenas that were previously the preserve of men (Byanyima, 1992).

This is not unique. In Eritrea, Zimbabwe and Algeria, women were active participants in nationalist struggles. Women participated in active combat and played supportive roles in intelligence, food provisioning and the general care economy, both in the guerrilla camps and in society at large. However, according to a number of observers, women in these countries were actively encouraged to revert to their traditional roles as soon as the struggle was over (Meintjes et al., 2001). These situations epitomise the inherent tensions of nationalism with regard to gender difference, as was the case for class and ethnic identity. Nationalism was only effective in mobilising the masses against a dominant colonial power; and once independence had been achieved, there was a gap in terms of how it could deliver to its varied social constituencies. Many liberation movements which promised benefits for women in the post-colonial period failed dramatically to live up to these expectations, which Hassim refers to as the legacy of 'dashed hopes, broken promises and unfulfilled commitments' (2002b:43).

In South Africa, this particular issue occupied centre stage in the women's struggle against apartheid. The South African case shows how women engaged actively with the inherent tensions between nationalism and feminism, perhaps with the benefit of being a latecomer in the achievement of liberation. Women (activists and guerrillas), both in exile and inside South Africa, demanded internal transformation that would recognise their right to an equal role in the political struggle beyond 'tea making' (Albertyn, Goldblatt, Hassim, Mbatha & Meinjtes, 1999:8; Hassim, 2002a). Women, particularly in the ANC, consciously critiqued the acute misogyny of nationalism as it had manifested itself in independence struggles in Africa:

> They argued that the liberation of women could not be separated from national liberation — that it was an integral part of how liberation was defined. These arguments were strengthened by the experiences of women in Mozambique, Zimbabwe and Angola in the 1980s which showed that the position of women did not automatically improve after independence, despite rhetorical commitment by political leaders… The practice of drawing women into active politics during the liberation struggles gave way to more patriarchal politics underpinned by dominant ideological constructions of women's position as subordinate to men (Albertyn et al., 1999:8).

Uganda's case provides a unique outcome of a nationalist struggle. Byanyima offers an insider's view to the effect:

> Ugandan women were not invited to take part in the national resistance war; they forced their way in. There was no women's movement in Uganda to encourage them, no leaders' speeches about women's emancipation, no consciousness-raising groups.

> The objective of the struggle – human rights, democracy and nationalism – were clear and close to women's hearts… The guerrilla war provided women the best opportunity, since Uganda's borders were first drawn, to be politically active (1992:42).

There was no real women's movement in Uganda, all budding women's organisations at the time having been banned through the 1978 decree that established the National Council of Women (NCW) (Tripp, 2000). When Obote's UPC took power in 1980, the NCW was manipulated to serve as the ruling party's women's wing. In a detailed study, Tripp (2000) describes the various struggles by women to resist the creation of the NCW as well as its manipulation by Obote II (2000:47-52). However, there is little evidence to suggest that women constituted an autonomous force in either the Amin or Obote II regimes (1972-1986). Uganda therefore demonstrates a sharp contrast to countries like South Africa, where women's autonomous and vibrant organisations in suburbs, townships and rural areas established a strong women's voice in the struggle against apartheid and its aftermath (Meintjes, 2001). It further contrasts with the independence struggle of Eritrea, in which the socialist project specifically recruited women for active combat, and yet encouraged a 'roll-back' to the traditional pre-war gender order when the war was finally won.

In Uganda the struggle against dictatorship and anarchy made possible a specific nationalist project, not with a homogenising discourse as at independence, but rather on the basis of a much more open and less pre-determinable terrain and political outcome. This view takes as its starting point the situation of a country emerging out of unimaginable state repression, civil war and economic decadence, what Doornbos rightly referred to as 'a starting from scratch predicament' to the whole nation (1988:257). The book entitled *Uganda Now: Between Decay and Development*, published in 1988, two years after the end of the guerrilla war, captured this predicament. The introduction opened thus:

> It is now 25 years since Uganda ceased to be a British colonial dependency. In these years Uganda has come to symbolise Third Word Disaster in its direst form. Famine; tyranny; widespread infringements of human rights, amounting at times to genocide;

AIDS; malaria; cholera; typhoid; and a massive breakdown of government medical services; corruption, black marketeering, economic collapse; tribalism, civil war, state collapse... there seem to be just too many causes of the country's troubles (Hansen & Twaddle, 1988:1).

The total collapse of the state meant that society was virtually revitalised from below. At the time it took to power in 1986, the NRM was primarily a guerrilla army, only given coherence by its overwhelming loyalty to the person of Museveni and its one priority of seizing power. It did not have structures to inherit nor did it have any 'formal internal structure for electing leaders or debating policies' (Goetz, 2002:567). Goetz views this as purely negative, contributing to the dominance of patronage politics rather than clear structures of accountability. A contrary view could be advanced to the effect that the fragility of the post-guerrilla political and economic environment, coupled with the initial fluidity within the NRM, could have been exploited by emerging and newly organised social forces to stake a claim. The politics of mobilisation hence connected women to the broader national question in a very loose manner. Women combatants had not had a chance to articulate a position on internal representation of women, or on gender equity, by the time of the takeover (Goetz, 2003b). But a group of women was able, at least, to demand access in the period immediately after the war. This is how I view the gains in women's public presence in Uganda though, as it will be demonstrated, these gains were paradoxically constrained by the very politics of mobilisation.

The one clear political gain for women — increased presence in governance structures — could also be usefully understood from the perspective of 'moment of opportunity'. The takeover by the NRM coincided internationally with the end of the United Nations Women's Decade and the conference in Nairobi at the end of 1985. This was the height of the Women in Development (WID) crusade that sought to integrate women into the development process. Among the Nairobi Forward Looking Strategies was a general position of consensus about the participation of women into decision-making structures (Snyder

& Tadesse, 1995). Some of the Ugandan women who attended the Nairobi conference returned to develop a new organisational terrain, which specifically focused on forming non-governmental organisations (NGOs) to advance women's interests. One such organisation formed in this period was Action for Development (ACFODE), which conferred with other women's organisations to generate a list of demands and mobilised to lobby Museveni soon after the takeover (ACFODE, 1995; Goetz, 2002:555). In what Goetz describes as a 'hastily compiled women's manifesto', women

> ...called for the creation of a women's ministry, for every ministry to have a women's desk, for women's representation in local government at all levels, and for the repeal of the law linking the National Council of Women to the government (2002:555).

The demands were made within a liberal framework, with a simplistic view of women's exclusion from public politics on the basis of individual-based strategies. The reasons for these minimalist strategies can be located in the fact that the women's movement was still in its infancy, having been retarded, in particular, by authoritarianism and civil strife. But it can also be argued that the very simplicity of women's demands made at a moment when the regime was still 'finding its feet' provided a critical opening. The simple access questions placed on the political agenda of a country emerging out of civil strife created a 'spark'. Initially, the president responded by appointing women who were strong NRM supporters to very prominent positions.[5] In addition to what women had demanded regarding representation of women at all levels of the RC system, 34 dedicated seats for women in the national assembly, the NRC, were added, that is one for each district (Goetz, 2003b:117).

In 1994 another mobilisation phase presented itself in the form of the constitution-making process. While other countries in the region simply amended their constitutions through existing parliaments to allow for political pluralism, Uganda had an elected Constituent Assembly (CA) to debate and to promulgate the new constitution (Makara & Tukahebwa, 1996). As shall be discussed in Chapter Four, the specific quota for women in local government stemmed from this process. The one-third representation of women in local government is one of the gains of constitutional mobilisation.

On the whole, the political gains of women were seen to benefit only a few elite urban or privileged women, without necessarily transforming the nature of women's engagement with the state. The general argument is that some women merely joined public politics under the tutelage of high-command patronage, thereby creating them as mere clients of the NRM, beholden to the regime, as it were (Oloka-Onyango, 1998; Goetz, 2003b).[6] The backlash of executive patronage continues to play out in many ways, significant of which is open opposition to the women's struggle, following the enactment of the new constitution, for property rights and equity in domestic relations.[7] However, Tripp (2000) gives a completely opposite view. In her analysis, Tripp views the NRM period as one in which women's 'associational autonomy' thrived in the form of a multiplicity of NGOs, professional bodies, self-help, faith-based and community-based organisations (CBOs). Since 1986, major women's organisations such as the Forum for Women in Democracy (FOWODE) and Uganda Women Lawyers Association (FIDA-U) as well as umbrella organisations such as the Uganda Women's Network (UWONET) and the National Association of Women's Organisations in Uganda (NAOWU), have arisen and have advanced the gender equity lobby in various ways. For Tripp, the synergy of these organisations has ensured autonomy and guarded against state patronage.

The position taken up by Tripp may gloss over the political question of women as a constituency drawn into public politics initially through a specific process of mobilisation. Debates in the wake of the new constitution (1995) revolved around the question of how far the gender question in Uganda could advance beyond mobilisation politics to substantial political engagement. With the move to a multiparty political dispensation, it will be interesting to see how this mobilisation dynamic plays out in intra- and inter-party gender politics and the specific agency of women thereof.

On to Decentralisation

Decentralisation in contemporary Uganda must also be understood within the framework of mobilisation politics. When the NRM came to power in 1986, it suspended political parties in view of the country's history of turmoil and extreme disintegration. Because political parties were viewed as a source of division and a major contributor to the civil unrest (Kwesiga, 1995; Tripp, 2002), a highly inclusive coalition termed 'broad-based' government was established initially. This broad-based coalition government appointed some of the major actors in political parties to cabinet positions. An alternative mode of political participation was also established through a system of individual merit.

The no-party system therefore officially removed structured political participation in the form of party political competition and formally permitted any person willing to stand for office to declare his or her candidature. The key elements of the no–party system in Uganda hence constituted electoral politics, individual merit contests and strict restrictions on political party activities (Carbone, 2001:12). Legally, non-partisan elections meant that, for both national and local elections, every aspirant was able to stand and was voted for upon personal merit (Furley & Katarikawe, 1999:11).

Critics likened the no-party system to a one-party state, while the regime was at pains to distinguish the system as a Uganda-appropriate version of popular democracy that allowed for consultation and inclusiveness while minimising ethnic conflict (Goetz, 2002; Oloka, 1999). This was the substance of debate in Uganda in the 1990s, a move from revolutionary politics to consolidation. Barya, for example, asserts that the no-party arrangement was intended to be a combination of political and social forces to resolve a political crisis and was by its very nature a temporary arrangement (1999:32). However, during the constitution-making process, the NRM sought to assign the no-party arrangement a permanent status and renamed it the 'Movement System' in juxtaposition to multipartyism. The passing of the Movement Act 1997 and the subsequent referendum of 29 June 2000, gave the Movement System 'privileged constitutional status', described as 'the country's political system which prohibits parties from functioning through elections... until a national majority recalls the system through a referendum' (Goetz, 2003b:113).

Focusing on the decentralisation of the 1990s,[8] a number of observers view it as paradoxical for the NRM to make claims of local democracy while thwarting political competition at national level (Crook, 2001; Barya, 2003). Hence many a scholar located the reasons for decentralisation in two explanations. One is the regime's pursuit of hegemonic patrimonialism, as elsewhere in Africa — an attempt to deepen the government's hegemony (Mutizwa-Manginza & Conyers, 1996; Hillebrand, 1996). Saito, for instance, argues that decentralisation was adopted as a mechanism to improve service delivery which, in turn, would increase people's support for the NRM and subsequently keep it in power (Saito, 2000).

Furthermore, there is a critique on the fragmentary nature of decentralisation in Uganda. Crook, for example, argues that the district focus and the lack of political bodies between the district councils and the national level 'deliberately fragmented potential local power bases into smaller, weaker, non-politically significant units' (Crook, 2001:10). For Crook, this system of fragmented units augured well for the no-party presidentialism of the time, with enormous power vested within the presidency, creating competition for presidential favours, and hence diffusing any institutional bases around which ethnic or sub-national political identities could reform themselves (Crook, 2001). In this way, decentralisation was viewed as a strategy by which the regime sought to diffuse the conflict at the centre through the creation of 'small states' at local level. However, this is a question that cannot be dealt with in a vacuum. The political history of Uganda, replete with civil strife and ethnic tensions, has much to say about a political strategy that attempts to avoid institutional mechanisms that permit ethnic identities to thrive. But to most observers, this very history was used as an excuse to avoid political options that could otherwise deepen democracy in Uganda's politics.

The second aspect, the donor good-governance agenda, relates to political conditionalities attached to aid (Doornbos, 1999). For instance,

Doornbos argues that the good governance theme has been related closely to strategies of institutional globalisation and 'its relaunch appears intended to provide a handle for the formulation of political conditionalities' (1999:35). Goetz also asserts:

> Decentralisation is one of the cornerstones of the contemporary good governance agenda …Policy reform therefore has targeted the public sector for radical surgery and along with sharp reductions in the extent of government action in the economy has come support for programmes which decentralise government to local levels and devolve responsibility for service delivery and local planning as well (2000:3).

However, emerging research illustrates that decentralisation in Uganda was not entirely driven by donor agendas (Livingstone Charlton, 2000; Saito, 2001; Francis & James, 2003). Rather than argue, for instance, that decentralisation in Uganda was donor-driven, I agree with Makara, who places the donor dimension in an already existing process, by arguing:

> There is no doubt that some donor agencies …are convinced that good governance is closely associated with the empowerment of local communities to participate in decision making and development programmes …This has served to strengthen the policy makers' commitment to the policy (cited in Lind & Cappon, 2001:7).

The argument here is that Uganda's history of turmoil, mass struggle and the nature of reconstruction shaped the nature of decentralisation. As a number of scholars have observed, the introduction of the RC system changed the structure of local rule (Mamdani, 1996; Tukaheebwa, 1998; Tamale, 1999). According to Mamdani, the RC system was the single most important political achievement of the NRM (1996:215). The commitment of the NRM to local government reform was also demonstrated by the institution of a commission of inquiry into the local government system, in the same year as the takeover.[9]

This book argues, on the one hand, that the kind of mobilisation politics brought about by the guerrilla struggle and the events that followed served as a very significant watershed in terms of women's political participation as well as repositioning gender power relations in political space. The present decentralisation is largely based on the RC first established during the civil war of 1981-1985, and this is what makes the analysis of mobilisation politics that animated the struggle important. The inclusion of women and other groups such as the youth and people with disabilities in very specific ways is part of broader reforms introduced in the aftermath of the war. Conversely, the expansion of women's representation in local government has happened within the context of decentralisation rather than because of it (as shall be explicated in Chapter Four).

The analysis conceptualises women as social agents specifically disadvantaged on the basis of gender. Hence the women's agency is situated within the consideration of other social (perhaps more powerful) actors. The populist stance that is called the politics of mobilisation, together with the specific mode of inclusion, impacts on the nature of women's presence and their specific positioning in decentralisation. The specific place of the no-party arrangement in women's representation is highlighted; and it is argued that, whereas the temporary suspension of party competition enabled women to access political structures, the ways in which the movement system worked for women as political actors had critical implications for their citizenship. The transition to multiparty politics has not shown any change. Nowhere is the 'no change' slogan more relevant than in relation to women. Mobilisation politics filtered through the transition and it remains to be seen what will happen.

Notes

1. The colonial and post-colonial crises of the Ugandan state are well documented (Mamdani, 1983, 1996; Wrigley, 1988; Kanyeihamba, 1988). The inherent tensions of the post-colonial state plunged Uganda into political crisis barely four years after independence. But the major blow was the military takeover in 1971 and the depredations of the Amin regime. The country collapsed into tyranny, anarchy and civil war for over two decades. This crisis formed the broader context of the rise of the guerrilla struggle.

2. These were elections organised in the aftermath of the war that ousted Amin, bringing back Obote, who had been toppled by Amin himself. The conditions surrounding the elections and the tensions in the political arrangements put in place afterwards have been documented by various scholars (Mamdani, 1996; Low, 1988).

3. It is beyond the scope of the book to go into greater detail to uncover the different dynamics and the ways in which the women's question was framed within the entire NRM struggle/war.

4. For example, the Ten Point Programme, which was a kind of manifesto (for the legitimation of the regime that had assumed power through the barrel of the gun), makes no mention of gender equity or its equivalent.

5. Gertrude Njuba, a high-level combatant in the Resistance Army, was appointed as deputy minister of industry, Betty Bigombe was given the vital task of leading the project of pacification in the north where there was resistance against the new government, Victoria Sekitoleko became minister of agriculture. In 1988, Museveni appointed two women as lawyers to the Constitutional Commission (Goetz, 2002:117).

6. This relationship has been specifically exemplified by the presidential elections in 1996 and 2001, wherein women were constructed as a homogenous group and vote bank for Museveni. An elite-engineered discourse, this time on the downside, accentuates the object identity of women as a homogenous and unproblematic constituency. In the wake of the 2001 presidential elections, a group of women in the capital constituted themselves into a mysterious organisation known as the Women's Movement for the Return of Kaguta (WORK), in a sense, speaking for the whole women's movement in Uganda. WORK ran advertisements which signified the status of women vis-à-vis the regime, as collective wives of the incumbent (*The New Vision*, 9 January 2001). In what Goetz rightly characterises as 'grateful sycophancy' WORK 'enjoined women to vote for Museveni' because of what he had done for them (Goetz, 2003b:121).

7. Kawamara-Mishambi and Ovonji-Odida (2003) document the experience of the campaign to advance women's property rights in the 1998 Land Act. In considering what came to be known popularly as the 'lost clause', the authors demonstrate the enormous resistance to women's efforts to include a provision on spousal co-ownership of land in the land law. The intention of the clause was that family land – homestead land on which a family resided or from which it derived its sustenance – should be vested jointly in husband and wife/wives, and be owned as such (ibid:161). The provision was passed in parliament but it did not appear in the published Land Act (2003:162). Women parliamentarians as well as women's organisations challenged the 'omission' but to no avail. The reform of the land law in 2002 presented an opportunity for the principle of women's right to land was to be reconsidered. The important point to consider here is that president Museveni came out openly to oppose the clause on the basis of what he saw as women's dubious intention to grab men's land (ibid.). The president's stance clearly indicated that the gender transformative or redistributive (Kabeer, 1999) political agenda was complex and could not be predicated on state patronage.

8. The history of Uganda's local government has been documented (Mamdani, 1996; Tukaheebwa, 1998; Goloba-Mutebi, 1999). Briefly, local government in Uganda, as in other African countries, projects a pendulum pattern over time, between centralisation and decentralisation (Mamdani, 1996; Wunch & Olowu, 1990). It is normally characterised by four main periods, viz. despotic decentralisation, 1900-1949 (pre-war British indirect rule); administrative decentralisation, 1949-1966 (limited local government reforms); centralisation, 1966-1993 (crisis of independent state); and 'democratic decentralisation', 1993 to date (Bazaara, 2001:15). These periods correspond roughly with the political history of Uganda, particularly relating to the well-documented impact and legacy of colonialism (Mamdani, 1996; Karugire, 1980; Mutibwa, 1992; Goloba-Mutebi, 1999).

9. The commission was constituted by respectable academics and high-level civil servants. Many of the recommendations contained in the report of the inquiry are reflected in the decentralisation framework of the 1990s.

2

Framing the Debate: Some Useful Conceptual Considerations on Gender and Decentralisation

> Decentralisation has quietly become a fashion of our time…it appeals to people of the left, the centre and the right, and to groups, which disagree with each other on a number of other issues (Manor, 1999:1).

Local democracy, it is often argued, results from the downward transfer of authority from the centre to the local levels, hence creating a system of governance in which citizens possess the right to hold local public officials to account through elections, collective action and other democratic means (Craig, 2001:522). This, in return, supposedly results in a more responsive state apparatus, responsive to local needs and aspirations, thus producing more effective systems of governance (Reddy, 1999; Crook & Manor, 1998). In sum, local government is viewed as the level of democracy that is closest to the people (Reddy, 1999), 'extending the work of democracy' and fulfilling 'democratic aspirations' (Zouankeu, 1994). And as Manor rightly states, 'no discussion of democracy would be considered complete without some reference to decentralisation', in the new millennium (1999:5).

The conceptual debates dealt with here seek to place enthusiasm about decentralisation in a gendered perspective and offer a gendered approach to local democracy. This will foster understanding about the ways in which gender determines women's and men's involvement in local-level politics and the consequences of their exercise of full citizenship. Questions about women's representation and political effectiveness, coupled with how these relate to the public/private distinction, are examined, specifically focusing on electoral and council experiences. Political space is explored within the national context of quotas or reserved seats for women (from above), a form of state feminism, as well as the broad climate of mobilisation or movement politics.

The challenge that comes to mind immediately is how to determine the boundaries of political space. The conceptual choice of this book follows Wolin's distinction between politics and the political to the effect that, whereas politics is continuous, ceaseless and endless, the political is episodic (1996:31). In this case, the political is a subset of politics. Politics is a broad arena of conflict, negotiation and consensus. In particular, the influence of feminist thinking has widened the conception of politics beyond the conventional definitions within mainstream political science that were narrow and concerned with government (Waylen, 1996b). This broadened definition of politics includes both everyday struggles in the home, community and civil society and contests within state-defined arenas. In short, politics includes nearly everything about human interaction. In this study, the specific interest is to examine the gendered patterns of power and authority at specific points in local politics.

This book focuses on political space as a specific arena of political contestation where competition for social legitimacy, the right to full citizenship, is played out. Issues relating to the broader legitimacy of women as political actors, not simply around issues such as voter turnout but rather around the transformation of political space that would afford women the status of being part of the norm rather than the exception, are examined. 'Political space is not only something taken up, assumed or filled, but something that can be created, opened and reshaped' (Cornwall, 2002:56). Hence, the concept of political space allows for the treatment of gender power relations in local-level politics without necessarily compelling one to follow evaluative technocratic approaches so characteristic of studies on decentralisation. This political space is therefore taken to refer to a fluid arena of contestation in public life on the basis of which identities are played out. Focusing mainly on electoral and council experiences (without presupposing that this is all decentralisation and political space involves), this analysis examines the emerging gendered patterns of political engagement in the context of decentralisation.

What does a gendered understanding of local democracy entail? Local democracy is clearly a popular concept in the decentralisation debate. The first thing that strikes a reader is that, despite the popularity of decentralisation as a field of study and public sector reform issue, it is grossly under-theorised, and remains largely unproblematised. Studies on decentralisation tend to place a heavy premium on structure, focusing on big and/or dominant actors, almost entirely employing the typology propounded by Rondinelli (1981) (see Appendix 2) for technocratic evaluative purposes. Most studies begin with the 'ritual' of laying out the typologies of devolution, deconcentration, delegation, in some instances adding privatisation, and then moving on to consider whether or not the country in question has implemented decentralisation (Borhaug, 1994; Nsibambi, 1998; Mapetla & Rembe, 1989; Makara, 1997).

According to Borhaug (1994), literature on decentralisation is generally characterised by a vague and general conceptual framework and this is why, for instance, there seems to be no competing 'schools' that contest each other (1994:11). Both pro- and anti-decentralisation arguments often 'rest on simplistic generalisation and often bear little relation to the specificities of actual contexts' (Gasper, 1991, cited by Swilling, 1997:9). This for-and-against argument tends to take the form of a shopping list and holds little possibility for deeper theoretical engagement (see Box No. 2.1)

Box No. 2.1   Decentralisation: Arguments For and Against

For	Against
Promotes democracy because it provides better opportunities for local residents to participate in decision-making	Undermines democracy by empowering local elites, beyond the reach or concern of centre power
Increases efficiency in delivery of public services, delegation of responsibility, avoids bottlenecks and bureaucracy	Worsens delivery of services in the absence of effective controls and oversight of standards
Leads to higher quality of public services, because of local accountability and sensitivity to local needs	Quality of services deteriorates owing to lack of local capacity and insufficient resources
Enhances social and economic development, which relies on local knowledge	Gains arising from participation by locals are offset by risks of increased corruption and inequalities between regions
Increases transparency, accountability, and the response capacity of government institutions	Promises too much and overloads capacity of local governments
Allows greater political representation of diverse political, ethnic, religious and cultural groups in decision-making	Creates new or ignites dormant ethnic and religious rivalries
Increases political stability and national unity by allowing citizens to control public programmes better at the local level	Weakens states because it can increase regional inequalities or lead to separatism or undermine national financial governance
Spawns new political ideas, leads to more creative and innovative programmes	Gains in creativity offset by risk of empowering conservative local elites

Source: International Council for Human Rights Policy (ICHRP) (2002) Local Rule: Decentralisation and Human Rights, Geneva.

Slater, citing Curbelo (1986), ascribes the popularity of the concept of decentralisation to a combination of elements. These are its capacity to conceal more than it reveals, its identification with long established sentiments, its forcible justification of purely technocratic points of view and the political instrumentality it potentially engenders (1989:593). Emphasis on technical, special and administrative aspects has projected decentralisation as being more of a managerial concern than a political one (Schonwalder, 1997; Bryld, 2000). Instrumentalism is underlined by emphasis on decentralisation as a 'one-size-fits-all solution to development problems'. Rondinelli, for example, argues that meeting the basic needs of the poorest groups requires widespread participation in decision-making, and decentralisation is advocated as a way of soliciting that participation (1981:133). Hence, decentralisation as a field has remained largely under-theorised owing to the technocratic thrust of policy evaluation within which it has been discussed and studied (Souza, 1997). Olowu states succinctly that the popularity of decentralisation in both scholarly and policy circles 'has not been for the best for it has made the term become slippery such that it can mean all things to all people' (Olowu, 2001:2).

In this, the emphasis has been on managerial aspects of government and the different levels of authority. With the exception of recent literature, which focused on participation and citizenship,[1] a number of studies on decentralisation are cast in such broad terms as to conceal the power dynamics at the level of community politics, in the process glossing over the intricate subtexts. Consequently, literature on decentralisation is predominantly gender-blind, presenting a 'gender neutral' analysis of such questions as efficiency, accountability and service delivery that ignore the differentiated way these matters impact on men and women and the relationship between them. In the specific case of Uganda, this is true for the major pioneering work by a number of political scientists, entitled *Decentralisation and Civil Society in Uganda.*[2] The book addresses whether or not decentralisation empowered local governments in terms of finance, human resources and service delivery. It is cast largely in general and gender-neutral terms.

Suffice it to say that a gender analysis of the decentralisation process in a country like Uganda faces a dilemma regarding whether or not to proceed to analyse the potential for gender in decentralisation, equality where even the general benefits of decentralisation are highly debatable. The question is whether or not one can talk about decentralisation when real power, financial or otherwise, is still concentrated at the centre. A number of observers suggest that decentralisation in Uganda is a sham, based on such measurements as autonomy, control and command of resources as well as content of citizen participation (Francis & James, 2003; Goloba-Mutebi, 1999; Mabirizi, 2001). In this regard, then, how does one examine questions of gender equity where real power has not been devolved?

Uganda's long period of civil war since the early 1970s implies a dimension of destruction and societal breakdown, which means that many of the service provision structures became largely dysfunctional. The rehabilitation process in the post -1986 era was successful in areas such as main roads, major schools and health centres, but services that relate to the immediate needs of households and individuals are still inadequate, even in urban areas. The resources controlled by local governments are meagre and this is why some observers point out that local governments are 'mere talk shops' (Olowu, 1999:288), since they lack adequate resources to function autonomously and effectively. This means that service delivery, a more or less generic yardstick of local government functionality, does not necessarily take centre stage, although it remains crucial. Is the case for a gendered study of decentralisation therefore lost?

Ann Marie Goetz (1998) provides a way out of the impasse. Talking about gender and democracy, Goetz argues that gender equality cannot be seen merely as a by-product of social change, but that it is critical to the achievement of the very goals in question. One does not wait for democracy to happen and then proceed to examine the gender equality question. Hence, democracy itself is contingent upon the gendered nature of equality. Who represents 'the people' is gendered, who votes for whom is gendered, and the whole arena of resource allocation is also gendered. Hence, in this case, gender as 'a constitutive element of social relationships and a way of signifying relationships of power' (Scott, 1986, cited in Goetz, 1992:9) is constitutive of and not contingent upon local democracy. In this sense power becomes the basis of how different collectivities are located within the political process and the subsequent claims (material or symbolic) they are able to make. Even in the context of a weak financial base, there is a basis for understanding the politics of distributing scarce resources, who is in and who is out.

Indeed, there is a whole gendered terrain of constructing claims and social legitimacy, even in the context of scarce financial resources.

With the above understanding, the conceptualisation of local democracy should of necessity include an analysis of gender equality, bearing in mind that what is normally referred to as 'community' is also differentiated by gender, class, nationality, religion and region, amongst other variables. In this sense, the understanding of community is not that of a unitary entity per se, but rather a set of relationships and a process (Hunt, 1996, in Khadiagala, 2000), within which dominant categories have wide discretionary powers to define morals and fidelity. For Hunt (1996), this process entails:

> ... a series of social practices that constitute closures, boundaries and divisions that create insiders and outsiders... delineate who has the right to set the rules and determine the morality which guides social conduct and the legitimacy of claims (cited in Khadiagala, 2000:59).

Griffin rightly argues that, in some cases (if not most), 'power at the local level is more concentrated, more elitist and applied more ruthlessly against the poor than at the centre' (1981:225). Indeed, this has far-reaching gender implications (Luckham, Goetz & Kaldor, 2000). Goetz argues that elites in control of local government may be more overtly and defensively patriarchal than at national level (2003:71). This validates the question of local elite capture, with regard to which numerous scholars have pointed out that one of the dangers of decentralisation is that it may simply empower local elites, and worse, perpetuate existing inequalities (Craig, 2001:525; Ahikire, 2002).

This means that local democracy cannot be taken as a given or even assumed to exist from the powers given to local governments. Localised democracy, for instance, may have the effect of re-arming patriarchal forces that would otherwise be under attack nationally. There is always a need to understand local-level processes critically and to discern the various mechanisms of inclusion and exclusion. And, conversely, it is not possible to dismiss outright even top-down decentralisation processes. Referring to Kenya, for example, Oloo (2002) observes that, notwithstanding its limited and top-down nature, decentralisation could lead to the emergence of space that could be filled by a vibrant civil society. The same could be said for specific gender equity lobbies. In this way, local democracy becomes a process of contestation rather than something bestowed upon the community, concurring with Guidry and Sawyer, who see 'democracy as a journey rather than a destination' (2003:274). And this is why an alternative approach to localising democracy is presented, to refer not to a product but rather to a continuous interactive process between various actors, men and women, losers and beneficiaries.

How does the local political landscape unfold and how does an understanding of gender enhance our appreciation of what is going on at local level?   In order to broaden the frontiers of local democracy within a gender perspective, it is imperative that the discussion moves beyond dichotomies.

On Presence

In 1989, Rosalind Boyd wrote an article entitled 'Empowerment of Women in Uganda: Real or Symbolic?' (Boyd, 1989). Boyd underlined the fact that NRM initiatives, particularly affirmative action in political structures, had introduced significant gender changes but that gender-based discrimination remained deeply entrenched. Boyd focused her analysis on questions of infrastructure, gender-based attitudes and the state versus autonomous organisations as routes to empowerment. The conclusion reached was that affirmative action and related initiatives in Uganda post-1986 had resulted in some change in gender relations but that traditional relations of power were largely intact. In the RCs, for example, women still struggle against subordination (1989:111). In effect, Boyd seemed to advance the position that the empowerment of women in Uganda was symbolic rather than real.

These concerns are still pertinent. Indeed, they partly provide a rationale for this book: to understand the politics of inclusion and the extent to which gender equality is being realised. However, it is important that the debate is reframed to allow for a much more useful conceptualisation of gender and politics in concrete realities.

The distinction between real or symbolic creates an unnecessary dichotomy. Yet the real and the symbolic are necessary ingredients for transforming gender relations in a polity. In this regard also, the casual way the concept of empowerment is employed tends to present women not as social agents but as passive bystanders in society. It tends to individualise gender-based power as well. Hence, this analysis avoids the dichotomisation and conceptual slippage embedded within the concept of empowerment. Pieterse (1992) validates this decision to avoid the concept, by observing thus:

> Part of the appeal for empowerment is the aura of power, but it does not necessarily problematise power. It can denote anything from individual self-aggrandisement assertion to upward mobility through adaptation and conformism to established rules. Accordingly, empowerment may carry conservative implications or more precisely, it is politically neutral (1992:11).

Pieterse alerts readers to the fact that the unproblematised use of the term 'empowerment' engenders discourses that divorce actors from the political context of other social actors within a particular set of institutional relations. The need to shift from looking at women as individualised objects to which the state acts, to conceptualisation of women as social agents, is what gives impetus to this inquiry. It requires theorisation of gender, considering it as a system of power that accords different political resources to different women and men.

That women do not and cannot constitute a homogenous category is a long-standing debate in feminist theory (Whitehead, 1984).[3] Yet, it is also important to underline the fact that because the study of gender is primarily predicated on concern about the subordination of women, the identity of woman, the subaltern, is highlighted and given prominence. A gender analysis nevertheless moves beyond focusing on women as a category, to examining the dynamics of gender-based power, which then highlights different women's locations in political space. Baylies and Bujra (1993) provide a useful way of considering gender relations as embedded in a continual process of negotiation and articulation. This is the approach adopted to analyse the democratic potential of decentralisation in Uganda.

There are two major questions in this regard. On the one hand is the question about women's agency and, on the other, the capacity of political institutions to accommodate formerly excluded actors. In addressing this question reference is made to Goetz (2003a), who observes that for adequate gender analysis of political institutions, it is useful to look at two aspects: one, the voice as the demand side of women on state structures, and the other, as the supply side relating to the gender capacity of institutions. To Goetz, the focus on these two aspects enables us to understand that although voice is crucial, it does not always lead to fair gender outcomes because political institutions can have strong gender biases which undermine the impact of women's voice and presence in decision-making (2003a:35). In other words, the 'rules of the game' (Goetz, 2003a) and their differential gender impact on the exercise of citizenship are very relevant here.

The question of women's voice is what is translated to refer to women's strategic presence or effectiveness in local-level politics. The interface between decentralisation and the numerical increase of women open up two areas that are linked closely, and these are gender equity and local democracy. On the one hand, the polity had high expectations of decentralisation as a process that would enable local participation, encouraging and enhancing a form of local democracy. On the other hand, decentralisation in Uganda happened hand in hand with the numerical increase of women through a form of 'electoral engineering' (Goetz, 2003a), rather than a natural process from within the electoral community.

Representation of women at local government level prompted questions of whether or not it mattered to women whether they were in decision-making positions, stemming from the assumption that women were better placed to represent women's interests and to bring about gender equity policies and implementation. These questions will be approached with a more critical lens.

The question as to whether or not it matters that women are part of state structures, has been a matter of great debate within feminist inquiry globally. The debate centres specifically on national structures or legislatures, but is equally relevant to local government. Pornima and Vonod Vyasulu (1999) ask, in relation to the Indian experience, whether reserving positions for women only is enough to achieve democratic change. With reference to Uganda and South Africa, Goetz argues that 'a numerical expansion of women in politics may not translate into effective representation of their interests in development policy making' (1998b:1). In relation to the Philippines, Atienza rather emphatically asserts:

> Empowerment is not measured solely by the number of women in high positions or in individual achievement. It should be viewed in the context of collective power of women to make relevant contributions in decision making, accompanied by changing views of both men and women regarding their roles in society (2000: 42).

Several scholars seem to agree on one thing, at least. Numbers are not enough and are an imperfect measure of women's effectiveness. The volume edited by Karam entitled *Women in Parliament: Beyond Numbers*, talks directly to this debate. Karam introduces the debate by observing thus:

> We need to look beyond the often asked question of how to increase the numbers of women in parliament, and move towards presenting examples and experiences of how women can impact on the political process while working through a parliamentary structure (1998:9).

Anne Philips (1991), in an earlier attempt to systematise the debate on women's representation in decision-making, provided three major principles that have been advanced to make a case for women in public politics. The first relates to democratic justice, namely that since women constitute roughly half the population, they are entitled to comparable numerical representation in those bodies that govern society. In other words, exclusion of women from politics is unfair (Hassim, 2002:104).

Second is a question of resource utilisation that argues that valuable resources are wasted when women are not involved merely because women have different values to men. This stems from the 'ethics of care school' (Albertyn et al., 2002:39), according to which the participation of women is supposed to transform the content of politics towards a caring and more humane society. This school of thought assigns women a role of 'cleaning up' politics. It is also heavily embedded in instrumentalist assumptions within the WID (Women in Development) perspective. Arguably, while this position has been criticised on the basis of its theoretical underpinnings, it happens to be the most popular at the level of practice owing to its de-radicalised and unthreatening outlook (as shown in Chapters 5 and 6 of this book).

The third principle is based on interest representation, focusing on the fact that women and men have different political interests because of the gender differentials in society generally (Philips, 1991:75). At another level, representation of women has been raised with regard to the legitimacy of democracies, to the effect that 'democratic deliberation and aggregation are most legitimate when political interests are represented in the decision-making assembly in proportion to their representation among the population' (Mansbridge, 1999 cited in Albertyn et al., 2002:38).

On the whole, the interests-based argument has received most attention, relating to how women can go beyond presence in decision-making structures and engage on behalf of women's rights and liberation (Corrin, 1999). Goetz (1998b), for instance, sought to make a clear distinction between a numerical increase of women and representation of their interests. In the same vein, Tamale (1999) who employs Pitkin's (1967) distinction between 'standing for' and 'acting for' representation, observes that women in Uganda's parliament fall largely within the descriptive mode of representation. Although Tamale acknowledges the difficulty of actualising the 'acting for' representation; she envisages the possibilities of focusing on the common oppression and subordination that women suffer as a group (1999:75) without assuming that all women are the same.

However Razavi (2000) suggests that such arguments are based on an implicit assumption that women can more effectively contribute to the formulation of women-friendly policies than men because they are somehow better able to represent women's interests. A key question has something to do with the constitution of women's interests, since women are at the same time differentiated along other social cleavages such as class, race, nationality, religion and age (Razavi, 2000). What constitutes women's interests or what passes as women-friendly legislation are highly debatable issues (Reynolds, 1999:3). Similarly, for Phillips, the interest-based view attributes too much power to nature and essentialises women, what she termed as 'identity-essentialism' (cited in Benhabib, 1996:10). To Phillips, this leaves the justice reasoning as the most tenable.

Feminist scholars in Southern Africa have found such debates less rewarding. In a volume entitled *One Woman One Vote* (Fick, Meintjes & Simons, 2002) feminist scholars in South Africa seek to revisit conventional feminist debates. Hassim, for example, makes a critique of such debates because these debates tend to construct women as a coherent group leading to the replacement of electoral politics with unnecessary debates about the premises of various arguments (Hassim, 2002a: 104). Making use of ideas advanced by pragmatic feminist scholars like Lovenduski and Dahlerup, Hassim re-examines the case for the numerical representation of women, and states a succinctly:

> The likelihood of gender inequality becoming a policy issue is in direct proportion to the number of women representatives... Though some women representatives may have neither the ability nor the inclination to address gender inequalities, this scatter shot strategy suggests their cumulative weight will impact on parliament. This argument is valuable because it sidesteps the controversial areas of normative judgements about fairness, as well as the essentialist arguments about women's difference... The demand for greater representation in its broadest formulation does not pre-judge the ways in which gender inequalities will be taken up by representatives... The issue is rather one of access to arenas of public decision making so that various interests of women can be debated and acted upon. Without broad representation, it is unlikely in fact that the complexities of gender inequalities can be fully appreciated in policy terms (2002:104-5).

The above argument is based on the idea that women as a differentiated category cannot be assumed to have a monolithic agenda that is identifiable in simplistic terms, since women's objective interests often differ on the basis of class, religion, nationality and many other sources of social cleavage. Besides, women do not necessarily subscribe to similar ideologies just because they are women (Lister, 1997; Philips, 1995).

However, rather than engage in cyclical arguments on difference, Hassim's argument seems to borrow a leaf from Jonasdottir (1988), who suggests that there is a need to focus on women's shared formal interest in access to political power rather than the content of any shared interests. This, in the understanding of political space, can be conceived as women's shared exclusion from full citizenship (Lister, 1997). A conception of shared exclusion can, indeed, avoid essentialist assumptions about women. Perspectives from the developing world context increasingly acknowledge that the either-or question, embedded in the descriptive versus substantive representation argument, is unnecessary and detractive (Goetz & Hassim, 2003; Tamale, 1999). Even Phillips (1996), a leading proponent of the 'presence versus ideas' project, submits that political presence is the first step and mechanisms should be devised to address the problem of group exclusion without necessarily fixing the boundaries or character of each group.

These and other arguments confirm that it matters that women are part of decision-making structures. This observation is made on the basis of both the justice argument as well as the fact that a greater number of women means that their cumulative weight will have an impact. One cannot be isolated from the other. Also, there is an 'ideological impact of women's office holding which may have an effect of undermining conventional definitions of relative status of men and women' (Ahikire, 1994a:79). As will be demonstrated in Chapter Five, the presence of more women in the electoral process has expanded the issues around which power is contested. To borrow from Agarwal (1997), issues such as those related to people's marital status and other private arrangements have moved from the 'doxa' (the norm) to the 'hetodoxy' (the arena of contestation and discourse) (1997:15). This is a fascinating process.

There is an additional dimension to women's access to formal structures. This relates to the fear of co-option or incorporation into a state–organised enterprise, projecting the state as essentially patriarchal (Oloka-Onyango, 1998; Mies, 1986, cited in Goetz, 2003b) and the more often cited danger of elite opportunism, on the part of women. But as a number of scholars have rightly argued, the state is not necessarily a unitary structure but a differentiated set of institutions. Experiences of other African countries such as Eritrea and Tanzania indicate that affirmative action for women in politics has been a significant factor which cannot be ignored (Madanda, 2003; Tanzarn, 2003). In this sense, a form of state feminism works to break down some of the significant barriers to women (Stetson & Manzur, 1995). This means that the state should rather be seen as a site of struggle (Rai, 2000). While the state has, for the most part, acted to reinforce female subordination, space can exist within it to act to change gender relations (Alvares, 1989, cited in Waylen, 1996b:104). This is especially true for periods of transition, which often present new opportunities and constraints (Ahikire, 1994b; Razavi, 2000; Hassim, 2002b). Such a stance also overcomes extreme separatism which treats women as a special category, and brings them back into the social processes in which women live and act.

Nonetheless, focus should not only be on those women who access formal structures but also on the whole institutional arrangement, including the capacity of civil society organisations and broader citizen engagement (Meintjes, 1996). This is particularly true at the local level. In relation to South Africa, for example, Coetzee and Naidoo observe that many gains in local government were due mainly to interventions by organisations and gender equity lobbies at the national level (2002). This is the view of the present examination of the local government system in Uganda. More women as candidates and representatives in local assemblies increase the possibility of broader political integration of women and the possibility that women's strategic representation will go beyond individual representatives.

The second major aspect of women's political effectiveness is the very politics of inclusion, or the mechanisms through which women access decision-making structures. Of particular importance in this regard is the role of electoral mechanisms, and the question of quotas. Major debates have been conducted around whether or not electoral systems matter, and there seems to be consensus that proportional representative (PR) systems are generally better for women than majoritarian ones. Globally, PR systems have proved to bring in more women because of the detached way in which the vote is exercised, such that a voter selects a party rather than a candidate, thereby having an effect of 'de-localising ' the vote (Matland, 1998; Meintjes & Simons, 2002; Ballington, 2002; Goetz, 1998). Examples the world over demonstrate that more women have been elected to legislatures through some form of PR system (e.g. South Africa, New Zealand and Ireland) than through majoritarian systems such as in India and the United Kingdom (Matland, 1998:68).

Nonetheless, there is still recognition that 'the electoral system is only as good as the commitment of parties to diversity (Meintjes & Simons, 2002:162). In other words, the context of electoral politics remains significant. Parties have a role to play, especially at the level of selection. This links directly to the question of quotas. Ballington (2002) observes that Scandinavian countries (with an average of 38.7% female representatives in parliament), contrast sharply with other countries — even those that use the PR list system. As a result of years of activism and pressure by women, coupled with the general nature of social development in Scandinavia, parties use internal quota systems to ensure nomination of women as candidates. Ballington (2002) goes on to argue that, besides the PR list system in South Africa, the relatively high numerical representation of women in parliament and local government is predicated on the gender commitment of the ANC [4] (as the dominant party) since it came to power in 1994. Female candidates had been placed in 'not-so-winnable positions' on the list (Ballington, 2002: 88).

Yet, the question of quotas is far from settled. Apart from general liberal arguments against quotas on account of interference with individual freedoms, there is concern about ghettoisation of women in public politics by quotas. This was relevant to a country like Uganda in the time it was governed by a 'no-party system'. Affirmative action for women is a highly debated issue in Uganda (Tamale, 1999; Kasente, 1994). As South African women battled with the question of women's representation, there was concern that quotas would perpetuate separate status for women. They, for example, rejected the Ugandan model, which entails separate and additive positions for women. One Democratic Party activist, Dene Smuts, is quoted as having said: 'When you send a person into public life under a quota system, you automatically send her with a question hanging over her head about her competence' (Gevisser, 1994, cited in Ballington, 2002:91). Opportunely, the PR list system agreed upon in the negotiated settlement to address the question of minorities and social inequalities in a post-apartheid South Africa, enabled the ANC in 1994 to implement a quota without weighing heavily on individual women. In the subsequent elections, many other parties found they could not ignore completely the question of quotas for women. On the whole, quotas are necessary to cut through deep-rooted cultural negativity about women. The question is how to implement it. As Dahlerup states, a quota system works best when the burden of recruitment is placed 'not on the individual woman but rather on those who control the recruitment process' (1998:92). The relevance of these debates will form the core of Chapter Four which will elaborate on the relatively unique quotas for women in Uganda's local government system.

The Private/Public

It has been argued that both developed and developing countries have higher rates of participation by women at the local government level than at the national level. The reasons given are various, but most notably that local government tends to be an extension of what women are already doing in the community. Hence, it seems a natural step from community activity to the council (Drage, 1999). Other arguments suggest that local politics is more accessible to women and easier to combine with domestic and child-care responsibilities, compared to national politics that does not lend itself to being meshed with family life (Einhorn, 1993, cited in Razavi, 2000). Does this argument hold in the context of Uganda, where the entry of women has not emerged naturally, but rather through quotas directed from above?

The above observations enmesh with yet another longstanding debate in feminist thinking — that of the 'public and private divide'. Local government (more than national government) seems to create a space where the line between the public and private changes shape viscously and the boundaries shift continuously. The context of Uganda specifically presents unique processes that call for critical examination. Decentralisation, with the resultant political activity at the local level, has changed the public/private relationship. In gender terms, the change can be understood at three interrelated levels.

First, the 30 per cent mandatory quota for women at all levels of the five-tier system increased the numbers of women in formal structures remarkably. This had the effect of expanding the range of issues around which political power was contested. In terms of elections, for example, the presence of more women on the scene brought with it new issues in campaigns. The boundaries of the public and private domains were therefore redrawn.

The second level is that which is normally expected — the gatekeeping syndrome. Even when women had access to public decision-making structures, they were still constructed as outsiders to the public domain. As Sapiro put it:

> Individuals do not share equally in both spheres. Man for example has two statuses as a public person and as a private person... Woman, however is totally immersed in the private... and is judged by the single standard appropriate to that realm (1983:31).

The third level has to do with what can be called the pervasiveness of the 'public'. The ways in which political activity at local level tends to intertwine with people's lives resulted in a situation where even what people (especially women) would regard as private, could be dragged into the public space. In this case the powerful slogan 'the personal is political' advanced by radical feminism had more than one edge to it. In some cases it would seem that there is a need to understand concrete conditions under which some women may see the personal as personal, despite being political, and what this means in terms of local democracy. Rai (2000), for example, observed that rather than focusing on the issue of exclusion from the public sphere, emphasis should be on making the private public, i.e. to politicise issues that affect women in their daily lives. Yet, the view of some women, and possibly men, who see danger in the pervasiveness of the public requires about new thinking feminist concerns around the private sphere. Morris captures this challenge when she argues thus:

> ...it is impossible to think critically about central problems in democratic theory... among them the very possibility of citizens representing, or translating into a common language, what is most singular, secret, ineffable, internal, that is, private about themselves (2000:323).

Once again, we are faced with the challenge of going beyond dichotomies. The public/private divide is not self-evident, but appears contradictory. It is context-specific as well. In seeking to understand the gendered nature of local-level politics in Uganda, it is important that the concrete experiences of this public/private dynamic are studied.

It would seem unusual to seize on an almost worn-out and discredited conceptual tool in the analysis of gender and politics. The public/private divide has influenced much of western-oriented feminist thought on politics. Liberal feminism demanded equal opportunities for women in the public sphere without questioning the divide. Radical feminism, with the powerful slogan 'the personal is political', questioned the relegation of key relations that defined women's subjugation to the private and therefore out of bounds for social inquiry and activism. In a much stronger connection to the definition of the state, socialist feminist analyses of social policy demonstrated that the delimitation of the state's proper sphere involved active codification and policing (Goetz, 1992) of the boundaries between the public and private,

> ... where these boundaries also delineate gendered spheres of activity; where the paradigmatic subject of the public and economic arena is male, while that of the private and domestic arena is female... with evident men's physical monopoly of the public (Goetz, 1992: 10).

In current debates, however, there are more nuanced perspectives, with some voices from Southern Africa arguing that the public/private dichotomy is only central to western feminism and does not relate to the realities of the Third World (Bonnin, 2000). This debate seems to be moving in the direction of abolishing the private/public divide as a key conceptual tool in feminist political thought. This stance evidently stems from the limitation of the popular use and conceptualisation of these two spheres as binary opposites, which denies their interconnectedness and simplifies their relationship (Bonnin, 2000; Pateman, 1989). Hence, the problem ceases to be about the separation per se (Bhattacharjee, 1997). Assuming centrality is thus the issue of the interplay between the different constructions of the two spheres and the implications for the concrete exercise of citizenship in local arenas. The parameters of what is public as opposed to what is private are not only broad and porous; they are also fluid (Tetreault, 2001).

It is important to mention at this point that the consideration of the public/private distinction here does not assume a clear-cut division between men and women in the public and private respectively. On one hand, the development of capitalism and its clear-cut division between private and public, does not apply to in Africa. Furthermore, people constitute new meanings of public and private continuously, particularly at the local level. Far from being mere bearers of the public/private divide, men and women are constantly constructing and negotiating the boundaries as active agents.

Nancy Fraser (1992) expands the conceptual possibility by speaking of multiple 'publics' and corresponding 'privates', thereby questioning notions of a given public sphere. Taking off from, and making a critique of, the Habermasian view of the public sphere, Fraser demonstrates that public and private are not simply straightforward designations of societal spheres and there are no naturally given a priori boundaries

(1992:129). Fraser notes that there are several senses of public. It can mean four things: first, state-related; second, accessible to everyone; third, of concern to everyone; and finally, pertaining to the common good or shared interests. Each of these corresponds to a contrasting sense of 'private' (1992:128). The other major sense of the private in terms of gender is that pertaining to intimate domestic relations or personal life, including sexual life. Fraser's point of departure presents a perspective where the spheres are shaped continuously by discursive contestation, which suggests that such processes need to be understood in concrete historical reality. There is also the case of dominant and subordinated publics, whose interface needs to be properly conceptualised. This is the case, for instance, with some of the conservative spaces such as religion-based groupings and basic self-help projects, which are discussed in Chapter Six.[5] How to understand these alternative spaces without romanticising their capacities?

Beck talks of a 'hidden public' to explicate the patrimonial nature of politics and the influence of patronage networks on the political participation of women in Senegal. Regarding what Beck terms the differential access to all halls of power, she demonstrates that not all political resources are accessed through formal structures, and looks at the hidden public,

> ... as that part of the public sphere in which 'dyadic' relationships operate: personalised patron-client relationships based on the patron's control of the distribution of state resources that are negotiated outside the public forum (Beck, 2003:149).

The conception of a hidden public dispels the notion that everything in the public sphere is universal and apparent for all to see. It provides a basis for understanding the 'below the surface' dynamics and how formal inclusion may not always translate into adequate legitimacy in the political process. Nonetheless, this argument should not seem to romanticise the hidden public and to blindly seek to have women included in it, and 'serving as men' rather than challenging patronage politics (Beck, 2003:165). Looking at local councils in Uganda, there is indeed a hidden public, as shall be demonstrated in the chapters that follow. The questions to be posed are: Should women seek to access the hidden public and/or challenge it? What are the benefits? What are the costs, especially in view of the sexualised view (whether real or not) of patronage networks? This fear becomes real, bearing in mind that women's sexuality becomes an object for public discussion and attack when it is made public.

My view, therefore, is that rather than discarding the framework completely, the public/private divide is still important for feminist scholarship and action. In particular, it assumes new conceptual significance when dealing with issues of local government and democracy, which do not necessarily have to follow a dichotomous path. In this case one cannot assume, for instance, that the proximity of local government means that women are more effective at the community level than at the macro level. Indeed, in some cases, the contrary could apply, as evidence seems to suggest. The public/private divide is nonetheless a useful tool to guide understanding of the differential location of men and women in political space, provided that it is contextualised adequately rather than essentialised. The significance lies not in the boundary question but rather in the interconnectedness and its different manifestations in concrete situations. The closeness and interconnectedness of these spheres in local-level politics makes an even more compelling case for its problematisation.

Presence and Deliberation: The Gendered Exercise of Citizenship

Beyond national citizenship, defined at the level of a nation state, there is a dimension relating to the way complexities of representation, power and the claim to know are played out in the physical and social arenas opened up to citizen participation. Under the veil of formal equality, therefore, citizenship is a differentiated relationship of belonging, action and accountability between citizens and many different institutions that have influence over their lives (Jones & Gaventa, 2002).

In discussions about local democracy, deliberation is seen as a necessary condition for a fully realised democracy. Fishkin summarises this sentiment thus:

Without deliberation, democratic choices are not exercised in a meaningful way. If the preferences that determine the results of democratic procedures are unreflective or ignorant, they lose their claim to political authority... Deliberation is necessary if the claims of democracy are not to be delegitimated (cited in Stewart, 1996:49).

Deliberation has been problematised in two ways: one in relation to party discipline, where choices of decision-making are constrained by party policies and priorities (Stewart, 1996), and the second where local dynamics are at play, thereby muting the less influential and less articulate voices. The second concern speaks directly to the political positioning of women in local government in Uganda. The councils, as major arenas of decision-making, are predicated on deliberation as a mechanism for people to participate and collectively reach a consensus on a specific course of action. The general guiding philosophy of LCs is that policy and programme outcomes are a crystallisation of a range of views at various levels.

However, deliberation is informed by power and it is gendered. This does not refer to the mere fact of being more or less articulate, but rather the very institutional arrangement of participation. Though deliberation is a necessary component of local democracy, it is not enough in itself and its efficacy is largely dependent on the very politics of decision-making and the patterns of interaction in specific contexts. Deliberation can mask domination as social inequalities can infect deliberation, even in the absence of any formal exclusion (Fraser, 1997, cited in Hassim, 2003:101). In gender terms, this has a lot to do with local definitions of the proper roles of men and women.

The extent to which marginalised actors have access to critical political tools, for example, money, power and information (Craig, 2001:525) to effectively influence decisions, becomes significant here. And this is where meaningful citizenship becomes relevant, in that collectivities assume full legitimacy in deliberative spaces. Ddungu and Wabwire argue rightly in relation to women's placement in formal political participation in Uganda that discussion and decision-making are not enough. They observe that it is equally important to understand the issues about which decisions are made, and thereby to locate the effective centres of power underlying the processes of decision-making (1991:40). This is the reason why some attempts by women to either create or maintain separate deliberative spaces should be put in perspective. What is its relevance and how do we understand such spaces, despite the fact it may not hold direct prospects for political leverage?

The specific orientation of this analysis is to understand local power dynamics as complex as opposed to unilinear.

It is easy to see women as victims because gender relations tend to be manifested in a manner akin to what Pateman refers to as the original 'sexual contract' (i.e. women's subjugation and men's freedom) (1988:2). This orientation is what Harding terms victimology — conceptions that create a false impression that women have only been victims and cannot be effective agents on behalf of themselves or others (Harding, 1987:5). To go beyond victimologies means that a different conception of power, one that always anticipates some space for contestation, or 'at the very least passive resistance', is required (Crehan, 1997:231). This does not at all imply that we lose sight of power regimes (Fraser, 1989). For example, systemic male privilege in political space cannot be ignored. However, power is seen in both its coercive nature and resistance to it, such that processes of contestation can be captured and understood adequately.

Notes

1. See, for example, Khadiagala (2000); Cornwall (2002); Agarwal (2001); Craig (2001); Goetz & Gaventa (2001); Cornwall (2003).
2. Edited by Nsibambi (1998).
3. The very use of the concept of gender has meant addressing the fact that all women are clearly not the same and their positions vary on the basis of class, race, religion, nationality and many other social cleavages. As Ann Whitehead summarises this debate, women are at once differentiated in the sense that the social relations between genders may vary among the women of any one society and, furthermore, women experience significant variation in their

situations in those wider areas of political, economic and social subordination and inequality which are not confined to gender (Whitehead, 1984).

4. The ANC's commitment to an internal quota was not automatic but rather a direct result of women's activism during the transition period in the 1990s.

5. This is where, for instance, the feminist literature's famous distinction between spaces that address practical and strategic needs becomes relevant. In the characterisation first advanced by Molyneux (1985), practical needs refer to those based on the women's and men's traditional gender roles, and addressing them does change their situation but tends to leave their social position (in terms of power relations) intact. Strategic needs, on the other hand, are those that relate to the transformation of social position, changing the power relations between men and women, for example. The practical and strategic distinction is situated within the larger debate of WID and GAD (Gender and Development) as broad approaches to development. WID, the first approach to emerge in development literature and practice, advocates women's integration into the development process, while GAD recognises the importance of redistributing power in social relations (Goetz, 1997).

3

The Local Government System in Uganda: Mapping out Structures and their Gender Dimensions

This chapter maps out the structure of the Ugandan local government system and sets out key signifiers for understanding the gendered nature of local politics. It focuses on the specific location of women in the different structures. Outlined here is the fact that, although the new pattern of local government saw a relative increase in citizen participation, including mandatory positions for women, in practice real power continued to manifest itself in a predominantly elite and male form. In particular, the existence of indistinct structures and positions for women constructs women as secondary citizens, hence further marginalising them, albeit in a whole new way. Yet it is acknowledged that there are, indeed, opportunities for women and other social actors to participate, opportunities that were not hitherto available. Paradoxically, it is clear that a form of democratic community engagement is being nurtured. The existence of what can be referred to as simultaneous spaces of gendered inclusion and exclusion as they are unfolding in Uganda's decentralisation is an interesting process to examine and understand.

People's relationships to local government can be divided into three dimensions. The first relates to elected representatives, the councillors, who constitute the political leadership. The second has to do with local state employees, the technical or implementation arm of local government. Third are people who are consumers of local government's goods and services, i.e. the larger community (Button, 1984).

This book's overall interest lies in political leadership, its key gendered subtexts and how it impacts on the realisation of local democracy. However, to fully appreciate the gendered location of elected local representatives, the broad structural interplay of these three aspects, as provided for by the legal framework in Uganda, is considered. The potential of this system of local government and, in particular, its gendered aspects in the whole terrain of political space, are analysed.

The local government system in Uganda is relatively complex, with multiple layers of local authority. It is further differentiated on the basis of the rural/urban divide, where urban councils have slightly different structures. This chapter relates largely to local government structures in the rural context, as derived from visits to districts.

The Framework

Decentralisation in Uganda is regulated under the Uganda Constitution and the Local Governments Act (LGA), 1997. Article 176 (b) of the 1995 Constitution stipulates that decentralisation shall be the principle applying to all levels of local government and, in particular, from higher to lower local government units, to ensure people's participation and democratic control in decision-making.

Objectives of the LGA 1997

a)   to give full effect to the decentralisation of functions, powers, responsibilities and services at all levels of local government;

b)   to ensure democratic participation in, and control of, decision-making by the people concerned;

c)   to establish a democratic, political and gender-sensitive administrative set-up in local governments;

d)   to establish sources of revenue and financial accountability; and

e)   to provide for election of local councils.

Launching the decentralisation programme in 1992, the president of Uganda, Yoweri Museveni, noted that though the RC system had eliminated some of the problems in relation to local authority and people's participation, it was a limited deconcentration. The limitations of the RC system were that it had dual systems of local administration and lacked clear mechanisms of accountability. Seeking to place the new initiative within a historical context, the president pointed out that, throughout the post-independence period, local government in Uganda had been decimated by governments seeking to monopolise and control the distribution of resources at local level (Republic of Uganda:1992:1-2).

Without a doubt, the decentralisation process established a new configuration of roles, powers and responsibilities for local institutions. Local government units were legally empowered to mobilise resources and utilise them as they deemed fit, employ staff for the effective delivery of services and exercise political and administrative authority, as long as this was consistent with the constitution (Kasumba, 1997; Ashaba-Aheebwa, 1996). It marked a relative departure from the inherited British colonial system of 'decentralised despotism' as Mamdani put it, where 'every moment of power, legislative, executive, judicial and administrative was combined in one official', the chief (1996:54). Kisubi (1996) suggests that the decentralisation policy was aimed at undoing the harm done to local systems of governance by over-centralisation. He suggests its purpose was to 'invigorate local initiatives and local democratic processes so as to enhance local capabilities for self-governance and service delivery in order to achieve sustainable development' (1996:84). The fieldwork for this study exposed that people's understanding of decentralisation involved a new configuration of power, at least at the general level. The local discourse, using such terms as *okuzza obuyinza mu bantu* (returning power to the people), *Okwemaririra* (full decision-making power) is indicative of how people viewed decentralisation.

The LGA (1997) set out in explicit terms that one of its objectives was to establish a democratic, political and gender-sensitive administrative set-up in local government. The LGA is written largely in a gender-inclusive language, which differs sharply from the Local Government Statute (1993), which preceded it, which had an overly masculine character and symbolically represented all actors as male. Suffice it to note, as will be explained in the next chapter, that women's activism during the constitution-making process shaped the language of the 1995 Constitution. This, in turn, had a positive impact on the nature of gender-inclusive language in all legal instruments that stemmed from it.

The most notable gendered feature in the LGA (1997) relates to the mandatory one-third representation of women in councils at all levels.[1] The effect was that at every local council level, women comprised a minimum of 30 per cent, a numerical proportion internationally acknowledged as adding up to a critical mass that could influence policy processes. Participation by other marginalised groups, such as disabled and the youth, was also guaranteed. Hence the LGA (1997) moved a step away from the single-female representative in the former RC system, to 30 per cent of the councils.

The system of local councils, though based on the RC system, presented major changes. The RCs were transformed into more conventional local government units known as local councils (LCs). Under Section 4 of the LGA (1997), the apex of the local government system is the district, a body corporate. There are no intermediate levels between the national and the local government. Below the district is the lower local government, the sub-county level (LC3), also a body corporate. Local governments and lower local governments as body corporates have the right to sue or be sued. The remaining levels constitute administrative units (LC1, LC2 and LC4). However, it is still a hierarchical structure, from the lowest LC1 (village) to the highest LC5 (district), as shown below:

Box No.   3.1   The Local Council Structure in Uganda

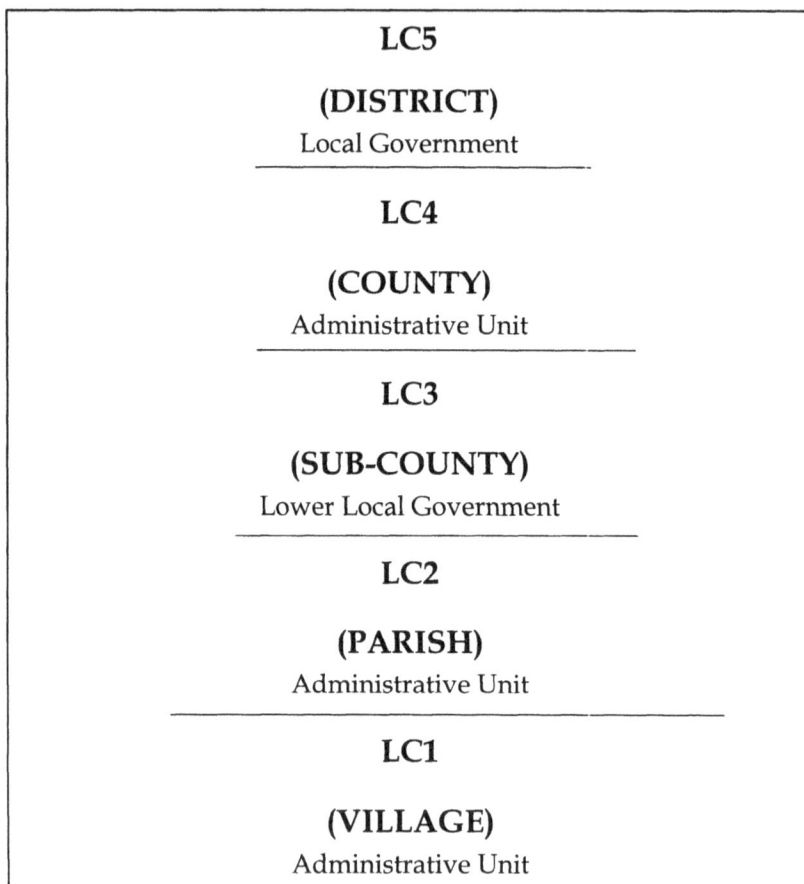

LC5
(DISTRICT)
Local Government
LC4
(COUNTY)
Administrative Unit
LC3
(SUB-COUNTY)
Lower Local Government
LC2
(PARISH)
Administrative Unit
LC1
(VILLAGE)
Administrative Unit

The Local Government (District/LC5)

According to the LGA (1997), a council is the highest political authority at each level of local government. At LC5, the district council is composed of the chairperson, councillors elected from each of the sub-counties and women councillors elected through a separate constituency system (to be elaborated on in the next chapter). The electorate for the chairperson comprises the entire district, while that of councillors is sub-county-based. All are elected through universal adult suffrage. The special councillors for the youth and people with disabilities (PWDs) are elected through their respective organisations, the Youth Councils and the National Union for People with Disabilities (NUDIPU), respectively. The district council is presided over by a full-time Executive Committee. The district Executive Committee performs the day-to-day executive functions of the council, such as initiation and formulation of policy, overseeing implementation, including financial regulation and probity (LGA, 1997, 17 (1)). The District Executive Committee consists of the chairperson, a speaker and deputy, elected from among the members of the district council, as well as the vice-chairperson and secretaries (one-third of whom must be women), nominated by the chairperson and approved by the district council.

The one-third provision for women on the district executive committee was made in the LGA Amendment of 2001. Initially, the provision was that at least one of the offices of secretary should be held by a female, followed by a specification that the chairperson should assign one of the secretaries to be responsible for health and children's welfare. The 2001 Amendments further detailed the one-third representation requirement for women with regard to statutory bodies. These were the District Service Commission, the appointing authority, the Local Government Public Accounts Committee, responsible for overseeing financial accountability, and the District Tender Board, in charge of procurement of goods and services. The provisions specified a minimum of one-third representation by women, a new development that changed the face of statutory committees. This change broadened reservation to include non-elective bodies, which are nevertheless key facets of the local government system.

These provisions established a principle of gender balance in terms of numbers. During a district council meeting in Mukono (12 June 2003), the vice-chairperson tabled reports by the District Service Commission and the District Tender Board and noted that the 2001 Amendment had necessitated a change in the composition of members of these bodies. Whereas hitherto there was only one woman on the District Service Commission, the proposal tabled was for three women and three men.

A particularly interesting process was that the names of the women were consistently presented first, perhaps owing to the fact that their inclusion was fundamental to the change in the composition of the bodies. However, it is significant that the chairpersons proposed for all the bodies were still all male. Suffice it to note that a new tradition of balancing numbers (women vs. men) is without a doubt taking root in Uganda. An official from the ministry of Local Government put the principle of gender balance in perspective by observing that, even where no legal requirement existed, there was a tendency, especially at local level, to achieve a gender balance in various posts and activities. As shall be demonstrated in the latter chapters, this gender balancing was still circumscribed, in that women tended to fulfil deputising roles. Nevertheless, the imperative need for balancing numbers, albeit circumscribed by patriarchal definitions, is a development worth noting and exploring.

The technical arm, headed by a chief administrative officer (CAO) under the new dispensation, was to be appointed by the respective local government rather than the central government, as was the case before. Civil servants were to be appointed through a standard system of merit and competition within the mechanism of the District Service Commission (DSC). While representation of women in the political sphere was guaranteed, this did not apply to the technical arena among civil servants. Here a huge gender disparity existed, with men dominating most of the positions of authority, such as heads of department, while women were concentrated in the lower echelons of district staff, as copy typists and cleaners. A gender audit carried out in ten districts in 2002 found apparent gender disparities in strategic technical positions such as CAO and heads of department in the district, with female representation less than 5 per cent, and even zero in some cases (DWGS, 2002).[2]

The Lower Local Government (Sub-county/LC3)
Unique to the system in Uganda was that, although it is a hierarchical one, the lower local government was not the county (LC4), the tier immediately below the district (LC5), but rather the sub-county (LC3).

The Sub-county Council is constituted in the same way as the district. There is a chairperson elected by the entire sub-county as the electorate, and the councils on the basis of the parishes in a specific sub-county. Again all are elected through universal adult suffrage. The technical staff at this level are constituted mainly of extension staff headed by a sub-county chief, who is posted by the district.

The sub-county is the level of actual implementation of district programmes. Francis and James (2003), however, observe that taxation, rather than service delivery, was the main way in which local administration manifested itself in the lives of community members at this level. Hence, villagers generally felt ambivalent about the sub-county, whose officials were identified mainly by graduated tax collection drives (Francis & James, 2003:329). Considered at through a gender lens, this observation illuminates significant dynamics about people's relation to the local government. According to the law, eligibility to pay graduated tax covers every male person of or above the apparent age of 18 years who, on the first day of the financial year, resides within a specific council's area of jurisdiction, and a female person of or above the apparent age of 18 years engaged in any gainful employment or business (LGA, 1997, Fifth Schedule 2(1)). Since few women are gainfully employed or in business in a rural context, the sub-county, with its overriding image of a collector of graduated tax, thence projects a masculine face.

The official discourse on graduated tax, however, differed from the reality. During a discussion with a group of men and women in Kanjuki village, Mukono District (November 1999), people observed that graduated tax was paid by men in name rather than in substance. In reality, graduated tax was experienced as a household tax because, in rural areas, assessment was done on the basis of assets such as houses, acreage, crops (annual and perennial) and animals. This meant that women, and in some cases children, influenced graduated tax. Evidence from a number of districts also suggested that the bulk of graduated tax was paid by women 'on men's behalf'. For example, the sub-county chief of Goma indicated that women were the principal payers of graduated tax. This, he said, was especially manifest when men were arrested for defaulting, in which case women would flock to the sub-county offices to pay the tax and effect their husbands' release. Following the abolition of graduated tax in the wake of the 2006 general elections, it will be interesting to explore the new image of the sub-county and how people — men and women — interface with it.

Administrative Units

The county (LC4), parish (LC2) and village (LC1) are governed by Executive Committees with the main tasks spelt out as assistance in the implementation of district programmes, mobilisation, communication, and maintenance of law and order generally. They are lean on civil servants — assistant chief administrative officer county (LC4) and a parish chief at parish (LC2), and none at village (LC1) level.

With respect to each administrative unit, there is a ten-person Executive Committee on which women have to occupy a minimum of four positions. At village (LC1) level the Committee is composed of a chairperson, a vice-chairperson, also secretary for children's welfare, a general secretary and secretaries for information, education and mobilisation, security, finance, production and environmental protection. The chairperson of the Women's Councils at village level is the secretary for Women and Public Health Coordinator; the chairperson of the Youth Council at village level is also secretary for Youths; and the chairperson of the Organisation for Persons with Disabilities at the village level is also secretary for People with Disabilities. Before the 2001 Amendment, people were elected to these posts by everyone residing in the village aged 18 and above. They were elected through the method of lining up behind the candidate. The amendment brought a big change. Only the chairperson was to be elected by secret ballot and he or she, in turn, nominated people to the Executive Committee.

At parish (LC2) level, all Village Executive Committees in a parish form the electoral college and elect another Executive Committee (with similar positions at that level). At county (LC4) level the elected representatives at sub-county (LC3) level constitute the electoral college from which an Executive Committee is elected. In other words, with regard to administrative units, the LC system is in many ways similar to the old RC system regarding election and modes of representation, where the lower tier executive formed the electoral college for the one above it. In practice, the parish and county levels have a minimal role in the local government structure. In the 2001/2002 LC elections, the constitution of councils at these two levels was deferred to a later date that was not specified. Accordingly, the Minister of Local Government announced that the government would consider abolishing the parish and county levels as structures of the local government system (*The New Vision*, 12 June 2002).

Functions of an Administrative Unit Council as laid out in the LGA (1997)

a)   to draw attention of the District Chairperson, the Chief Administrative Officer and the Assistant Chief Administrative Officer at the County level or Chief at the Parish level to any matter that rouses their concern;

b)   at the County level to advise the area Members of Parliament on all matters pertaining to the county;

c)   at the County and Parish levels to resolve problems or disputes referred to it by relevant Sub-county or Village Councils;

d)   to resolve problems identified at that level;

e)   to monitor the delivery of services within its area of jurisdiction;

f)   to assist in the maintenance of law, order and security;

g)   to carry out any functions that may be assigned to it by the District Council or higher local government councils; and

h)   to carry out any other function conferred by law or incidental above (LGA, 1997 Sect. 49).

Alongside the mainstream Local Councils are parallel structures. First, there are Women Councils (WCs), and Youth Councils (YCs); and before the transition to the multiparty political system, there were Movement organs whose purpose and function remained obscure.[4] Women and Youth Councils are structures that largely form a mobilisation arena for the government because, though they operate at local level, they are within the ambit of a central government ministry, the Ministry of Gender, Labour and Social Development. The WCs, for instance, are a structure parallel to the LCs, made up of councils at village, parish, sub-county, county and district levels, with an Executive Committee of five at each level, culminating in a National Women's Council. These councils were constituted following the enactment of the Women and Youth Council Statute of 1993, in circumstances largely considered grotesque and interpreted by many as an attempt by the NRM to control various sectors of society and to halt associational autonomy (Tripp, 2001a).

The powers and functions of local governments as set out in the LGA (1997) mean that local governments are, first and foremost, legally vested with planning and legislative functions. The District (LC5) Council, as the supreme organ in local government, has powers to enact district laws as long as they are not inconsistent with the constitution or any other law made by the national legislature. This power is to be exercised by passing local bills into ordinances. The LGA (1997) permits local governments to budget and make development plans; and allows them to levy, charge, and collect fees and taxes, including rates, royalties, stamp duties, personal graduated tax and registration and licensing fees (Republic of Uganda, 1998:4).

According to the LGA (1997) the District Council has powers and responsibilities to prepare a comprehensive and integrated development plan incorporating plans of lower-level local governments which, in turn, prepare plans incorporating those of lower councils (administrative units) in their areas of jurisdiction (36 (3)). The planning process is guided by the local government planning and budgeting cycle, governed by the LG financial year that runs from July 1 to the end of June.

The planning function is the nerve centre of decentralised local governance and in terms of policy, there is a framework for bottom-up identification of priorities and incorporating the development plans from village to district level. Village and parish councils (i.e. all adults of 18 years and above residing in the village/parish) are convened in what is termed a budget conference, and priorities are identified and sent through to the sub-county (LC3). The sub-county council is supposed to prioritise further so as to enable the Sub-County Technical

Committee to come up with a plan. The district budget conference takes place finally to aggregate priorities from all the sub-counties.

Summary of Powers and Functions of Local Governments in Uganda

- Make policy and regulate the delivery of devolved services
- Make development plans based on locally-determined priorities
- Raise revenue, including determining and implementing revenue raising mechanisms
- Make, approve and execute own budgets
- Alter or create new boundaries
- Appoint statutory committees, boards and commissions for personnel, land, procurement and accountability
- Establish or abolish offices in the public services of a District or Urban Council, including payroll and pension
- Make ordinances and bye-laws that are consistent with the Constitution and other existing laws
- Have responsibility to manage a broad range of services including primary, secondary trade, special and technical education, hospitals other than hospitals providing referral and medical training, health centres, construction and maintenance of feeder roads; provision and maintenance of water supplies; agricultural extension services; land administration; and community development.

To capture the status of women in the decentralisation process adequately, there is a need to consider the political framework of decentralisation. Goloba-Mutebi (1999) questions the value of participation in Uganda's local government system, considering that the community seems to have little impact on the nature of service delivery in key sectors such as health and education. Goloba-Mutebi's analysis is set in very broad terms and his critical review of participation is not disaggregated by gender, but it is nevertheless valid. There is, on the one hand, the participation principle sustained from the mobilisation politics of the 1980s and 1990s and, on the other, the developmentalist mode focused on achieving poverty reduction targets and efficiency (Francis & James, 2003). The gender dimension of this duality is mapped out in the section that follow.

The Gendered Dual Mode: The Inclusive Patronage and the Exclusive Technocratic Modes

This section characterises women's positionality in a decentralised Uganda by employing the concept of the dual mode as advanced by Francis and James (2003). Accordingly, the decentralisation framework in Uganda is at once ambiguous and based on potentially conflicting ideologies of development. On the one hand, there is the overriding language of participatory planning and empowerment of local people. On the other hand, there is the prioritisation of poverty reduction driven by national targets. Francis and James seek to understand this as a dual mode — the former as the patronage mode and the latter as the technocratic mode:

> Under a technocratic mode, conditional funding from the centre is earmarked for particular programmes but with little local participation. In contrast, the patronage mode is an elaborate system of local 'bottom up' planning but with limited resources which are largely consumed in administrative costs and political emoluments… the technocratic mode is driven by targets and is closely associated with poverty reduction plans… the patronage mode draws on the language of participatory planning, but in the context of lack of resources and capture by local elites.

The categorisation by Francis and James (2003), though on the most general level, provides a useful starting point for understanding the level of women's inclusion and exclusion. Women were principally included in the patronage mode and largely excluded from the technocratic mode, where resource allocation primarily takes place. Uganda's decentralisation, in a way, resonates with symbolic politics, as described by Button (1984), of depoliticisation, but which creates an illusion of political action.

Nonetheless, it is necessary to consider the possibility of these two modes intersecting at some point, and to identify any potential for enhancement of gender equality at local level, from the view that gender justice is a process as opposed to an end result.

The technocratic field revolves around the key issue of finance and resource allocation. Finance, as many scholars of decentralisation observe (Cheema and Rondinelli, 1983; Olowu, 2001), is significant for illuminating relative powers of local governments and the degree to which democratic decentralisation has taken place. In Uganda, finance and arenas of broader resource allocation were seen to be in the tight grip of the technical mode, within which people's participation is at best minimal. This reveals a contradictory reality and calls into question the whole elaborate bottom–up planning framework of local governments.

According to many observers, local authorities lacked real financial power. For example, a visiting president of the Zimbabwean Association of Rural District Councils observed that Uganda's central government had retained the major sources of revenue and had only decentralised minimal sources, such as graduated tax and trade licensing, which did not derive substantial revenue (*The New Vision*, 7 October 1999). Though local governments complained when graduated tax was abolished, performance indicators for a number of districts showed the number of defaulters had been increasing since 1993. The Three-year Development Plan for Mukono District reveals the trends clearly (see Table 3.1 below).

Table 3.1 Revenue Performance, Mukono District for Years 1993-1996

Financial Year	Estimates in UG Shs.	Actual Receipts in UG Shs.	No. Tax Payers Registered	No. Paid	Number of Defaulters
93/94	1,845,583,000	1,359,321,000	115,516	109,687	5,829
94/95	2,249,492,000	2,037904,000	121,945	99,504	22,441
95/96	1,945,456,000	1,407,567,000	125,902	108,980	16,922

Source: Mukono District, Three-year Development Plan, 1993-1997.

Factors that explain the trend visible in Table 3.1 include inelastic domestic revenue, a small number of taxpayers which did not increase in relation to the increasing population, as well as low taxable rates due to unemployment and under-employment. Inadequate and delayed payment of taxes, coupled with tax evasion[4] and inadequate accountability, theft and embezzlement of public funds were seen to compound the matter.

Further, the limitation on local revenue was traced through the fact that central government retained control over the major sources of revenue, such as natural resources. According to the Second Schedule of the LGA (1997), the central government retained functions related to land, mines, minerals and water resources and the environment, as well as responsibility for national parks and policies for forests and game reserves.

The above trends in local revenue meant that the most stable source of revenue for local government was central government transfers (Livingstone & Charlton, 2000). Central government transfers were divided into three types: conditional grants, meant to be utilised, in the words of one official from the ministry of local government, 'according to what it was exactly meant for'. Unconditional grants, over which local governments had power or discretion of allocation for efficient service delivery as they deemed fit; and equalisation grants, aimed at achieving a national average.[5] Conditional funding dominates, constituting nearly 80% of all central transfers (see Table 3.2).

Table 3.2 : Transfers from Central Government to Local Government (UG Shs. Bn.)

	1997-1998		1998-1999		1999-2000		2000-2001	
	UG Shs. bn	%	UG Shs bn	%	UG Shs. bn	%	UG Shs. bn	%
Conditional Grants	54	24	64	23	67	17	79	15
Conditional Grants Recurrent	168	75	202	71	275	71	321	63
Conditional Grants Development	2	1	19	7	45	12	107	21
Unconditional Grants	0	0	0	0	2	0	4	1
Total	224	100	285	101	389	100	511	100

Source: Fancis & James (2003).

One district chairperson was quoted as saying that that decentralisation was doomed to fail because conditional grants were promoted at the expense of unconditional grants. In his view, such conditional grants with strings attached abuse the decentralisation process, as local authorities had no say over the money:

> We (at the districts) are postal messengers promoting conditional grants at the expense of unconditional grants… districts have burning issues which demand funding, but due to the conditionality of the money released from the centre, those issues cannot be addressed (*The Crusader Newspaper,* 30 January, 1999).

The Ministry of Local Government linked financial transfers to local governments to specific purposes in the form of conditional grants because local governments were apparently not allocating adequate resources to government priority areas, among which poverty eradication.[6] One official from the ministry asserted that central government had been compelled to award a large part of development grants as conditional grants due to the meagre resources and the fact that most of these funds come from donor support. While government's view was that the approach of conditional grants was transitional, aimed at achieving minimum national standards (Republic of Uganda, 1998), local governments claimed they were constrained in identifying meaningful priorities based on the specific needs of communities in relation to funds received as central government transfers.

The above funding framework reflected directly into district budgets. Considering the budget framework for Mukono District 1997-2000, it is clear that central government transfers formed the bulk of local government revenue sources and, of these, conditional grants formed the highest percentage, as shown in Table 3.3 below:

Table 3.3: Mukono District Revenue Sources and Performance 1997-2000

	1997/1998		1998/1999		1999/2000[7]	
Source of funding	Estimated Shs. (000)	Receipts Shs. (000)	Estimated Shs. (000)	Receipts Shs. (000)	Estimated Shs. (000)	Receipts Shs. (000)
Unconditional Grants	2,370,570	2,639,507	3,221,656	3,180,164	3,264,450	1,632,229
Conditional Grants	7,417,161	794,097	9,953,596	9,818,059	11,532,591	5,187,174
Donor Funds	2,085,879	1,446,995	2,884,089	1,759,946	3,678,824	1,086,915
Local Revenue	3,045,104	1,820,546	3,330,446	2,445,285	4,424,878	480,363
Total	**14,918,714**	**13,881,145**	**19,405,645**	**17,203,454**	**22,900,743**	**8,386,681**

Source: Mukono District Council 2000/2001-2002/2003, Budget Framework.

As shown in Table 3.3, conditional grants formed well over 50% of the revenue sources for the district while central government transfers together with donor funds constituted 85% to 90% of the total budget receipts. This meant that, in Mukono, local government functioning in terms of planning was limited, since most of these grants came with regulations and constraints to guide their utilisation. Similar observations apply to the financial position of district councils elsewhere. In Zimbabwe, Mutizwa-Mangiza and Conyers note, for instance, that councils' heavy reliance on central government financial allocations for both capital and, recurrent expenditure eroded financial autonomy and, in their view, the very essence of decentralisation in Zimbabwe (1996:87).[8]

The trend in Table 3.3 seemed to be exacerbated by the aloof and technical thrust of district civil servants. During the preparation of budget estimates for the financial year 2001/2002, the director of health care in Mukono made a presentation to the Sectoral Committee for Health and Community Services and indicated that the budget estimates he presented for the financial year 2001/02 were influenced by the following:

1. Budget Call Circular by the Directorate of finance and planning

2. Budget Framework paper by Ministry of Finance and Economic Planning

3. Policies and Priority Health Programmes by Ministry of Health

4. Donor concerns on poverty alleviation strategies.

In other words, the impetus for planning was largely external to the district council, the otherwise supreme organ of the system. In Sectoral Committee meetings I attended, it was not uncommon to hear technical staff stress, in their presentations, that they were following guidelines set by the ministry. One sensed that, in some cases, this claim was used as an excuse to avoid critical issues raised by the councillors. It was also remarked in a sectoral meeting in Mukono, that some heads of department did not respect sectoral committees, to the extent that they either absented themselves without apology or did not bother to prepare adequately.

But the accusation was not unilateral. Technical staff also accused councillors of emphasising politics at the expense of development. For instance, as implementors, technical staff claimed that regulations which made them subordinate to local councillors 'had made it difficult to impose discipline in revenue collection. Politicians at all levels encourage default,' in the view of many civil servants (Francis & James, 2003:330). During a training workshop in Kumi,[9] it was interesting to witness accusations and counter accusations, with technical staff insisting that councillors were engaged in 'empty fire', i.e. they assumed enormous power and authority, yet they were technically ignorant.

Is politics antithetical to development? Civil servants are generally of the view that politicians are more interested in votes than in people's development. A community development officer illustrated his viewpoint. He said that before decentralisation, the chief ensured that households adhered to minimum standards of hygiene, such as having a pit latrine and a compost pit. Food security was also enforced through a policy which expected each household to have a barn (*ekitara*) for storing harvest. According to the community development officer, these initiatives did not exist anymore. Household hygiene had deteriorated, in his view because politicians would not motivate people into such directions. Motivated by the fear of losing votes, politicians were allegedly even hampering district programmes. Interestingly, such top-down policies as the one on hygiene also regulated intra-household relations. Men, as heads of households, were answerable for such matters. During the fieldwork for this study, the researcher came across two women who had taken their husbands to the LC courts because they had failed to construct pit latrines. The wife dug small pits for the children to relieve themselves in the banana plantation. The neighbours complained that this practice was posing a health hazard, but the husband paid no heed. The wife then went to the village (LC1) court, which dismissed her case. The case was only resolved at sub-county (LC3) level. The man was finally forced to construct a pit latrine. Indeed, this struggle would not have arisen if minimum standards had been enforced.

However, some people believed that participation at local level was yeilding results. In a discussion (February 2003) in Kanungu, district councillors pointed out that one positive aspect of decentralisation was that it had brought power down to the local level and people could express their views and identify local needs. In some villages, the 25% of local revenue returned to the village level had been used to improve water sources and other problems identified by the communities themselves. In other cases, however, local power dynamics were at play and the men tended to dominate processes such as the budget conference, such that the priorities identified did not reflect the needs of the majority. The general trend identified was that these budget conferences became less and less meaningful to the general populace as the relationship between the priorities set and actual service delivery became more remote.

Another significant aspect of the technocratic mode is corruption, especially in the lucrative area of tendering. Reports of corruption in the tendering process are common in local newspapers and NGO reports.

A survey by Uganda Debt Network (UDN), an NGO monitoring issues of accountability in the conduct of government business, conducted in the districts of Soroti, Kumi and Kaberamaido, found that millions of shillings under the School Facilitation Grant (SFG) had been lost to shoddy work. SFG funds were set aside by central government to improve and expand primary school facilities, especially through construction of classrooms. A number of schools were in a sorry state, according to the report, with roofs blown off by the wind even before the buildings had been completed. The report further observed: 'In some cases it seems that the shoddy work was carried out with the collusion of some high ranking district officers' (UDN, 2002). It was alleged that this state of affairs had benefited some councillors, especially men with informal networks, who fronted particular companies where they evidently had vested interests.[10] One contractor in Arua District was quoted during open discussion before the Tender Board:

> To call a spade a spade: you need backing from someone in the Tender Board before you will be awarded a building contract (Republic of Uganda, Project Document, DDP Pilot, 1997:38).[11]

An official from the ministry of local government, however, sought to put the issue of corruption into perspective. To him, the problem of corruption had little to do with decentralisation. Rather, corruption should be seen as a broader problem of development. Perhaps the evaluative mode in which decentralisation is approached has meant that everything happening at the local level – particularly on the negative side, is attributed to decentralisation. This particular comment redirected leads to an analysis of decentralisation in more fluid as opposed to rigid casual terms. The fact that corruption and irregularities persisted despite decentralisation should not be surprising since, in the first place, the same people tender and the same elite group vet tenders as prior to decentralisation. By implication, therefore, what should be at stake is finding solutions to corruption in general and addressing it as a national question.

Apart from corruption as an irregularity, the tendering process technically excluded the poor and the less influential. For example, the Tender Notice for Mukono District gazetted on 2 July 2002 had 23 items to be tendered, which included construction, maintenance and procurement of goods. Except for two items, the rest of the requirements favoured established companies or businesses (see Box below).

Requirements for Tender Applications Mukono District Council,

2001/2002 Tender Notice, July 2, 2001

1. A copy of the general receipt for the non-refundable fees
2. Samples (items to be supplied where applicable)
3. A valid trade licence (2001/02)
4. Certificate of incorporation
5. Income tax clearance
6. Documentary evidence of past performance
7. Bankers
8. Physical and postal address
9. Terms of payment must be indicated
10. All prices quoted must be in Uganda Shillings and must indicate VAT separately
11. Tin number must be indicated
12. VAT registration copy

Source: *The New Vision* 2 July 2001.

The closing date for the notice was July 17, about two weeks after the notice. The tender notice was for the whole year, meaning that the Tender Board could keep on calling on the same tenderers as the need arose. Yet the tender notices are supposed to correspond to the priorities identified in the council budget. In order to compete successfully, those who tender have to have access to information prior to the notice, so as to prepare all the required documents.

Communities also strongly criticised the fact that they were far removed from the process of tendering. In a group discussion at Misindye in Mukono (August 2001), the example of construction of pit latrines was given. It was observed that contracts were awarded to people from outside the local community to construct pit latrines at high cost, whereas local people could construct them at half the cost.

Community development workers were of the view that participation would have been meaningful if the poor had been mobilised to provide some of the goods and services that did not require heavy machinery and financial input, such as the supply of plant material, piglets, simple furniture, construction of pit latrines and basic water sources. It was observed that the procurement process largely benefited the rich and technically excluded the poor, particularly women. In their view, the rigid formal rules and technicalities functioned to conceal the heavily guarded lucrative ground for the Tender Board and the elite business community. Instead, community participation was advocated in less lucrative arenas or where free labour was anticipated, for example, water committees.

Critical to the decentralisation process in Uganda is the question of territoriality, the fusion of identity with specific territories. The notion of territory has far-reaching implications for citizenship generally and for gender identity in particular. The Commission of Inquiry set up in 1989 to investigate the system of local government gave as a general recommendation, that decentralisation in Uganda should lie between deconcentration and full-blooded devolution, because the latter would have a disintegrative effect in view of the country's fragile history (S.2). This is what Barya relates to when he argues that, while it is important that most services are controlled at the local level, decentralisation should be handled carefully and democratically to 'avoid situations where dominant or historically or strategically advantaged nationalities exploit or disadvantage other nationalities' (1996:136). The notions of territoriality and homogeneity that are embedded within the logic of decentralisation in Uganda tended to create more distancing than inclusive discourses. This raises questions about how local ethnic identity becomes operable and how gender operates to construct these identities.

The LGA (1997) allows local governments to manage their cultural affairs. This opened up space for expression of rights and belonging, resulting in the quest for formation of new districts constituted of a people formerly subsumed under dominant cultures (Kayunga, 2001).

Within ten years, between 1992 and 2002, eleven new districts were created. In 2005 thirteen more districts were added to make a total of 69 (see Appendix iv).

The very notion of people determining their own destiny and the impulse towards cultural homogeneity is problematic in the context of Uganda, a country with a very complex ethnic composition and heterogeneity. Specifically, it has far-reaching gender implications. For women who, as a result of marriage, often reside in districts other than their own, the quest for homogeneity would automatically rob them of social legitimacy in the respective local governments. For example, the power of the districts to employ staff encouraged what was locally known as the 'son of the soil syndrome'. Within District Service Commissions, the tendency was for each district to employ people who regarded a particular district as their native home (Kayunga, 2000). During the 2001 LC elections, one of the salient issues in Mukono related to eliminating foreigners and giving jobs to 'sons of the soil'. If this kind of localised discourse were allowed to flourish, it could marginalise people and communities perceived as non-native in the specific districts. This is what some critics have termed 'ethnic nation building' (*The Monitor*, 8 July 1997).[12]   In this regard, civil servants suffered the 'freezing effect' of decentralisation. A civil servant was stuck in a district and at the level at which decentralisation found him or her (Kyomuhendo, 1994).

This is a complex report of how local ethnic identity becomes operable at the local level, contradicting the efforts of nation-building towards a unitary citizenship. How does gender intersect? As will be demonstrated in the analysis of elections and council experiences, women are more often disqualified as direct biological expressions of the local clan or ethnic body, because most adult women reside in conjugal rather than natal homes. Also, as Mbatha (2003) observes in a study of local government in South Africa, the salience of ethnic politics further diminishes the prospect that gender equality concerns will be treated seriously. Without implying that all of custom is negative, there is a need to re-theorise decentralisation, to take into account possible disintegrative effects and how to address it.

The decentralisation process in Uganda can be said to demonstrate simultaneous spaces of inclusion and exclusion. It is, however, important to observe that the process is still evolving and dependent on the balance of social forces, such as interest groups (including women), civil society, councils, as well as central government. At this point, therefore, the focus is not on specific end results but rather on the democratic potential of the process and how, for instance, gender is played out in the different arenas of political space at the local level.

Women, Patronage and the Legacy of Mobilisation in Local Government

Beyond the general level, where the technocratic mode seems to exclude the poor and the less influential, there are ways in which women are marginalised further by specific patronage mechanisms. This is analysed by considering the role and place of parallel structures and the discourse of women as part of the 'marginalised' or 'vulnerable' groups.

By their formal description, Women Councils (WCs) are developmental and not political structures symbolically defining the former out of politics, as if 'developmental' were an uncontested terrain. The WCs are supposed to foster women's development through mobilisation and participation in income-generating projects. WCs also formed part of the electoral colleges for women district representatives to parliament at the time. Beyond this general level, however, their roles and status are ambiguous. To many, these councils (WCs in particular) were merely diversionary. Winnie Byanyima, then a member of parliament and a woman, had no kind words for Women Councils. She said:

> I don't like them [Women Councils]. I want them scrapped. I want women to go for real power. Any structure that is parallel, that takes them away from the real power and takes their time, which they have so little of, is diversional. The real place where women should be running and influencing the local government... I want women to participate in government like men in the councils (cited in Tripp, 2001a:125-6).

The relationship between these (Women and Youth) Councils and LCs is precarious. For instance, at village (LC 1) and parish (LC 2) levels, the chairperson of the WC is legally part of the Executive Committee; but at local government levels, WCs have no legal existence and they are only allowed as observers in district and sub-county council meetings. Since these councils are under the ambit of a central ministry, they cannot make a demand on local governments. At local government level, their roles are unclear. Only some minimum consensus seems to have been built in specific instances. For example, in a number of districts, these councils are provided with token resources to organise the International Women's Day and Youth Day. This is, however, not mandatory.

In a discussion, the chairperson of Youth Council in Mukono District cited president Museveni who, in defense of the councils, said that 'if you want to spray cows, you put them in a crush'. This chairperson said:

> Women and Youth Councils are supposed to just give marginalised groups an address (or point of contact). They are mobilisation vehicles because if a politician wants to capture women or youth, he or she gives money to the relevant chairperson who will easily do the mobilisation (interview, July 2001).

The views of the youth chairperson seemed to endorse patronage politics in the sense that he saw women and youth as clients of national and district politicians. This, perhaps, stemmed from the larger structuring of people's understanding of the political system.

Yet, these structures are not without influence and effect. The WCs, like other non-political organisations, such as church and singing groups, can act as training spaces for women in leadership, or arenas of 'political apprenticeship' (Goetz, 2003b:125). Though not adequate, the WCs seemed to open a window to the otherwise airtight recruitment system of leadership that mostly favoured men. For instance, the deputy speaker and secretary for finance, Mukono District Council (1998-2002) were formerly in WCs. The deputy speaker, in particular, explicitly connected her presence in the District Council to her participation in the WC.

Case: Deputy Speaker: The Road to the District Council - via the WC

I was born in Kiboga District; my father was a sub-county chief. After my first degree I contested in the RC system and became the RC4 general secretary and subsequently became a district councillor. I was encouraged to stand for parliament and got through to the then NRC and subsequently to the CA. I then married a man who hails from Mukono District and when I stood in Mukono I lost on those very grounds of marriage that I was a foreigner. I started to mobilise women's groups and joined WC and came to the district as the chairperson. When decentralisation was introduced I contested in the LC system because I knew the status of the WC. By this time I was already known to the people, and was elected as councillor and further elected unopposed as deputy speaker (interview, Mukono, 2000).

The above case demonstrates how participation in seemingly insignificant structures helped this particular woman to overcome some of the gender-specific modes of exclusion and barriers to legitimate authority. But the question that may arise is: at what cost are such structures, which are symbolically and materially alienated from mainstream political praxis, beneficial to women? A number of women at the local level were asked whether WCs should be disbanded. The majority proposed that the WCs needed to be resourced adequately and their roles streamlined. Their view is that the WCs offered space for women to pursue their agenda beside male-dominated LCs. In practice though WCs could be seen as a diverting of women's energies, further distancing women from mainstream contestation in local government. The WCs seemed to 'impose a double duty of political participation on women, as women are also enjoined to engage with the local government system' (Goetz, 2003b:125).

The other phenomenon resulting from intense politicisation in the 1980s and the years that followed the NRM takeover, was the emergence of a discourse on 'marginalised groups'. In contemporary Uganda marginalised or disadvantaged groups are defined to include women, the youth and people with disabilities, and sometimes children. Concern was expressed about marginalised groups in national policy documents, such as the Poverty Eradication Action Programme (PEAP) and the Plan for Modernisation of Agriculture (PMA). At the local level, a district document would not be complete without a mention of the marginalised, also referred to as vulnerable, groups. This, indeed, is a positive development, that political structures are sensitive to the fact that marginalisation existed.

Yet the language of marginality is not without problems. The lumping together of women and youth, for example, has far-reaching political significance. Evidently, the discourse infantilises. It is not uncommon to hear comparisons of youth and women, as if these identities have similar social bases. In one of the sectoral committee meetings in Mukono, it was observed that the youth, as opposed to women, were a difficult group to deal with, because they wanted projects that offered quick returns and their priorities were always shifting. An example was given that it was very hard to plan for the youth because you might offer them clonal coffee when they were actually interested in brick-making. Since this observation was made in comparison with women, one might therefore infer from it that planning for women was unproblematic and they would embrace whatever project was brought to them. Here inspiration is drawn from Barrett (1992) who argued that language constructs meanings, rather than merely expressing it. This book argues that such a discourse constructs women as mere recipients, rather than major actors in the political system. Implications of such and similar discourses are that women increasingly become constructed as clients of local government as opposed to actors and shapers in it.

At a practical level, the view that women would take any project planned on their behalf increased the failure rate of a number of projects. A female councillor in Kanungu District reported her experience (February 2003). There was a programme to distribute clonal coffee seedlings in the district. She acquired some and planted it on one of the family plots. But the husband had other plans for the plot and he planted woodlots in the same plot. Consequently the coffee trees wilted. This story reveales flaws in the whole construction of women as 'unproblematic' consumers of local government services.

The discourse on women as unproblematic participants could therefore have far-reaching implications for how women would proceed to make claims on the system and how these claims could be received. The language employed in policy documents and general political discourse seem to depoliticise the gender question, and define women as intrinsically vulnerable — together with children, people with disabilities and youth. The status accorded to women then becomes problematic. To group women with youth, for example, is to give them the status of minors. The difference, though, is that the youth will become elders — true citizens. Women, by being defined specifically as 'other' as 'minor', will have that status forever.

Furthermore, 'marginalised groups' fall under the ambit of an equally marginalised directorate — of gender and community services. A number of districts exhibited an almost consistent pattern namely that this directorate was the least resourced directorate. When decisions had to be made regarding the scrapping of a sectoral committee in the District Council, community services was the first in line to be scrapped and pegged onto other sectors, with the rationale that it was a cross-cutting issue.[13] In Kumi and Mukono, the sector of community services was combined with health where, in actual fact, it was subsumed and underrated. According to the community development officer of Kumi District, the cross-cutting nature of gender ended up translating into a lack of concrete programmes and hence minimal budget allocations and programme commitment. Technical staff working in these directorates observed that even the meagre funds allocated were not actually released as budgeted. The conclusion is that the language used for marginalised groups mainly served the purpose of including women as subjects of patronage, which involved them being regarded as secondary citizens.

The decentralisation process in Uganda could be said to demonstrate simultaneous spaces of inclusion and exclusion. It is, however, important to observe that the process is still evolving and dependent on the balance of social forces, such as interest groups (including women), civil society, councils, as well as central government. At this point, therefore, the focus is not on specific end results but rather on the democratic potential of the process and how, for instance, gender is played out in the different arenas of political space at the local level.

The chapters that follow attempt to problematise the inclusion of women within the institutional framework described above, in relation to processes of legitimation, especially with regard to leadership and gendered local governance. Experiences of women, particularly with regard to electoral processes and leadership, and the possible reconfigurations of authority engendered by this very process, are examined, as well as how representation of women's interests can be addressed in the context of the local government system in Uganda.

Notes

1. The actual constitution of the one-third women at the different levels of local councils is examined in Chapter Four.

2. A gender audit was carried out in 2002 by the Department of Women and Gender Studies (DWGS), Makerere University, to assess gender capacities of local governments. The capacities evaluated were awareness and understanding of gender, the skills required to translate this awareness into practice, representation on decision-making bodies, planning and resource allocation, among others.

3. There is a resident district commissioner (RDC) in every district. Though not a structure as such, the RDC is provided for in the Local Governments Act, as a presidential appointee and not part of the elected representatives of the district, whose function it is to represent the president and government in the district, especially in matters of security and any other matters of national importance (LGA 1997 Part VII).

4. For Mukono District, which involves a large part of Lake Victoria, this is a critical problem. Through a discussion (January 2000), councillors in Ngogwe Sub-county bordering the lake, observed that taxpayers (men) often migrate to islands at the time of tax assessment and collection. The islands, though part of the district, are not easily accessible.

5. Equalisation grants are supposed to be remitted to disadvantaged local governments in order to minimise disparities.

6. Government Priority Programme Areas (PPAs) include primary education, roads, primary health care, agricultural extension and rural water supply (Decentralisation Secretariat, 1997).
7. The 1999/2000 cash receipts refer to the first six months of the financial year.
8. The space available does not allow for a detailed examination of the question of autonomy as it relates to the debate of decentralisation. However, it is worth noting that many critics of decentralisation view this as a more or less positive aspect, as it could serve to check the powers of the local elite (see for example, Khadiagala, 2000; Bryld, 2000).
9. A workshop on gender training and skills development for decentralisation, carried out by the Department of Women and Gender Studies, Makerere University, Kumi District, 17-20 December 2001.
10. One Ogole called on the IGG (Inspector General of Government) to probe Lira District Tender Board: 'The officers are abusing their offices without fear. They award tenders unfairly. Most of the district work done has been shoddy... This defeats the purpose of decentralisation, which is to empower the poor' (*The New Vision*, 13 September 2001).
11. The study did not attempt to verify these claims, firstly because records of the Tender Board are confidential. Pursuing this question would have also shifted the research into more complex directions, whereas the major aim was to capture gendered aspects of political space in a relatively normalised environment.
12. A personnel officer in Kabarole District observed that, in his view, decentralisation was creating and nurturing intolerance against non-indigenous district residents. He asserted that prejudice against 'strangers' undermined the progress of the country as a whole.
13. This trend seems to fit well into the national and international discourse of gender mainstreaming, but mainstreaming is a concept that is often used without a concrete understanding of what it entails in terms of actual mechanisms for addressing gender gaps.

4

From Exclusion to Directed Inclusion: Women and the Question of Quotas in Uganda

The previous chapter sketched the contours of the local government system in Uganda, specifically mapping the location of women. The explicit provisions for women's representation contained in both the Constitution (1995) and the LGA (1997) ensure the presence of women in local government leadership and decision-making structures. This chapter analyses the mode and effects of that inclusion. Through what process did explicit provisions about women come into place? What informed the nature of the specific inclusion of women in local government structures? This process is traced through the constitution-making process, and a review of the relevant debates in the Constituent Assembly (CA) (1994/5), a body that debated the new constitution.

Reviewing how the inclusion provisions translate into actual electoral mechanisms, the directed nature of women's presence is examined. Women's inclusion as directed is conceptualised with reference to Molyneux, who, in her analysis of women's mobilisation, makes a distinction between independent movements and directed mobilisations (1998:229). Directed mobilisations, according to Molyneux (1998), occur in a context of greater control by a higher authority and where genuine negotiation over goals is limited. Analysing women's political participation in Peru, Blondet (2002) examined a similar phenomenon that she termed the 'Devil's Deal' in Fujimori's regime in the 1990s. Blodent's conclusion is that what happened in Peru was a machismo project to mobilise women to expand support for the regime. However, this stance attributes too much power to state leaders and by the same token discounts women of possessing any social agency. The sense in which the term 'directed inclusion' is used in Uganda's case is therefore to denote a dynamic process involving women struggling and achieving relative 'access' gains within a highly state-controlled process.

The conclusion of the chapter takes a comparative approach. Experiences from South Africa and India, two other countries where women have accessed local government structures in relatively large numbers in the recent past, are compared. The comparison is aimed at clarifying the unique nature of Uganda's political system and explaining how this informs the specific mechanisms for addressing questions of gender equality in political representation.

Tracing the Inclusion Debate in the Constituent Assembly (CA 1994)

Constitutional change was one of the major facets of the fundamental change that the NRM promised on assuming power in 1986. Accordingly, a Constitutional Commission was appointed by the president in 1989. The Commission completed its work of consulting the people and presented a Report and Draft Constitution in 1992 (Republic of Uganda, 1999). Elections to the CA were held in March 1994 and the CA debated the draft constitution for 16 months (Bazaara, 2003). Bazaara (2003) notes that both critics and supporters of the NRM alike agree that the 1995 Constitution was the result of the most participatory process in the history of Uganda.[1] Specifically, with regard to the gender dimension, Tamale, citing the *Chicago Tribune* (1 December 1996) considers the 1995 constitution to be one of the most "woman friendly" constitutions worldwide (1999:116).

During the CA, local government was one of the critical issues debated. In its report, the committee that was charged with deliberating on local government stated that discussions had been guided, first by the principle of decentralisation and, secondly by the desire to empower the people. The main points aired related to the principle of 'power to the people', local government financial autonomy and local government's power to make laws (Republic of Uganda, 1995b). The debate about decentralisation or federalism focused on whether smaller or larger units would ensure people's power and participation against what was termed the experience of the exercise of power from the centre. It was seen as a critical question for power in a political system. In particular, the majority of delegates from the central region of Buganda threw their weight behind federalism as opposed to decentralisation. Partly, this was because Buganda had enjoyed federal status prior to the Republican Constitution of 1967. One delegate, Mr. Apolo Nsibambi (a presidential nominee) argued that decentralisation was essentially borrowed power, whereas the federal model conferred constitutional powers on local government and thus the capacity to plan in a predictable manner. Federalism, he argued, would empower people by creating constitutional arrangements and making it possible for people to concretise power (Republic of Uganda, 1995b:3,602). 'Too much blood has been shed in this country and in other parts of Africa. We have no option but to empower people…', Nsibambi asserted.

In the CA, local government and its related institutional arrangements were seen as key factors in the transition to and quest for stable and enduring political arrangements. The House was generally agreed on transferring the principle of power to the people. Contributing to the debate, Hope Mwesigye, a female delegate, submitted that since the House had already passed a provision guaranteeing that Uganda would be governed and guided by democratic principles which empowered and encouraged people's effective participation, there was a need to 'take the level of government to as low a level as possible to enable people to participate effectively' (Republic of Uganda, 1995b:3,619). According to the record, a total of 35 delegates contributed to the debate, with 19 delegates (all male) supporting the motion for a federal system. Fifteen delegates, 12 male and 3 female, opposed the motion. In the end, decentralisation carried the day partly owing to the overwhelming NRM power bloc in the CA.[2] The votes of the female delegates against federalism was generally attributed to their support for the NRM (Oloka-Onyango, 1998). However, there could have been an additional factor relating to a fear of regional power, and the difficulties associated with advancing a gender equality agenda under more or less ethnic arrangements (Goetz, 2003b).

Flowing into the debate on people's participation was the issue of women's representation. Katenta Apuuli, the chairperson of Committee Four that deliberated on the chapter on local government, presented the committee amendments to the draft, one of which related to membership of councils. Article 205 Clause (2) paragraph (b) read in part: 'one third of the membership of each local government council shall be reserved for women,' and paragraph (c), 'any law enacted by virtue of this article shall provide for affirmative action in favour of marginalised and disadvantaged groups' (Republic of Uganda, 30 March, 1995b:3,704).

Reactions to the amendment ranged from lukewarm reception to outright objection. Brig. Kyaligonza moved a motion to oppose the amendment, arguing that since affirmative action had been enshrined in the constitution, there was no reason for reserving one-third of the membership for women. He said:

> Women as their right should have equal participatory democracy. After all they are the majority, and in our national objectives, Mr. Chairman, national objective No. 9, it is already mentioned in clause (3) that all people of Uganda shall have access to leadership positions at all levels subject only to the constitution and other laws in Uganda. Mr. Chairman, the rationale for favouring this group the committee is regarding as marginalised, is unreasonable on the grounds that women or all citizens have equal rights to compete in leadership positions... this participatory democracy should not be pushed too much in terms of favouritism, so people should stand on their own right and be elected accordingly (ibid:3, 707).

Another member had similar concerns:

> I find this particular provision as an excessive and detrimental approach to what has been dubbed affirmative action (ibid: 3,707).

Women delegates spoke up to defend the amendment on women's representation, which was on the verge of being deleted. Jeninah Ntabgoba reacted thus:

> I start with heartache in reply to Brig. Kyaligonza who hides behind the support of the marginalised groups according to his references

and then he ends up abusing women's rights at the same time... I would like to inform the Hon. Kyaligonza that any forum without women will come out without sound results; therefore, this one-third is not as a big fraction to scare him. In fact I would ask him to increase the number... (ibid: 3,707).

Winfred Masiko, another female delegate, said that participatory democracy might sound virtuous, but had not delivered much in real terms and specific instruments to enable women to participate in all levels of governance, particularly at the local level. She referred to constitutions of Morocco and Nepal, which provided for specific quotas for the chamber of representatives and members of parliament respectively. Victoria Ssebagereka concurred with Masiko's submission and added that, instead of one-third it should have actually read 'at least one-third' and, in her view, this would encourage women from non-participation into taking part in the decision-making process. She said:

> I know right now RC1 up to RC5 there is one woman representative and the ideas of women which are brought in those councils are normally suffocated because you have one woman against eight men. But if they are six women or if they are four women... when a woman brings an idea and men are against it at least there will be more voices to support that idea... I call upon all men supporting the women's cause. Please do not let this (motion) go through (ibid: 3,709).

In the above submission, Ssebagereka advanced the idea that increased numbers of women would enhance the gender capacity of local government structures in the direction of supporting more women-friendly policies and programmes. Evidently, this assertion is contentious. The gender capacity of institutions does not always necessarily correspond to the numbers of women therein although the question of numbers cannot be discounted completely. However, it was fair enough for the women delegates to anchor their lobby in numbers.

During the debate, female delegates were constantly interrupted by their male counterparts. Janet Okorimoe had to appeal to the chair for protection 'Mr Chairman, protect me from Hon. Atwoma, I have even moved away from him but he is still harassing me.' The chair had to appeal to the delegate to 'leave the young lady alone' (ibid.: 3,712). In another instance, the chair advised one male delegate a sexist remark in itself!, 'Please do not heckle the Hon. member' (ibid.: 3,713). One male member who had been part of Committee Four that recommended the amendment, turned around, and said that, having heard from the floor, he thought that the Committee might have been too generous or too inconsistent (ibid.: 3,714). In response, a female delegate rose and objected strongly to what she saw as an overly misogynist or anti-woman approach in most male delegates, decrying the fact that some male members had been overheard saying that men who supported women should have gone back to 'put on dresses' (ibid.: 3,713). The debate turned into a contest between men and women, although quite a number of men did support the amendment.

Complicating the matter of the amendment was the question of how the one–third representation would be obtained. Several questions were raised, including whether the one-third women would be appointed to council; would male delegates be asked to stand down in favour of female delegates; and what formula would be applied to calculate women's representation? One delegate asked whether specific sub-counties would be told and directed to permit only women to represent them. For some delegates, establishing constitutional percentages would, in the long run, work against the interests of women, since it could set a limit of one-third to the seats women could occupy.

The majority of the women delegates based their arguments on non-threatening and instrumentalist grounds—that having a reasonable number of women in local government was good for development. This is reminiscent of arguments found in United Nations and development documents to the effect that development goals could not be achieved without the full participation of women (Karl, 1995). Some of the men who supported the amendment held similar views, for instance, that since women formed the bulk of the population at the local level, local governments would gain by tapping into the experiences of women who confronted livelihood problems on a day-to-day basis.

Some women delegates, though, also addressed the question of power and subordination. Lagada, for example, appealed:

> I believe in this assembly we have the cream of Ugandan men who are woman friendly... I am appealing to the members that, when we are thinking about the women, let us think about what our culture, what our society for the last over two hundred years has done to the women... Mr Chairman, I think the Hon. women delegates who are here who stood in this last CA Elections in the counties against men will bear witness that they probably had to surmount a lot more odds than their male counterparts. When you are a woman and you are standing in an election you are not only going to be judged for yourself or for your sins, you are also going to be judged for the sins of your husband... majority at the grassroots ... still believe that men are the ones... more fit for politics (Republic of Uganda, 1995b:3,710-1).

A total of 15 delegates contributed to this particular debate; seven women and eight men. Only four men actually opposed the clause of female representation, but they made their contributions in a strong and sometimes derogatory manner that threatened to swing the mood of the whole assembly. The female delegates and the voices of the men who opposed the amendment were more concerned with development, 'appealing to basic logic' (Tamale, 1999:117).[3] Wandira Kazibwe, for instance, ended her submission with the strong statement, "Mr Chairman I beg vehemently, and I really want to vehemently oppose the motion on this floor" (ibid.: 3,717). The amendment for a one-third quota for women at all levels of local government was retained in the end, and the motion to delete the amendment was rejected.

It can be argued, however, that the apprehension about the formula and envisaged implementation problems were realistic in view of the absence of an opposition voice and organised competition in Uganda's political system at the time. But in many respects, the one-third female representation on all councils was indeed a significant gain. It ensured and guaranteed the presence of women in local government structures in numbers that had never been achieved before. Moreover, one-third women representation was not the limit, since they could also contest the general parish and sub-county seats.

The above gains were attributable partly to the efforts of women inside and outside the Assembly in the constitution-making process (Tamale, 1999). According to Tamale, the draft constitution, the basic document for CA debates, had not proposed any sex quota at the local government level. The language was generally gender-blind too (1999:116). The CA was a skewed assembly, with token numbers of female delegates. The tokenism was not merely about the numbers (50 out of 286 delegates) but also related to what Tamale (1999) views as chauvinism and patriarchy. What, therefore, accounts for the range of achievements of the constitution?

Two specific developments emerged during the CA. One was the formation of the Women's Caucus, a loose but consistent and issue-based association of female delegates; and the other was the establishment of the Gender Information Centre (GIC), which provided support to women delegates in particular.[4] The GIC acted as a forum for meeting and discussion as well as a focal point for lobbying, strategy and consensus-building (Nakirunda, 2000). Women's organisations such as ACFODE, UWONET and NAOWU together with the Ministry of Gender, Labour and Social Development, organised seminars for female voters and CA delegates. It is well documented that the synergy between the women's organisations, the Ministry of Gender and the Women's Caucus inside the CA made an impact unrivalled in the history of Ugandan politics and the women's movement (Tamale, 1999).

A report on the CA by the Ministry of Gender, Labour and Social Development, stated:

> The efforts of the Ministry of Gender and Community Development, Women NGOs and all who wanted the new constitution to be gender sensitive were rewarded with a document which meets their expectation. Uganda now leads the way in Africa by coming up with a constitution which lays a firm foundation for the advancement and emancipation of women (Republic of Uganda, 1995b).

The one-third reservation of seats for women in local government as one of the clear gains of the above process opened up a new set of questions. This chapter now turns to the specific policy provisions for elections and practical constitution of the one-third women's quota, in order to provide a basis for adequate analysis of the directed nature of women's inclusion.

The Policy of One-third Women's Representation: Peculiarities of Uganda's Quota System

Reserving seats for women within the existing constituencies would have meant that some sub-counties and parishes would be forced to have a woman as their representative. That would be dictational and show disregard for the democratic right to choose (interview with former CA delegate, November 1999).

The above statement was made by the deputy speaker of Mukono District (a woman) who had been a CA delegate and a member of Committee Four that dealt with the chapter on local government. Although almost all current literature on the Ugandan situation talks about the one-third reservation for women, in actual fact it is not so much a reservation as an accretion, as will be illustrated.

Under the Local Governments Act (1997), women are elected separately, as are other categories of youth and PWDs. The one-third for women is derived as follows: At district and sub-county levels, the chairperson, directly elected councillors and representatives for youth and PWDs are taken as the two-thirds (LGA, 1997 Part III [ii]). The total number is thus determined by the original number of sub-counties or parishes, with the addition of the four PWD and youth representatives. The female councillors as a category are added to this number through a separate election. This does not, however, preclude women from standing for election in the direct election of councillors. All voters vote for all categories except the PWD and youth. This fact has led to the differentiation between the councillors and the women councillors.

Thus women councillors have a different constituency from the directly elected councillors and require specific demarcation of electoral areas. According to the LGA (1997):

The population quota of women representatives shall be determined by the requirement of women constituting a third of any Local Council being considered (Part X, Article 109 (3)).

In Article 111, the Act provides:

Whenever there are fewer women seats than lower Local Government units, the electoral areas for women councillors… may bring together two or more Local Council Units using a population quota determined by the Electoral Commission.

A report by the Electoral Commission (EC) on the 1997/8 election demonstrated the complexity of determining the one-third quota for women. The total number of the directly elected councillors and the four councillors, two representing the youth and two representing the PWDs, were divided by two to get the number of seats required for women (Republic of Uganda, 1999:2). The result of this calculation did not always coincide with the existing number of sub-counties or parishes and hence new constituencies had to be created. The report gave the example of Kiboga District. It had 14 seats for the directly elected councillors and, together with the youth and PWDs this made 18, giving nine as seats for women. In order to calculate women's representation for the entire district (i.e. the 14 sub-counties) small sub-counties adjacent to each other were combined to create only nine seats for women (Republic of Uganda, 1999:2). Big sub-counties or parishes were subdivided in the same way, in some cases according to a specific calculation. In other cases, if the resultant number of seats for women was a rational number, it was corrected upwards or downwards to the next integer. For example 3.5 was corrected to four (Republic of Uganda, 1999:2-3). Two examples are given, one district and one sub-county, to illustrate this arrangement, in the box below.

Inclusion Mechanisms for Women at District and Sub-county Levels

Example 1: District level: The Case of Mukono District Council 1997-2001

Mukono District: 32 sub-counties and 5 town councils (hence 37 constituencies)

     37 directly elected councillors

     2 PWD reps (1 male and 1 female)

     2 Youth representatives (1 male and 1 female)

     1 district chairperson

Sub-total: 42 taken as two-thirds of Council (divided by 2 to get 21 seats)

     21 women elected (added)

     37 constituencies reorganised to create 21 women's constituencies

Example 2: Sub-county level: The Case of Bukinda, Kabale District 1997-2001

Bukinda S/c: 6 parishes (6 parish constituencies)

     6 directly elected councillors

     2 PWDs (1 male and 1 female)

     2 Youth representatives (1 male and 1 female)

     1 chairperson

Sub-total: 11 taken as two-thirds of Council (divided by 2 to get 5.5 seats)

     5 women elected (added)

     6 parishes reorganised to create 5 women's constituencies

---

Source: Fieldwork, 2000.

The situation with administrative units i.e. LC4, LC2 and LC1 was different. Elections were conducted on the basis of the established ten positions of the executive committee and in this case, the electorate had to ensure that at least four of these positions were occupied by women. With the 2001 Amendment, where the chairperson was to nominate people to the executive committee, the particular chairperson was obliged to nominate at least four women. At this level, therefore, the term 'reservation' applied because the positions were fixed.

The electoral system for the several tiers and multiple layers of representatives is equally complex. There are elections by universal adult suffrage, as well as elections by electoral colleges and interest groups. Until 2001, LC elections were conducted in two ways, through the ballot box and by the electorate lining up behind the candidate or his or her representative or portrait. In popular parlance the latter is referred to as 'election by lining up'. There were amendments along the way and by 2001 secret ballot was universal. Below is a table that shows the elections of various positions at different levels.

Table 4.1 Types of Elections for Different Positions

Level	Position	Type of election	Nature of Election 1998	Nature of Election 2001/2
LC5	Chairperson	Adult Suffrage	Secret ballot	Secret ballot
	Direct councillors	Adult Suffrage	Secret ballot	Secret ballot
	Women councillors	Adult Suffrage	Lining up	Secret ballot
	Youth	Electoral College	Lining up	Secret ballot
	PWDs	Electoral College	Lining up	Secret ballot
LC4	Chairperson	Adult Suffrage	Lining up	Secret ballot
	Executive Committee	Adult Suffrage	Lining up	Secret ballot
LC3	Chairperson	Adult Suffrage	Secret ballot	Secret ballot
	Direct councillors	Adult Suffrage	Lining up	Secret ballot
	Women councillors	Adult Suffrage	Lining up	Secret ballot
	Youth	Electoral College	Lining up	Secret ballot
	PWDs	Electoral College	Lining up	Secret ballot
LC2	Chairperson	Electoral College	Lining up	Secret ballot
	Executive Committee	Electoral College	Lining up	Secret ballot
LC1	Chairperson	Adult Suffrage	Lining up	Secret ballot
	Executive Committee	Adult Suffrage	Lining up	Appointment by Chairperson elect

Source: Fieldwork notes (1998-2002).

Analysis reveals that provisions of the LGA (1997) were initially related closely to the relative legal importance attached to the different positions. The most critical positions, according to the local government framework, namely the chairpersons of the district and sub-county councils, as well as directly elected councillors at district level, were accorded high status by being elected by secret ballot from the outset. Those of female councillors, both at district and sub-county level, and all elections in lower councils, were originally designed to be conducted through the lining up system. Whereas lining up was popularised in the years of mobilisation and reconstruction (1986-89) as being a transparent and cost effective measure to combat election rigging, it lost its legitimacy over time. With the 2001/2 elections, lining up was abolished at all levels on the basis of its cumbersome nature.[5]   This eased the election process, but for women councillors, questions still remained in terms of the separate and unique electoral space.

In summary, though the term 'reservation' is employed in legal documents and academic writing, what has happened in Uganda is not reservation at all levels but rather a combination of reservation and accretion. Actual reservation occurs at the level of administrative units (village (LC1), parish (LC2) and county (LC 4)). At district (LC5) and sub-county (LC 3), the two major decision-making levels, women were included by expanding the council by accretion.

Translating Directed Inclusion into Electoral Mechanisms

How the directed inclusion of women translates into official electoral mechanisms is significant because its effect is to define women as separate, distinct and largely secondary citizens. The question of status or positionality begins at the lowest level of the formal election discourse. Apart from the administrative units, where categories of chairperson and the executive are gender-neutral, representation at the sub-county (LC3) and district (LC5) level has very specific categorisation that attaches specificity to women in particular. The categories used to distinguish candidates in these LC contests as chairpersons, directly elected councillor and women councillor are distinctions that have led to a division that constructs women as secondary citizens.

Candidates for directly-elected councillors named themselves according to the constituency e.g. councillor LC5 (representing a specific sub-county) or LC3 (representing a specific parish). The women councillor seat, on the other hand, was riddled with confusion with combined or divided sub-counties. Important was that constituencies for the women councillor seat were unpredictable and could easily be altered by such changes as the creation of a new district. For example, a new district known as Kayunga was created out of Mukono District, and in the 2002 elections, some women had to repeat the nomination exercise because the Electoral Commission realised later that the one-third quota for women had not been achieved. The announcement was made within a space of one day and it was only those who had access to information networks who turned up the next day for the renomination exercise. Not only did it mean that the previously nominated candidates had to repeat the exercise, it also meant that new candidates had to come forward because new constituencies had been created. According to an officer of the EC, Mukono District, the short notice of the announcement meant that some women could not meet the deadline and elections had to be postponed in those cases where no woman came forward for nomination.

Secondly, women voted in on a quota basis are formally referred to as women councillors (LGA 1997, Part X). In a legal sense, this means that they are representatives who are women (in their biological being) rather than representatives of women (as a social category). There was confusion about the use of this label. Campaign posters showed and caused confusion. The labels of the positions being contested by female candidates were varied, ranging from councillor for women, woman councillor, women councillor, to women's representative. This led to confusion and differentiation in the role and place of women councillors as opposed to those who stood for the mainstream electoral posts. The ghettoisation of women councillors created a 'second class' of candidates and, as shall become clear in the next chapter, this significantly factored into the subordinate position of women in the LC elections.

In 1998 there were evident problems with the womens' polls. As was reported in one of the local newspapers, many polls flopped and new dates had to be set. In the case of Mukono, voting failed to take off because 'Voters shunned polling stations' (*Sunday Vision*, 19

April 1998). After three attempts at rescheduling, the EC decided to endorse all results including those where there was failure to raise quorums.[6] According to the *Sunday Vision* (19 April, 1998), voters shunned womens' polls because they were simply tired of voting - there had been too many elections and hence widespread voter fatigue. 'They voted for the president, members of parliament and even LC3 chairmen', 'Even tomorrow they are supposed to vote', the newspaper commentary observed. The official explanation for the failure was poor voter education. Other views were that men thought it was only women who were supposed to vote for other women; yet another view was that women district councilors were themselves to blame because they did not do as much campaigning as men did (*Sunday Vision*, ibid.). This, indeed, was a direct consequence of an add-on system that did not integrate women within the mainstream electoral mechanism.

The 'add-on' system was also grossly misunderstood and misrepresented. The way through which women's representatives came to sub-county and district councils is clearly misunderstood and demeaned, even by the top leaders in the system. It was assumed that women representatives were not required to canvass for votes as in the case of general sub-county and district elections. For instance, the view of the chairperson of Kabale District was that 'mass adult suffrage makes a politician, which most women in the district council are not' The LC3 chairperson of Bukinda Sub-county in Kabale District (for the first term of 1998-2001) asserted that *"kyenda bareke abakazi batuutuke nkabandi,"* meaning: Women should also be left to tussle it out and sweat like the others' – the others being men. The general view was that women sailed through the easy way, without having to prove themselves. The implication was that they were not legitimate leaders and this pointed to a serious structural weakness in their very mode of inclusion.

The 2001/2 polls took place under an amended law that attempted, among other things, to address the confusion around womens' polls. This time, local government elections for the chairpersons, councillors and women councillors took place on the same day. The issue of quorums and other associated problems were eliminated. However, there was still a sustained marginalisation of the post of women councillors in the general discourse. At the polling stations, there were separate booths; one for the chairpersons, another for councillors and the third represented as 'the women's quota'. The EC voter education posters were important pointers, and constituted a gendered discourse of its own, influencing and endorsing the public's view of women's political roles as a 'bit on the side'(Hassim, Metelerkamp & Jodes, 1987). Notable among these posters was one on the arrangement of the polling station as shown in Figure 4.1.

Fig 4.1: EC Poster suggesting hierarchy of voting

Polling Station Poster Distributed by the Uganda Electoral Commission

The placing of the voting tables as in the Figure 4.1, illustrated a particular hierarchy, in itself creating a special discourse. The chairpersons came at the top of the ladder where the voter began. Next in line were councillors (the directly elected) and finally, on the way out, was the 'women's quota'- the term women councillors was not even used. This arrangement had far-reaching political significance. The term 'women's quota' signified an addition to the mainstream. While the amended law united the election of women councillors with the election of chairpersons and directly-elected councillors, the actual mechanism maintained the status of 'the other' for women councillors.

At the level of councillors, the term 'directly-elected councillor' formally distinguished these councillors from the affirmative action seats for women, the youth and people with disabilities (PWDs). However, the youth and PWDs were elected by their own organisations and were thereby subjected to a process of group representation rather than universal suffrage. In other words, the youth and PWDs did not suffer the repercussions of affirmative action because they were elected by their own members - the Youth Councils and NUDIPU respectively. Women councillors, elected by universal suffrage, similar to the directly-elected councillors, was the only group chosen by the general electorate but brought into the contest as a 'tamed species'. This subjected women to unique processes of community politics, as will be shown in the next chapter.

The women councillor provision established a distinctive discourse of separate and unequal interests, reflected in the delineation of women's and men's seats. Reports by the NEMGROUP (the NGO Election Monitoring Group) cited examples of how women themselves viewed their positions especially in the case of the general seats. Many of them embraced the ghetto of women's seats. 'The government has given us an opportunity to occupy leadership positions through the women councils. Why should I leave these seats to compete for men's seats?' said one female candidate in Masindi District. Another prospective female candidate in Iganga District had a similar view: 'Why should I stand for men's seats when there are seats reserved for women?' (NEMGROUP, 2002:30). According to the law, a directly-elected councillor could be a man or woman, suggesting that women had a double vote. However, the direct seat retained its male character as election results for the first LC elections indicate (see Table 4.2).

Table 4.2 : Directly-Elected Councillors by Gender 1998

Level/Category of Councillor	Total No.	Females	Males	% Female
District	886	23	863	2.6
Municipality	111	5	106	4.5
Sub-county/Municipal Division	4,270	51	4,219	1.2
City Division	133	6	127	4.5
Town	41	4	37	9.8
Total	**5,441**	**89**	**5,352**	**1.6**

Source: Republic of Uganda, 1999, a report on Local Governments Councils' Elections 1997/1998, EC.

The national average of women in directly-elected councillor positions was below two per cent. The question arises: Are women contesting the open seats and losing? Or are women only constesting the special seats? Looking at the figures from a number of districts given in Table 4.3, the situation varies. In the districts of Mbale, Mbarara and Lira, for example, the number of women in the race (and even winning) was well above the national average. However, generally, the situation was that only a few women stood for the directly-elected councillor seats. The urbanised constituencies tended to have more women standing for the direct seats - and winning - than rural settings, as indicated by the differentials between the town/city (urban) and the sub-county percentages of women given above. The urban–rural difference has also been noted in the case of South Africa, where rural councils tended to have few women compared to metropolitan councils (Coetzee & Naidoo, 2002). This phenomenon requires more focused research but it could be argued that the urban environment neutralises cultural negativity towards women to a degree by delocalising government power. In rural areas, women in public politics are conceived as unnatural. They occupy a space traditionally identified as male as opposed to female. Hence women's public role in the rural sphere is much more contested. In urban areas, women's participation is, in any case less conspicuous as women are already significant public actors in the economy.

Table 4.3 : Women in the Directly Elected Councilor (LC5) Contest 2001: Figures from Selected Districts

District	Total No. of Candidates	No. of Women Who Stood	No. of Women Who Won	% of Women in the Race
Mukono	78	4	2	5
Kabale	25	1	-	0.04
Mbale	110	10	5	9
Mbarara	89	12	6	13
Nakasongola	40	3	2	7.5
Pallisa	120	-	-	0
Katakwi	28	2	-	7.1
Sembabule	62	4	1	6.4
Masindi	82	1	-	1.2
Lira	71	9	6	12.6
Total	**705**	**46**	**22**	**6.5**

Source: NEMGROUP Monitoring Reports (2002).

The implication of the add-on arrangement has therefore indirectly been to create different spaces for men and women in local politics. The EC report on the 1997/8 elections reasoned that some women misunderstood the women quota of one-third as meaning that women, 'were barred from standing on the general ticket' (Republic of Uganda, 1999:21). However, this may not be as much a case of misunderstanding as a logical outcome of the very nature of women's reserved positions.

Because mainstream elections retained a male character, a woman candidate contesting a direct seat was symbolically constructed as an aberration. She needed to justify her candidature. By the same token, those women who stood for direct seats were given greater esteem and referred to in the general discourse as 'those women who dared to stand against men'. To emphasise this point, one woman standing in Wakiso District placed additional information on her campaign poster to the effect that she was contesting with men: 'Nvuganya na baami babiri' (I am contesting with two men). This brings forth yet another debate about the conceptualisation of women's political agency, where the goal is measuring up to men. If 'measuring up' becomes the norm, women will have to be absorbed into the masculine politics rather than challenging the male-defined political space.

Quotas: Comparing Uganda with India and South Africa

> Let me say bluntly that I do not like quotas. It smacks of Indian reservation, it smacks of ghettos. But, having said that, I absolutely feel that the quota is totally necessary. If the quota had not been introduced, I really wonder where we would be standing today. The only logical explanation we could give is that this is how it was in the past. Because women did not have access to positions of power, obviously women were to be considered inferior. Of course we know this is not true…What is a quota about…quota is simply setting right what was wrong from the very beginning (M. Boniva, International Secretary of the Italian Socialist Party, May 1989 cited in Abzug & Kelber, 1994:39).

The above quotation reflects two major perspectives about quotas for women. The question of quotas has been subjected to robust feminist debate with minimal agreement, as was mentioned in Chapter Two. Whereas the concept of setting specific numbers for women is widely accepted, apprehension abounds about its effect of ghettoisation. This is because the redress of past discrimination is often turned on its head, to imply inferiority of the concerned social actors, in this case, women.

Yet, there is general agreement that specific mechanisms are needed to get women into decision-making positions. What is therefore at stake is the very nature of those mechanisms in terms of which instruments are best at delivering effective and legitimate political power. Uganda, India and South Africa offer fascinating comparisons in this regard.

The three countries had some similarities as they implemented quotas for local government elections to varying degrees in the late 1990s. The major points of comparison related to the formal measures of inclusion, the actual implementation and the merits and demerits of each case. The comparison is aimed at further clarifying the very unique character of women's inclusion in Uganda.

Quotas in the three countries have taken different forms. As in the case of Uganda, the reservation in India was constitutional. In India, the 73rd and 74th Constitutional Amendments of 1993 made it mandatory for local governments to include women (Rai & Sharma, 2000). One-third of seats in local bodies (the Panchayats) were reserved for women. The Panchayat raj is an old system which had come to be dominated by the rural elite and bastions of privileged and patriarchal interests, manipulated by dominant political parties for political ends (Mayaram, 1999:3). The constitutional amendment was aimed at involving the oppressed sections of Indian society in local decision-making. The Panchayat raj is a three-tier system, the highest being the Zalla (district) Panchayat, the lowest, the Gram Panchayat with the Taluk as the intermediate and co-ordinating body (Vyasulu & Vyasulu, 1999). A unique feature of the new phase of the Panchayat was that a third of offices of chairpersons at the Gram Panchayat level were reserved for women. The new Panchayat system meant that existing constituencies were designated such that, in some constituencies, men were not allowed to contest election as chairperson at village level. Reserved positions rotate such that new constituencies are reserved in each round of elections.

In the South African case, the largest number of women ever was elected to local government without a formal quota, although the principle of gender equity is generally embedded within the new constitution. The ruling party, the ANC (African National Congress), adopted an informal 33 per cent quota policy on the electoral lists for national, provincial and local governments (Commission for Gender Equality (CGE) 1999). The principle of proportionality in electoral politics is embedded in the constitution but gender is not specified. Because of the ANC's quota, following the 1994 election, it had a substantial number of women representatives (90 out of 252) in the national assembly, well ahead of other parties.[8] This fact contributed greatly to the 27 per cent of women in the national assembly, which places South Africa seventh in the world (Albertyn et al., 2002). At local government level, where a mixed electoral system (PR and ward) prevails, PR brought in more female councillors than the ward system, reaching a total of 28.2 per cent female representation among all councillors (Pottie, 2000).

In Uganda, the inclusion of women in local governance has been, as in the case of India, embedded within the constitution explicitly by Article 180 (1) (b) on local government councils, which stipulates that one-third of each local government council shall be reserved for women. The LGA (1997) has explicit provisions for the election of women representatives, as already indicated. The peculiarity of the Ugandan system is the add-on arrangement, where the so-called reserved seats are actually in addition to mainstream seats. Whereas the numbers in the case of South Africa can vary, depending on the performance of women in the PR and ward elections, the situation in Uganda is that the minimum is set on 30 percent. The percentage of women in councils may go up if more women stand for the open seats, but it must not go down. What is clear is that the three countries have the numbers - Uganda and India, a minimum of 30 per cent and South Africa over 28 per cent. The issue at stake is the mechanisms – the politics of inclusion and the subsequent gendered implications for women as political subjects.

In the case of India and South Africa, the inclusion of women has meant that male privilege in elections has been undermined to a certain extent. The PR system, in particular, challenges and undermines the notion of voter preference for male candidates. In feminist understanding, this could be conceptualised as a move towards what Kabeer (1999) refers to as redistributive or transformation politics i.e. a transformation in the very definition of rights and citizenship, thereby changing the gendered nature of the polity. In South Africa, the PR system, selected by parties involved in the 1994 negotiated settlement as the fairest way of representing diversity, meant that the question of gender balance would be addressed as one of the many aspects of social inequalities in society (Meintjes & Simons, 2002). To this end, the power of the women's movement to lobby within a party structure (the ANC in particular) is noted (Meintjes & Simons, 2002), because political parties have been historically male-dominated and hostile to gender equity concerns (Razavi, 2000). South Africa's performance in PR provides an interesting case of women's influence in party politics second only to Scandinavia. Female ANC politicians pushed the ANC to commit itself to an internal quota, and the other parties cannot afford to ignore this if they are serious about winning votes.

India seems to have taken on the issue of women within a much broader framework of oppressed sections of society, including the untouchables and other lower castes. Women are given an explicit reservation to the extent that there is a concept of 'surrogate husbands', or proxy candidates i.e. cases where men were not able to stand and send their wives (supposedly to stand in for them). In the Indian case, the top position of the president of the village Panchayat is reserved for a woman on a rotational basis, according to the categories specified in the constitution. The EC specifies the required gender of the elected president in each Gram Panchayat at each election.

In Uganda, the method of reservation for women in local council representation, particularly at sub-county and district levels, raises a number of issues. One overriding weakness of the system is the separate nature of the representation, as discussed above. The dual system in Uganda provides an electoral system which includes women through a separate process that does not challenge the deep structures involving males and females as political subjects. The 'add-on' system grew out of and was conceived within the context of a no-party political dispensation. The principle of individual merit, with candidates contesting as individuals, means that any number of positions can be established without any significant transformation of the electoral or political system. However, the inclusion of women in positions signifying formal political participation within a context of a less than strong women's movement makes the Ugandan case unique (Goetz, 2003).

What are the implications of the electoral system for women? At a practical level, the guidelines for the election of women in Uganda are somewhat ambiguous. As at the national level, the electoral law and the practice of LC elections itself awards women a different status from men. Separate seats for women mean that they compete among themselves, while subjected to the adult suffrage vote. One significant effect is that women tend to draw on popular discourses of womanhood to win votes. Analysing parliamentary elections in Uganda, Tamale (1999) observes that the 'women-only' campaigns leaned heavily on moral aptness rather than articulation of issues, and some women tended to use the morality card against each other. In this way, the women-only competition separates women's political engagement from the mainstream of political competition (Goetz & Hassim, 2003:13). Inclusion occurs through exclusionary means – through the creation of separate spaces. The concrete manifestations of this women-only system is analysed in the next chapter, when the two local government elections held in 1998 and 2001-2 are discussed.

Therefore, do electoral systems matter? Meintjes and Simons (2002) pose this question with regard to South Africa and explore electoral models from a gender perspective. Examining the argument normally advanced, namely that PR systems are better for women, Meintjes and Simons (2002) argue that PR on its own does not seem to provide the solution. Other factors, including open or closed lists and positive measures such as quotas and economic empowerment have to come into play. But, on the whole, the nature of the electoral system is seen as an important variable in facilitating the presence of women in political structures, especially in the context of an androcentric political culture (Meintjes & Simons, 2002:164).

The differential in the local government elections in South Africa, in which fewer women won seats as ward councilors than PR seats, leads Pottie, for instance, to conclude:

> The consistent higher representation of women in the party list component of South Africa's local government elections indicates the strength of the PR electoral system to achieve electoral results

that reflect the desire to ensure that women are more equitably represented in elected bodies. By contrast, women's performance in the ward elections did not match the same share of seats achieved in the party lists (2001:10-11).

The local government experience of a mixed electoral system in South Africa indicates that the type of electoral system matters for numbers at least (Meintjes & Simons, 2002). And beyond the question of numbers, there is the view that women elected through mainstream mechanisms, as in the case of South Africa, have deeper location and legitimacy in the political process.

Yet Pinto Jayawardena argues:

> ...the Proportional Representation cannot be said, in isolation, to work for the betterment of women in politics. Its beneficial effects are heavily dependent on the type of party structures and the socio-cultural ethos within which it works itself out (2000:3).

Writing about Sri Lanka, Jayawardena casts doubt on the transformative potential of PR because the processes of selection are intricately intertwined with the politics of the country such that, if ever women are selected, the selection process itself is between and among the elite. In Sri Lanka, the political process is further complicated by intense conflict and violence. Her view is:

> Throughout, a privileged group of women have managed to enter and sustain themselves within the Sri Lankan political process. Their interests within this process have, however, not led to any significant empowering of their sisters...Women in the upper echelons of politics are more likely to become an elite group among women and develop their own vested interests (Jayawardena, 2000:4).[8]

Although Jayawardena conflates the question of numbers with the issue of effectiveness by looking at numbers as a deceptive 'empowerment' of percentages, she specifically raises the question of the PR system and the almost complete subordination of the individual to the will of the party. Nomination to the party list can be a highly gendered and class-based process.

According to Mayaram, the Indian system is fast realising a deficit. There was a backlash in India, with active female representatives being targeted for rape and other forms of abuse (2000). This happened because men had to forego political opportunities in favour of women. In many states, women representatives in Panchayat raj institutions were routinely denied access to records, or permission to sit with male Panchayat members. There were cases of women Panchayat members being refused access to information about meetings, as part of men's strategy to oust women for non-attendance. In extreme cases, there were violent demonstrations against the presence of women, involving parading elected women naked through the streets of villages (Goetz, 2000). To Omvedt (2000), the reservation and rotation system in India robs women of the opportunity to build political careers because a seat is 'declared open at each subsequent election' and thence 'rotated to another constituency'. Omvedt (2000) proposes that direct legal pressure on political parties to nominate women candidates is more sustainable and also much more predisposed to enabling women to build a political career and by implication, gain more political legitimacy - hitting, as she terms it, 'at the heart of women's exclusion from political power' (ibid.).

The political costs of Uganda's minimalist system are very clear. There is no redistribution of seats as in India. Because the involvement of women has not replaced or dented male privilege in the electoral contest, no major political choices have had to be made. As opposed to India, for example, women candidates for reserved seats do not replace would-be male aspirants; hence the kind of harassment reported in India does not exist. What exists in Uganda represents a different level of gatekeeping, with discourses that attempt to construct women as outsiders to political space, as will be argued in the coming chapters. The view is not 'politics as usual'. The patriarchal outlook of councils has been dented by participation by such large numbers of women. Some women contest open seats and based on the argument that a critical mass of women has the potential to effect change; the quota will have even greater potential for being politicised if more women win general seats.

On the whole, the system in Uganda includes women as individuals without providing adequate mechanisms for collective action. While individual women might be able to break gender, discriminative and oppressive barriers, it is more difficult to represent group interests because of the competitive nature of the women's quota system. In the next chapter, this mode of inclusion is discussed in relation to political identity and legitimacy with regard to local council elections.

Notes

1. Critics have raised questions about this seemingly consultative and participatory process. Oloka-Onyango (1998), for instance, contends that the mode of consultation was not transparent but rather one circumscribed by the regime's high-handed authority – from appointing members of the Commission, to the nature of questions posed during consultation and the final nature of the CA debate.

2. The NRM commanded a strong majority in the CA. First, the majority of elected members were strong supporters of the NRM. In addition, other categories such as presidential nominees were added to the NRM bloc.

3. Analysts observe that the success of the women's lobby in the CA was partly attributable to this kind of pragmatism, to tone down the language of their demands. This is believed to have mobilised quite a number of liberal men, who sometimes presented the women's case in a moderate manner. In other words, this pragmatism is viewed as having contributed greatly to forming alliances, especially with men in the Assembly (Tamale, 1999). This is a debatable issue which requires concrete inquiry, because questions may arise about the transformatory potential of such a strategy. In this case, however, there is tentative agreement that pragmatism could have been necessary in view of the power relations at play.

4. The GIC was established with the support of the DANIDA Constituent Assembly Project, under the auspices of the Ministry of Gender and Community Development.

5. The report by the EC on the 1997/8 LC elections notes that elections by lining up generated the biggest number of complaints. Candidates and voters complained about manipulative tendencies, intimidation and outright cheating. Candidates were also feared, because candidates could easily tell who had or had not voted for them. Furthermore, was very difficult to sustain the one-third requirement of all persons entitled to vote before elections could commence. The elections were disrupted by rain and other factors and where lines for certain candidates were long, voters who had already been counted could easily move from the front to the rear of the line (Republic of Uganda, 1999:17).

6. The UWONET documentation of women's experiences in Uganda's local council and local government elections reports clearly that 'on the whole, elections for district women councillors (1998) were a flop country wide. Originally these elections were gazetted for Saturday April 18, but due to the failure to raise a two-third quorum in many parts of the country, the electoral commission postponed the exercise to 19th, then to 26th April and finally to 17th May, 1998. The postponement however did not field better results either but instead caused a lot of confusion to the candidates and the voters…Many monitors reported that elections in many parts of the country went ahead without realising the quorum because the electoral officials insisted that they would never raise the legally stipulated quorum' (UWONET, 1998:48).

7. The Inkatha Freedom Party had 10 out of 43 women representatives, the National Party 9 out of 82. The Democratic Party and PAC had 1 each from seven and five respectively while the African Christian Democratic Party had none (CGE, 1998:6).

8. Women within the party pose serious threats to younger women striving to make a difference, in addition to strong family-based vote patterns in Sri Lanka.

5

Of Local Democracy and Grassroots Tyranny: Gender and Local Council (LC) Elections

One of the major pillars of the contemporary system of local government in Uganda is the fact that representatives at all levels are elected rather than appointed, hence promoting local democracy and autonomy. As expected, elections have proved to be a crucial aspect of political space and a critical legitimating process, where threads of local democracy and grassroots tyranny seem to be intertwined in very significant ways, especially when it comes to gender differences. The aim of this chapter is to analyse the terrain of elections, particularly in view of the space created for women in the general framework of local government.

Elections as a political activity present feminists with an opportunity to examine how the social dynamics and complex constructions of gender impact on the location of women's and men's spaces in public life. The LC elections, in particular, impel a search for explanations about women's and men's positioning within political space in the realm of public life. Here, the concept of public life, as Tetreault (2001) argues, does not presume distinct spaces between private and public, but rather a site of overlapping domains.

The interdependence of the private and public is particularly significant in situations when gendered definitions of status, rights and responsibilities are being contested and adjusted. Elections as a specific political process present one such situation. Local government elections in Uganda reveal the tendency for the threads of local democracy and grassroots tyranny to be part and parcel of the same electoral experience. Spaces for participation dynamically are intertwined with a re-assertion of cultural negativity and forceful patriarchal notions of womanhood. Grassroots tyranny means that, far from the notion that power to the community entails democratisation, the local may, in specific cases, be more oppressive. This chapter analyses the terrain of local elections in Uganda with particular focus on the space opened to women to exercise their democratic right. The points of reference relate to the local council elections of 1998 and 2001/2 that took place after the policy of decentralisation had been instituted.[1]

In the general literature on political space, periodic elections are generally viewed as a benchmark of democracy. According to Huntington, a political system is defined as democratic in so far as:

> Its most powerful collective decision makers are selected through periodic elections in which candidates freely compete for votes and in which virtually all the adult population is eligible to vote (cited in Waylen, 1994:332).

Adejumobi adds the notion of a social compact:

> Conceptually, election symbolises popular sovereignty and the expression of the `social pact' between the state and the people, which defines the basis of political authority, legitimacy and citizens' obligation. It is the kernel of political accountability and a means of ensuring reciprocity and exchange between governors and the governed (1998:43).

In the same breath, however, Adejumobi offers a critique of elections, particularly in the African context, as being a fading shadow of democracy and as merely a mechanism for providing a political framework for the justification and legitimation of autocratic rule.

March and Kaase (1979) refer to voting as:

> A unique form of political behaviour in the sense that it occurs only rarely, is highly biased by strong mechanisms of social control and social desirability enhanced by the rain-dance ritual of campaigning, and does not involve the voter in major informational or other costs (cited in Randall, 1982:51).

It is an undeniable fact that elections are viewed as one of the basic yardsticks in the process of building democratic institutions and hence democratic polities.

'Participation of the citizenry in elections and thereafter collective involvement of the elected officials in the decision-making process, are important ingredients for the gradual establishment of democracy' (Adar, 1999:341), at least institutionally (Luckham et al., 2000).

In other words, the very basic idea of empowering the population as an electorate to make a choice about who should govern has an element of democratisation, especially when these elections take place at the very local level. This is one observation on the decentralisation process in Uganda.

However, elections, with their ingrained component of competition for votes tend to create spaces that could be manipulated by already powerful sections of society, thereby advantaging themselves, to the relative detriment of the less powerful. For Adar (1999), it would indeed be simplistic to argue that elections always lead to democratic systems because elections can also serve as devices of social control. Despite these limitations, elections remain a significant indicator in any political system. Contrary to Goloba-Mutebi's (1999) assertion that elections are not a good measure of participation on the basis of their episodic nature, elections can present a prism through which a particular political culture is refracted. The question goes beyond whether or not elections are a measure of people's participation, and seeks to unravel the underlying discourses that inform the nature of different people's participation at the local level.

Local government elections in Uganda can be best analysed along a continuum. The basic idea of periodic elections establishes principles for a democratic culture. The fact that there are guaranteed mechanisms for social groups such as women, the youth and the disabled to participate, provides a basis for local democracy and emancipatory discourses in local spaces. As far as gender is concerned, the inclusion of women in electoral processes as contestants (albeit directed or manipulated from above) has forced a redefinition of public space at the local level, thereby fostering new gender identities. At the same time, however, elite and patriarchal mechanisms appear to have been strengthened by local electoral politics. The generally held view that it is easier for women to participate in politics at the local level because of more modest eligibility criteria and its closeness to the women's sphere of life (Evertzen, 2001; Drage, 1999) flies in the face of this evidence. Under what conditions does devolution of power to lower levels actually deliver democratic politics in general, and gender equality in particular?

This chapter proceeds by analysing the gendered nature of local council (LC) elections and the manner in which the contest manifests itself in the lived reality of men and women vying for leadership positions. The intricate position of local government and risks that localism poses to the character of the legitimating processes, that is, the different demands on men and women, is examined. In what is referred to as gendered mandates, an analysis of the way key aspects such as money, morality and marriage constitute a unique blend of local democracy and grassroots tyranny, is conducted. The chapter also examines gender differences in key posts in local government in Uganda.

Gendered Mandates: Money, Morality and Marriage in the Local Sphere

Decentralisation in Uganda and the structure of the local council elections guarantees participation for all. The mandatory affirmative action for women guarantees their participation in local government. The issue at stake is therefore not whether women participate, but rather the mode, quality and effect of that participation.

The analysis commences with campaigns, a critical starting point for political leadership.[2] Election campaigns in Uganda, whether at national or local levels, have tended to be more personality-based than programme-based (Goetz & Hassim, 2003). This situation seems to persist even when the system of individual merit has been officially scrapped. The outlook of the 2006 elections, though, held under a multiparty arrangement, did not show a substantial break with the individual merit mentality. Voters and candidates alike tended to draw more on individualised notions of politics, where personalities tended to overshadow party manifestos. In this context, gendered identities become a very significant aspect, as the individual person is under close scrutiny.

Campaigns facilitate mobilisation and the organisation of political support. The campaign period is a crucial time when voters, through their demands made in meetings and other fora, express what they require and expect from their leadership. Equally, the candidate has to demonstrate what she or he has to offer as a leader against other candidates. This is the origin of the notion of gendered mandates or the differential intersectional determinants for male and female candidates. Gendered mandates allow examination of the differences regarding expectations that communities have of men and women as local leaders.

Voter perceptions of who should rule tend to extend beyond formal requirements. Formally, the main requirements for local government positions are residence in the area and payment of a non-refundable nomination fee.[3] Only candidates for district chairpersons were required to have a minimum academic qualification of Advanced Level or its equivalent (Republic of Uganda, 1999).[4] No other positions had education requirements. Hence, education requirements, often listed as a basic barrier to women's political participation, had little significance here. Beyond the official requirements, local representatives were judged more on the personal and private, and this is where gender differences arise.

At the general level, community selection processes were informed by class, thus the importance of the question, 'who is she or he'. In rural contexts, women who assumed leadership roles were teachers, health workers or people engaged in trade, or wives of church and other opinion leaders in the community. Men also had to be of some prominence in the community as teachers, traders or retired civil servants. At a minimum, a person had to be slightly "above" the common peasant, though not necessarily part of the 'elite', to be elected as councillor (Banerjee, 1998). Experience of LC elections demonstrates that candidates have to address themselves to mandates beyond the more or less expected yardsticks. The study identified three key aspects, namely money, morality and marriage.

Money and Commercialisation of Elections

Asked whether she would stand for re-election for the 2002 local government elections, a woman councillor in Kabale District Council had this to say:

> I would be willing but I am afraid. Voters expect a lot of money and I am still indebted (April, 2000).

The financial implication and constraint of elections was aired by all the men and women interviewed. Apart from the minimum requirement of the nomination fee, there were additional costs. According to one male councillor, one such standard was the campaign poster. Candidates needed vibrant (coloured and expensive) campaign posters that would attract potential voters. The politics of posters have became a feature of elections and voters would discuss and compare the appearence of different candidates on their posters. For women, the aspect of beauty also crept into this competition and a poster could play a role in the success of a candidate.

Furthermore, voters and supporters preferred candidates with vehicles. On nomination day, a candidate should have at least one vehicle to move around in, and provide fuel for a fleet of motorcycles to create, at a minimum, the impression of a person of significance. Appearing at the nomination station on foot (especially for LC5) would not be acceptable.

However, the most profound issue relating to money had to do with vote buying or bribing voters. Following the 2001 presidential and parliamentary polls, vote buying became a more or less institutionalised affair at all levels of the electoral process. Apparently, the same voters are bribed by presidential candidates, by parliamentary candidates, and expect the same exchange during local council elections. Hence sponsoring a campaign was expensive and well out of reach of ordinary people, especially women.

The most common and apparent form of vote buying is through providing free alcohol to adult men and male youth. Come election time, peri-urban locations and trading centres are overly vibrant and entertaining, especially for the unemployed. In some cases, success was predicated on how well the candidate, whether male or female, satisfied this group. Reports indicate that women were bribed with soap, sugar, salt and blankets, items considered as tokens. One of the candidates in Mukono revealed that women were not 'difficult voters'. Once they decided on a particular candidate, they were not easily swayed by bribery.

Kizito, a male candidate who opted not to distribute money to voters, added another dimension. He viewed 'dishing out' money to voters as not only morally wrong but also absurd in view of the voting patterns in Uganda. Using his sub-county in Mukono District as a case, he argued that, though there were 32,000 eligible voters, only 8,000 actually voted. This meant that one would bribe people who would not vote in the final analysis. He did not regret that he had lost on this account. He observed that elections in Uganda were less about selecting people who would govern effectively, and more about the dispersal of bribes, money and alcohol.

What is the impact of this observed commercialisation of elections? In a workshop in Kumi District (18-21 December 2001), an observation was made that elections had impoverished a number of people, particularly men, who even sold their land in order to finance campaigns. Women, on the other hand, discussed their constraint in satisfying voters because they did not control household property. Views from Mukono District indicated that voters tended to demand more money from men than from women. In a discussion with a group of men at one candidates' meeting, it was revealed that voters' demands for money tended to match the general perceptions about men's and women's earning power. Since it was well known that women had limited sources of money, voters' demands on them were equally limited.

However, contrary to the general view that women did not have to bribe voters, women maintained that they faced a major problem, with voters holding them at ransom during the campaign period. In their view, some women faced a bigger burden because they had to campaign in more than one sub-county (in the case of the district councils). This case also exposed structural differences between men and women. While one female councillor cited having used 3,000,000 shillings to demonstrate the burden of election, a male counterpart laughed this off, implying that 3,000,000 shillings was petty compared to what men had actually spent – over 5,000,000 shillings, according to him. Impact lay not in the absolute numbers, as in the relative sources of income for men and women generally. While the source of income for the majority of women (especially in rural areas) was usually a salary for low-paying government employment (e.g. teachers and nurses) or small income-generating projects, men had a wider range of economic assets, ranging from land, cattle and medium-sized business enterprises, including tenders for government-related service provision.

Commercialisation of elections poses a huge dilemma to all participants and distorts local democracy. For women, this element increases the gender gap and compoundes the constraint of limited political resources. Yet, at the same time, the general view that female candidates lacked money to bribe voters also worked to further construct them as 'minors' in the electoral process. Similarly, not all men had money to sponsor campaigns. Hence the assumed `natural' male economic power was disadvantageous to some men.

The Question of Moral-Suasion in Community Politics

Election criteria seemed to penetrate to candidates' personal and private lives. Local politics is heavily imbued with moral contests and women were the most affected in this regard. As stated by Meintjes and Simons, who argue that women's citizenship is often structured around their identity as homemakers, mothers and sexual beings (2002:18), women's participation as candidates in local politics is encumbered by their femininity. This makes political space heavily skewed against women. Material from observations at one of the candidates' meetings attended during fieldwork is used to unravel these questions.

LC5 (Councillor) Campaigns in Mukono District: The Case of Nenyodde, Nakanyonyi Parish, Nabbale Sub-county (28 January 2002)

The chairperson LC2 Nakanyonyi opened the function by welcoming all present and called for orderly conduct on the part of the candidates and the gathering. The chairperson explained clearly that since candidate meetings were taking place at each parish in the sub-county, every person had an opportunity to pose questions to the candidates, at and in relation to their parish. Only residents of Nenyodde were supposed to participate and ask questions that day.[5] On the part of candidates, the chairperson called for a clean rally rather than mudslinging, which was termed *kusiga nziro* (dirt smearing). Thus candidates were enjoined to talk about what they had to offer rather than engage in a smear campaign against opponents. The rule was that each participant could ask only one question to each candidate.

The presiding officer then took over, called the meeting to order and introduced the candidates (four contesting the directly-elected councillor seat and two for the women councillor seat). The procedure was that the order of speaking would be determined by ballot, with each candidate speaking according to the position written on the paper that he or she had picked. The candidates were required to address the gathering for a maximum of ten minutes. The presiding officer then announced that the 'direct candidates' would talk first, followed by 'the women'.

Candidate 1 (Male - direct seat)

Musoke introduced himself as a 'son of the soil' and went on to recount his parents, grandparents and great-grandparents in some detail. He gave a number of reasons why he considered himself the most eligible candidate. One was that as a journalist, he was knowledgeable. Secondly, he was young and energetic. He attacked those candidates who had taken the trouble to write a manifesto. 'Does a councilor have money to finance a manifesto?' he asked. Musoke spoke about the tendering and contractual process in the district which, he said, was skewed and did not benefit *Banamukono* (people of Mukono), such as the building of the district headquarters, where even the porters were allegedly imported from Kenya, a neighbouring country. Finally, he introduced his wife, whom he referred to as his *olubirizi* (rib). He announced that he had never beaten her. He further asked whether anyone had seen him bringing family disputes to the LC. Musoke urged strongly that it was time for the aged to step aside and assume an advisory role – which was their rightful place and to 'let the youth lead because they have the energy'.

Candidate II (Male – direct seat)

Katerega introduced himself as a native of Nagalama, one of the parishes in the sub-county, and identified his cause as a youth concerned about the backward status of Nabbale Sub-county. He went on to critique the one-sidedness of most micro-finance programmes that tended to favour women. He suggested that when women failed to pay, it was men who suffered. In some cases men's property was apparently confiscated and families forced to abandon their homes. Katerega also reiterated the contest between the aged and the youth. Katerega was unmarried and hence did not spend time outlining his family situation.

Candidate III (Female and incumbent on the direct seat)

Kamya, the incumbent, opened by kneeling down and saying:

> *Ng'omukyala omuganda owawano kansoke nokubabuuzako bassebo ne banyabo mwasuzeyo mutyano?* (As a Muganda woman, let me begin by greeting you all, gentlemen and ladies. How are you all?)

She then introduced her husband by saying *simuleseyo ekka* (I have not left him at home). With that preamble, Kamya enumerated the roles of a councillor. In a very interactive way (moving around and making close eye contact with the audience), she addressed herself to the two critical issues apparently working against her candidature and these were her gender and age. Citing some of the concerns that *omukazi atwesimbyeko, ekifo kyabasajja* (the woman is encroaching on the men's seat); she rightly argued that the direct seat was not for men alone. The reserved seat for women existed, but it did not preclude women from standing for the open sub-county seat. As far as age was concerned, she argued: 'Yes I am an old woman' *(omukazi mukadde)* but quickly added: 'Age is wisdom; after all, what you need in a council is not muscle power but rather deliberative skills and competence.' Kamya assured voters that since she was seeking re-election for the same position of councilor, she was still the same person she was four years before, in the previous LC election.

Kamya presented her strong points. These were, first, that a woman of her age and status could not be corrupted thus assuring the electorate of her probity. Secondly, her children were mature and had constructed a house for her. Her third argument was that she was a good debator and that had enabled her to secure projects like a school, rehabilitation of roads and water sources in the sub-county (though the audience murmured in disagreement saying those were government projects and not hers). Concluding her address, Kamya knelt again saying, *Banange mbasaba akalulu* (I humbly request your vote).

Candidate IV (Male - direct seat)

Kizito identified himself as a youth and claimed to hail from a poor family, which he said indicated that he felt for the poor. He announced that his manifesto leaned heavily on president Museveni's manifesto for the 2001 presidential elections in which he pledged modernisation of agriculture, reduction of taxes (graduated tax) and general poverty eradication. Kizito also ambitiously pledged facilities like a community library and tele-centres. He pointed to his education level as a graduate and also elaborated how community development problems could be addressed. As this was quite inconceivable to people still grappling with issues of safe water and feeder roads, his speech caused laughter and ridicule. Lastly, he pledged his respect for the Kabaka, the King of Buganda, possibly as a strategy to capture local sentiments and to demonstrate 'closeness' to the Buganda identity. (Meanwhile some people in the audience murmured questions about Kizito's origins, *Naye Ssebo oliwawa* (But sir, where do you come from in the first place?).

Candidate V (Woman Councillor seat)

Jaya was introduced as one who was going to represent women (*agenda kukikilira abakyala*).[6] She commenced by kneeling and greeting the audience amidst clapping and ululation. She introduced herself, *Ndi mukyala mufumbo* (I am a married woman) and said she had been married for 20 years. She knelt again and introduced her husband (meanwhile some voices in the audience were urging her to 'speak up'). Jaya pledged to develop women in the two sub-counties she was to represent. Giving an example of chicken rearing, she observed that eggs from such a project would improve the nutrition of the children and husbands.[7] In what continued as a uniform interjection of kneeling down after each point made, Jaaya gave a performance that reflected her extreme subordination to culture and tradition. She announced that she was a woman of virtue (*omukazi wa mpisa nyo*), her home was open to everyone and that if elected she would uplift women in many areas such as *ebyemizanyo* (sports) and handicrafts. She concluded, pleading, *Banange mbasaba akalulu* (My friends, I request you to vote for me) and knelt down and bowed.

Candidate VI (Woman Councillor seat)

Lumaama also began her address by kneeling down, greeting and welcoming everybody. She introduced herself as *Omukyala mufumbo* (married woman) married for 23 years, to a man of virtue (*Omusajja owekisa nyo*). She then explained her education, revealing that she had pursued home economics because she knew a woman's role was to marry. Using the same subservient mode of kneeling between points as Jaaya, her opposition, Lumaama pointed out that her home (with her husband) was – *maka gabantu* (a respectable home) and as a mother, she cared for and about children. If elected she promised she would teach women *emisomo gya Senga*[8] modern cookery (*enfumba eyomulembe*), work on marketing of handicrafts and generally be an example to fellow women. She finally knelt amidst clapping and cheering.

The candidates' meeting at Nenyodde delivered powerful statements regarding how women and men are placed within the local political landscape. There were cultural variations in terms of how this actually manifested itself in campaigns across the country, but the basic trends were similar, varying more in degree than in substance. The fact that female candidates found it imperative to kneel before the voters was a signifier of the general status of women in the electoral process.

Kneeling before voters had become a more or less institutionalised practice, mandatory for women in the central region.[9] Traditionally, in Kiganda culture, women and girls are supposed to show respect to men and elders by kneeling down, whether to greet them or talk to them generally. This social practice has extended to the public space in a very powerful way, particularly with the onset of decentralisation. Before a woman candidate addresses a gathering, she has to kneel and greet the voters in a 'respectful' manner. In only one case a woman in Wakiso District lost the vote because she exaggerated the ritual. According to her contestant, she knelt everywhere; on the roadside and wherever she came across men and potential voters, until even the voters saw this as 'over-kneeling'. The symbolism in kneeling, though, is significant. Women who did this were recalling traditional respect and subservience towards men. Transferring the practice to modern politics represented articulation of a new subordination. The combination of tradition with modern forms of ritual behaviour created a new kind of subordination and secondary status, further entrenching the idea of the women councillors as 'a bit on the side' (Hassim at al., 1987).

For women to gain legitimacy and receive votes they had to prove that they were 'real' women despite the fact that they sought public office. At one of the candidates' meetings attended in Mukono District, one of two women contestants, a highly educated veterinary doctor who also lectured at one of the universities in Uganda, also knelt and requested votes. Some people cheered and screamed, though others were perplexed. A group of women wondered quietly how this professor could appear so subservient. Their views captured the signifying process: *Banange akalulu kakoseza! Olaba ne Professor naye bimuganidde?* (The power of the vote has even brought this professor down to her knees!) A man also quietly observed that it was ridiculous for this apparently well-educated woman (possibly nobody else in the rally had attained the same education as she), to kneel for votes.

The idea that kneeling only occurred in rural areas has to be dispelled. While civil servants in Mukono District argued that it was mostly people in the rural areas who emphasised these customs, in practice it occurred even in urban areas. To pursue this issue, a candidates' meeting for a town council was attended. One of the candidates for the woman councillor seat, highly educated with university education, had held a powerful position in the district and was also knowledgeable about the Local Governments Act (1997) and general functioning of the local government system. Concluding her campaign address, she knelt, saying: *Banange nva wagulu, nga mbafukamiridde, mbasaba akalulu* (I come down to my knees, I beg for your vote).

Demanding women to kneel can be interpreted as calculated not only to humiliate women but also to keep them in their place. Questions of subjectivity arise. How are female politicians constructing an identity for a female representative? Some women were asked how they felt about kneeling for votes. One of the women councillors in Mukono asserted:

> If you really want the vote you have to kneel for the voters. If you don't do it you stand to lose. They say *omukyala tatusamu kitibwa* (this woman does not respect us) (Interview, 16 September 1999).

Another woman admitted, 'Yes, I felt humiliated, but I had to do it. It is better to be humble and fight the system from within.' In other words, conformity with a demand like kneeling is regarded as a political tactic or strategic retreat that diverts the electorate from focusing too much on a candidate's person.

The view of the women was predominantly, as Vargas noted, that they could not fight all the battles at the same time (cited in Wieringa, 1994:841). Women's first battle was to access structures of public decision-making, and conformity to traditional rituals could make it easier for women to step into political space. These and other analyses serve to alert readers to the need to avoid stereotypes and to conceptualise social reality as potentially dynamic. In this case, kneeling during campaigns may assist women in getting 'a foot in the door' (Tripp, 2000).

However, how far do strategies such as kneeling for votes go to legitimise women in public life? Campaign rallies are free public gatherings, attended by people of all ages and walks of life. Adult women kneeling for everybody present could have far-reaching political significance for the identification of their collective identity as minors in the political system. In a discussion in Mukono District, one male councillor (a District Council speaker for the 1998-2002 term) argued that a candidate kneeling for votes was not an experience particular to women alone. He submitted that even men were required to do what he termed 'funny things', such as dancing, hugging and waving. A female councillor in Kanungu District said, *Oburuuru bwabantu bakye nibubi, nibutwarwa akantu kakye* (elections at local level are terrible. They are swayed by petty issues). She gave the example that people could, for instance, front a drunkard 'with all teeth and gums full of dregs of local brew', and demand that the candidate hug him to demonstrate that he or she is a 'person of the people'. However, morality demands directed at female candidates had a gendered character. Women were under pressure to prove that they were 'still' women through socially submissive acts such as kneeling before crowds of people.

Other examples of morality qualifiers in local politics were dress, generosity and religiosity. In the central region, the gomesi, a traditional gown worn by women, was almost mandatory, not only on the campaign podium, but also at community functions such as meetings, funerals and weddings. On nomination and campaign days women had to appear in gomesi.[10] In other parts of the country, a woman had to be seen to be in the habit of dressing respectably, particularly in long dresses, covering all parts - 'neck to heel' and 'neck to wrist' - preferably complete with a headscarf. Requirements and specifications of dress rarely applied to men, except if a particular man was excessively untidy.

On generosity, the question posed by voters was: 'Is that particular woman's home easy to access?' In one of the candidates' meetings in Mukono, a woman who had once accused someone of trespassing, was asked how wide her home's door was open. Trespass is an alien concept to rural Buganda and it is unheard of for someone to accuse another of trespass. The concerned woman lost the election, mainly on this account.

Generosity was not required of women alone. That expected of men however, positioned them in a different locale. Men's generosity was measured by their sociability in the men's clubs - bars and other social gatherings for men. Sociability was defined by men as mixing easily with people, and once in a while sharing alcohol. In Kabale, the only woman who had stood for an open sub-county seat (in the 1998 elections) was defeated and one explanation for the victory of her male opponent was that he was social and co-operative. He was said to be particularly helpful in times of difficulty, such as death, where he was quick to make radio announcements. Women are unable to mix in that manner. Their sociability is located back in the home. This is one of the reasons why canvassing for votes did not involve an even playing field for women.

For Christian-dominated communities, another opportunity for a woman to win votes was her level of participation in church activities. In the words of one male councillor in Kabale District: 'As a woman, if you do not go to church, forget about votes.' While men could afford to begin going to church when canvassing for votes, it was almost a mandatory condition for a woman to be a well-known churchgoer, actively participating in different church-related activities.

On Marriage and Belonging

In local politics, marriage is central to the legitimation processes. Appearing at the campaign podium with a husband is a big plus for a female candidate. It prevents voters from posing embarrassing questions such as whether or not a particular woman would become a 'loose' woman. An unmarried woman, on the other hand, was confronted with questions about whether or not she was a *Malaya* (prostitute). Some women were compelled to present wedding photographs to prove that they were 'properly married'. Consequently, a pattern emerged in councils that, except for women contesting the post of youth representative, all other women candidates are married.

Unmarried male youth, on the other hand, could contest and win direct councillor seats with relative ease.

There was a general feeling that unmarried women, if voted into leadership, would set a bad example for other women in the community. This view was especially prevalent at village (LC1) level. One of the election monitors observed that the Local Governments Amendment Act, 2001, had injected more conservatism in local-level politics by giving the chairperson more powers. As already noted, the original idea about popular participation engendered multiple elections, and at the village level all adults over 18 would vote for the 10 positions. The new amendment changed this, and only the chairperson was voted in by adult suffrage. The successful candidate then nominated the executive.

> Members of the executive committee at village and parish level shall be nominated by the chairpersons with the approval of their respective council with Local Governments Act 1997 (with 2001 Amendments).

The amendment reduced the long process, which could involve a full day or more of voting. But what implication did this change have for local participation? An official from the Ministry of Local Government intimated that even people in the ministry were opposed to the amendment, precisely because it undermined the democratic principles that decentralisation was trying to promote in the first place. This particular observation referred to the fact that this change tended to create autocracy at the local level, by concentrating power in the position of the chairperson. Other views advanced were that this was one way through which the Movement regime sought to entrench its hegemony at the local level. Critics saw this amendment as a reversion to colonial chiefs as channels of state patronage and repression, and in effect, a direct inversion of local democracy.

The 2001 Amendment also had specific gendered effects. According to election monitoring reports by ACFODE (2002), elections of LC 1 (village councils) were skewed. Apparently, chairpersons specifically selected women who were regarded as having 'stable marriages', in addition to such criteria as visibility in community activities and the church. Chairpersons believed that selecting 'respectable, married' women protected the chairpersons against allegations that they would have affairs with the women chosen. In addition, women who campaigned actively for the successful chairperson stood a better chance. The danger in this was the potential for clientalism rather than deepening local democracy.

Where men were asked what they would do or achieve in the councils, women were more often asked about what would happen to their husbands and children. During a group discussion in Misindye, Mukono District, one man commented that women's involvement in leadership was fine, but men were getting tired of eating cold food, because the wives were spending more time on LC activities. According to him, some women had devised a method of preparing food beforehand and leaving it in vacuum flasks, 'but she is not there to serve you, and flask food has a bad odour too', he said, causing laughter among the participants (20 July 2001).   This resonates with what Ddatta (1998) observed in India. She interviewed a man on women's participation in the Panchayat, who, though he had no problem with his wife being elected on the Panchayat raj, worried: 'Who will make the chapattis?' (Ddatta, 1998:2). Agarwal also quotes a man in Kanartaka, India, who said: 'We want our women to come to the Panchayats, but who will take care of our children?' (2001:1,638). In other words, women's political role interfered with domestic responsibilities, once again identifying a specific aspect of the private/public interplay.

Men too, had to convince voters of their suitability to fill public office. The most common question that men had to answer related to ethnic belonging. In some cases, they had to explain who their parents, grand- and great-grand parents were and, in some areas in the central region, identify where their dead ancestors were buried. While men's marital status and their private lifes were not judged with regard to councillor positions, it was a deciding factor for certain positions, such as chairperson, more specifically at village level. A report from Kabarole district cited one female voter as saying:

> How can we trust unmarried women and men with our husbands and wives? An unmarried chairman will definitely disturb our secretary for Women Affairs or secretary for Youth (NEMGROUP, 2001).

In Masindi District, a man who had separated from his wife lost the election because people argued that, since he had failed to manage that small unit (his family), how would he lead a whole village? Men with domestic problems who frequented LC1 courts also stood less chance of being elected as chairpersons. For this post, men with settled family relationships were seen to be more appropriate. Sixty per cent of disputes brought to the LC courts were domestic, relating to women, as main clients, seeking arbitration, either with regard to domestic property or violence (Khadiagala, 2000). In this case, one positive potential is that selecting men with stable home lives would indirectly influence the kind of men who ultimately govern.

Marriage was significant in another way. Apart form from being a basic yardstick for women (and men with regard to a few specific posts), marriage itself posed a limitation for women, particularly in the process of canvassing for votes. First and foremost, women had to be accountable to their husbands. There were cases where men literally prevented their wives from contesting elections (NEMGROUP, 2002). Also, in an interview, a former chairperson LC3 in Bukinda (Kabale) claimed that women were principally poor mobilisers, not because they were naturally like that, but rather owing to their positions and responsibilities. He argued that canvassing for votes was intensive and time consuming. Women's workload worked against them. Women could not abandon their social responsibilities to engage in campaign activities. Conversely, most of men's responsibilities could be postponed, restructured or even abandoned altogether for the period of intensive campaigning. Activities such as food preparation, childcare and other household chores normally performed by women are labour-intensive and not easily rescheduled, compared to men's activities, such as preparing land for cultivation, which can be rescheduled, in addition to the fact that the work is seasonal. Although domestic help may relieve some privileged women of day-to-day chores, in rural areas in particular, no woman could successfully absolve herself from domestic chores completely.[12]

Canvassing for votes generally and necessarily involved travelling at night. 'It is only at night that one can effectively look for votes. You have to distribute materials and money under the cover of darkness,' asserted a former LC3 chairperson. Thus, men had an advantage because they could move around freely. A woman, on the other hand, had to make sure that her husband was in full agreement. But this was not all. Intimidation and harassment could be used to scare off women, especially if they were engaged in a very competitive race. In Kabale, it was observed that some husbands would be warned:

> *Akakazi kawe kaashuba kugyenda ekiro turaza kukaata omutwe neinga tukahambe. Karepanka.* (If your wife continues to move at night we shall smash her head or rape her. She is so proud.)

The English translation cannot deliver the powerful embedded meanings of belittlement and disgrace in the use of the term *akakazi*, an inverted term of *omukazi* (woman/wife). Such belittlement of women's public presence further served to infuriate some husbands, causing them to curtail their wives' political ambitions.

A further question is whether candidates could use agents to overcome the gender-based disparity in campaigning and time required to canvass for votes. The argument against this was that for LC elections, voters wanted to be visited personally. Besides, one could not be sure that agents would deliver messages adequately. Referring to what he had to do to become a sub-county (LC3) chairperson for the 1998-2001 term, Turyamubona stated that of the 3,622 homes in his sub-county, there were only 71 that he did not visit personally. During some visits, he would participate in harvesting, transporting harvested crops such as potatoes and sorghum from the gardens and splitting firewood. He believed this gained him overwhelming support because he would be seen as someone who knew people's actual problems. He then asked:

Nogira ngu omukazi oshweirwe ebyo akabibasa? Bahurire ngu muka nanka ariyo nakora owabandi arikuroonda akaruuru? (Do you think a married woman - somebody's wife (sic) can manage to do all this? How would they hear that somebody's wife is working in other people's homes to solicit for votes?)

The discussion of money, morality and marriage demonstrates the complexity of community politics. Candidates confronted multiple demands beyond and above those relating to council business. In particular, women faced highly 'othering' and distancing discourses of morality that further negated their legitimacy in public space. A number of female councillors expressed dissatisfaction with the terrain that exposed a leader to the whims of the electorate (in a unique way with regard to women), raising concern over who apparently leads whom. Specifically, women entered politics with several messages: they were respectable women, they had the appropriate qualifications of motherhood and marriage, and possessed moral probity; and they had the necessary drive and public virtue to be public representatives, whether as direct or as women councillors. In this way, women entered public politics both because of their sex and in spite of their sex.

The selection process probably favoured conservative women. *Mukazi mufumbo ate muzadde* (wife and mother) was a major yardstick for women who stood for political office and this set a precedent which excluded contrary discourses about womanhood. This community power was not necessarily in the hands of men alone. In Kabale District, for instance, respondents argued that, in the two local council elections, women had been at the forefront of moves to ensure that fellow women standing for office conformed to the minimum standards of morality of womanhood. While discussing why women in Kabale did not stand for open seats, one man intimated that women often discouraged or criticised fellow women who attempted to stand for the highly competitive seats, giving them nicknames.[13]

How can this phenomenon be undertood? Is it a case of women opposing fellow women and lacking unity a a group? Sen reminds us that inequalities often survive precisely because the priviledged make allies of the deprived and 'the underdog comes to accept the legitimacy of the unequal order and becomes an implicit accomplice' (Sen, 1990, cited in Agarwal, 1997:22). This is the position taken in considering the issue of women's unity, on lack of it, bearing in mind that women are also a heterogeneous group.

The experience of women in the local sphere does not imply that women at the national level were spared these battles. While analysing Ugandan electoral processes, Tamale (1999) observed how marriage was used to subject women to moral probity:

> Women spent a great deal of campaign time convincing the electorate of their moral aptness to stand for political office rather than in the articulation of issues... Women encountered slurs regarding their marital status, sexuality and in (fidelity). A married woman was penalised for neglecting husband and family. A woman who was 'unattached' was put to task to prove that she was not a *Malaya* (prostitute) (1999:121-2).

Tamale (1999) expressed shock that female contestants themselves used the morality card against each other, but this should not be surprising. Women's actions have to be understood within the context of their subordination. Women employ the ideological constructions available to them as members of specific communities. One may well ask whether any alternative routes are available to women standing for office, to legitimise themselves in this meta-space. Does the campaign period offer opportunities for individual women to move certain norms into an 'arena of contestation and discourse' or the 'locus of confrontation and competing discourses' (Agarwal, 1997:15)? The unique nature of women-only contests is specifically relevant. The stage is choreographed to engage women in competition against each other and the result is one that constrains the possibility of transformation.

Evidence from the campaign meetings attended confirms some of the observations Tamale made with reference to parliamentary elections. In addition, it was observed that, in the local political landscape, morality was even more powerfully emphasised to shape women's public identity in terms of their conventional roles as wives, mothers and carers. In certain respects, national politics enables some fracturing of the discourse around which such factors may be negotiated. In local elections, everybody knows everybody else. The closeness and intimacy of the local limits the potential for ambiguity and negotiation, compared to the national arena.

The above examples show that women's agency is more limited and different from men's. The lived reality of gender roles prescribes what women and men can do. As was shown, each gender canvassed for votes in different ways, and the value ascribed to the contribution was different. Voters wanted candidates to understand the texture and context of their lives, so that their interests could be represented adequately. Thus the contest between candidates was deeply embedded within daily community life, including that of ideologies and beliefs about gender morality and the material needs of these communities. In essence, these concerns reflect the difficulties of altering conventions of gender divisions and raise questions about the larger transformation of women's and men's roles.

The Local and the Unbending Patriarchal Power

The interface between moral battles and commercialisation of elections, further compounded by the separate ballot box, produced a gender-specific political landscape. Far from the assertion that women find it easy to participate at the local level (Evertzen, 2001; Drage, 1999), it seems that, apart from the seats created from above, patriarchal construction of political power seems to be even more resilient at local level. Local government is without a doubt close to the people, but this does not translate automatically into power for the less privileged, especially as far as competition is concerned. With regard to women as a social category, there seem to be new ways in which subordination is constructed, thereby sustaining their secondary status. In other words, devolution of power per se may either leave patriarchal notions intact or aggravate them, depending on the situation. This is what is meant by the unbending nature of patriarchal power.

At a conference on Ugandan Women in Politics in 1998, the then minister of local government (Uganda), Mr Bidandi Ssali, asserted that, despite the increased participation of women, they had not gained access to positions that increased their capacity to influence policy (see Table 5.1 below).

Table 5.1: Women and Men in Local Government Positions

	1998 – 2001				2001 –2006			
Elected Positions	**Councils**	**M**	**F**	**% F**	**Councils**	**M**	**F**	**% F**
District (LC5) Chairperson	45	45	0	0.0	56	55	1	1.8
LC5 Vice Chairpersons	45	5	40	88.9	56	38	18	32.1
Mayors	14	14	0	0.0	14	13	1	7.1
Sub-county (LC3) Chairpersons*	860	851	9	1.0	416	410	6	1.4
Appointed Positions								
CAO	45	39	6	13.3	56	55	1	1.8
Town Clerk	63	62	1	1.6	-	-	-	-
RDC	45	35	10	22.2	56	47	9	16.1

*Total number of sub-counties are 953; only 416 are covered by this research.

Positions of influence in Uganda's local government system are basically the chairpersons of the district and the sub-county and it is not a coincidence that there are no women in these positions. To occupy a position of influence means that one has to contest highly competitive seats and, as already argued, the conditions are not favourable for women to do this. As the table below indicates, very few women contested key positions:

Table 5.2: Women and Men in Key LC Elections 2001/2

Position	No. of Candidates	Females	Males	% Female
District (LC5) Chairpersons	159	9	150	5.6
Sub-county (LC3) Chairpersons	2,709	91	2,618	0.04
Directly-elected (LC5) Councillors	2,671	70	2,601	0.03

Source: Uganda Electoral Commission Records (2002).

Graph 5.1: Women and Men in Key LC Elections

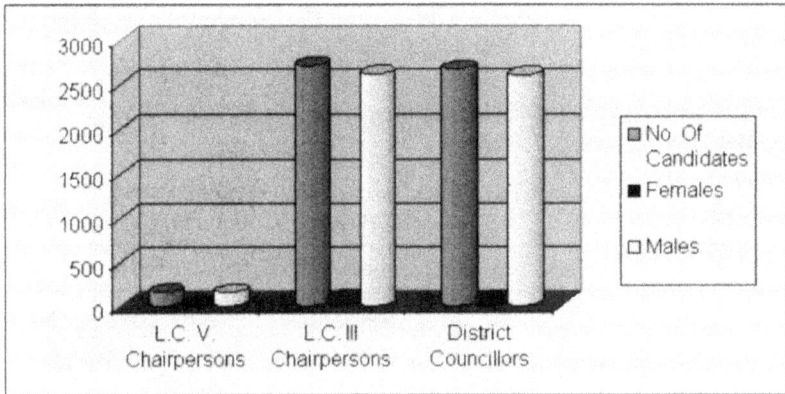

As can be seen from Table 5.2, the most powerful position in local government, that of the LC5 chairperson, was exclusively filled by males in 1998, and in 2001 there was one woman among 56 men. In 1998, two women stood; one in Hoima District (Taaka Awori, 2000) and the other in Kampala city (for mayor), but both lost.[14] In 2002, three women stood and one won in the new district of Kanungu.

A specific phenomenon emerging in the hierarchy of local government is the feminisation of the deputising role. For example, of 45 district vice-chairpersons in the 1998-2002 term 40 were women. In a number of districts, the post of deputy speaker was occupied by women, particularly in the second term of 2002-6. Whereas there were nine women among the 56 district speakers, female deputy speakers numbered 32 of 56. The pattern was replicated in lower local councils.[15]

The phenomenon of women's dominance in deputising roles can be interpreted in various ways. One is that it could mean that women are getting closer to the seat of power. According to one official in the ministry of local government, gender awareness in Uganda has increased to the point where people are conscious that, if a chairperson is a man, the deputy should be woman. The monitoring group in 2001/2, however, noted with concern what it termed as the deputising or 'viceship syndrome' affecting women (NEMGROUP, 2002). The trend emerging in local government mirrored marriage arrangements, with the male as the head and the female in a secondary role. Besides, in the case of the vice-chairperson at district level, it was the chairperson who nominated his deputy, further contributing to the clientelist and patronage relationships emerging at local level. The only legitimating moment was that the nomination had to be approved by two-thirds of all members of Council (LGA1997, Part III 19: (1)).

Chairperson and 'Chairman'

As already noted, women have a dismal record in highly competitive contests but, there is also the question of the politics of leadership and local definitions of legitimacy in key positions. These positions are chairpersons at the district (LC5), sub-county (LC3) and village (LC1) levels who are key icons in the local government system. In fact, much as the official discourse has adapted to embrace a more gender-inclusive naming, the title 'chairman' was pervasive and in popular use by the media, academics and everyone else. The use of the title 'chairperson' was often used when a woman held the position. However, there were so few women in this such position that the androcentrism of power is sustained. The 2001/2 election outcomes revealed a number of trends in this respect.

The District (LC5) Chairperson

The post of district (LC5) chairperson is the most powerful and prestigious, popularly referred to as 'the president' of the district. As shown by the figures in Table 5.2, this post is a male bastion. In 1998, all district chairpersons were male and in 2002 one woman joined the prestigious cadre. Predictions by people in Mukono, Kabale and Kumi districts were that a woman was not likely to stand for this post in the near future.[16] Three well-respected women councillors in Mukono District were asked whether they would consider standing for the post of district chairperson. Their responses were remarkably similar, beginning with a sigh and adding that 'our' people were not yet accustomed to having women in such powerful positions. In the run-up to the 2002 elections, the former secretary of finance of Mukono DC (a woman), was asked if she would contest the district chairperson seat, and she shuddered at the thought. In her view, it would be easier to run for parliament than stand for district chairperson. 'The people who elect us would not think that a woman can run a district, they even think we women should not tamper with the other general sub-county or parish seats.' She hastened to add: 'Heading a district requires a lot of experience. This man (meaning the then chairperson of Mukono District) literally knows every village in this district - and in detail!'

These and other views on district chairpersons prompted the author to consult Josephine Kasya, the only woman LC5 chairperson in the country. She was the chairperson of Kanungu, a new district created in 2002. She said that her political career shows that the presence of women in public politics can provide significant opportunities for other women to reach decision-making positions. The path she followed to reach the position of chairperson is set out below.

Case: The Political Career Path of Josephine Kasya, LC5 Chairperson, Kanungu District (2002-6)
Josephine Kasya was a teacher (Grade 3) and was also active in the church as a member of Mother's Union and in a community-based organisation called Bakyala Tweyombeke. This particular women's group ran a revolving fund that helped women to meet their practical needs such as buying clothes, plates and other household utensils. She was the vice-chairperson of this group. In the 1989 RC elections, she became secretary for women at RC3 and in 1992 she became women representative to RC5, representing her county in the old district of Rukungiri, before Kanungu was created. In the District Council there was an affirmative action seat for women and she took this unopposed. In 1993, Kasya contested the Constituent Assembly but was defeated. But she said: 'I have no regrets because the campaigns provided me with enormous exposure and interaction. People could not believe that a woman from such a marginalised/remote county (Kinkizi) could contest in such elections.'
In 1998, with the one-third reservation, she passed unopposed to become a councillor at LC5 where she was appointed secretary for Gender and Community Services. In 1999, there was a reshuffle within the Rukungiri District Executive and she became the vice-chairperson of the District Council. During this time the District Chairperson (Rutaro) was nominated chairperson of the Uganda Local Authorities Association and Kasya as the vice-chairperson effectively acted as chairperson, as provided for by the LGA (1997).
In 2001, six months before the second LC elections, Kinkizi was given and became district status known as Kanungu District. Following this, the representatives from Kinkizi were required to constitute a government for the interim period of six months. Through much lobbying and tactical politics, Kasya became the unopposed chairperson of the new district. During the six months interim period before the elections Kasya performed well, providing basic services in the district. At elections a man wanted to stand but her performance had won her support. Kasya says, 'Actually, I wanted to pull out, but people promised support and shying away would have betrayed them. Additionally I had something to show.' In the six months she had secured funds to construct an office block and purchase two vehicles and for provision of water. These achievements discouraged the opponent and Kasya once again passed unopposed to become the chairperson of Kanungu District for the 2002-6 term.

Kasya's case brings out a number of issues. First, whereas the affirmative action seats for women were seen as tokenism and limited in their capacity, here was an example of one woman had risen above these stereotypes. Affirmative action saw Kasya move from being a member of a community group to holding the prestigious post of district chairperson. In this sense, state feminism worked to break the glass ceiling. Secondly, how individuals or groups strategically position themselves in these structures in terms of networking, is important; they need to grasp opportunities to acquire power. A new district was created at a time when Kasya was not merely a vice-chairperson, but when she was strategically in charge of the Council (Rukungiri). The example demonstrates how she seized the opportunity, acquired support from both men and women, holding evening meetings and entertaining Council members. But at the same time, she had a track record of service provision.

How do we explain the fact that Kasya's path to political power was unopposed? What does this mean? Many observers in the district feel that going through unopposed can undermine one's political legitimacy. To be a proper politician, one has to jump through the hoops of contest, locally referred to as *akasengegya* (sieve). However, an alternative view could be that consensus can be achieved by lack of opposition. Competition can polarise people, particularly in local politics where other factors, such as proximity, are at play. This, contrary to women's supposed fear of competition (as discussed earlier with regard to women councillors) could constitute seeds of a different political culture.

During group discussions it was observed that people were coming to terms with a female leader. In some cases men were mortified to be ruled by a woman - *Okutegyekwa omukazi*. In one discussion in Nyakishenyi Parish, a church leader lamented:

> *Abantu boona nibagira ngu Kanungu tukakora eihano. Obwe shi abashaija bakahwayo twaza kutegyekwa omukazi?* (Most people are saying that we people of Kanungu committed a sacrilege. They ask whether there were no more men to allow ourselves to be ruled by a woman.)

But women in the discussion group cheered and said: *Naitwe katubategyekeho ako mwaraturuhize* (Let us also use this chance to rule you. You had made us tired). A number of women, especially female councillors, were happy with the situation and felt validated by the fact that a woman could occupy such a prestigious position. The implication was that a woman occupying such a position and a positive impact on women's collective identity. However, it was also interesting to note that some women felt uneasy about a woman ruling over their husbands, especially husbands who wanted, and were capable of, occupying the same office.

The other significant factor during the transition from the six months interim period was that much had been achieved for the new district. Kasya, as a chairperson of a new, remote district, had attracted support. In her own words, 'all doors seemed to be open'- even those of the ministries critical for service delivery, such as finance, works and housing and local government. Accordingly, people justified her unopposed election on the basis of her achievement:

> *Egi gavumenti neeyebembeza abakazi.* (In this government, women are ahead. A man cannot get as much from the central government.) 'If she can achieve this in six months what about a whole term of four years?'

Two views existed about whether Kasya would run for and win the second term. One was that she deserved the second term, and would consolidate gains for the district. The other was the opposite: 'She was just lucky to pass unopposed that time', said one opinion leader in Kanyantorogo Sub-county. 'There are many men eying the post now,' he added, implying that the time for the post be filled by its rightful occupiers (men) was long overdue. What was observed as people oscillated between the two positions was that gender biases were still deeply entrenched, but the moment of opportunity had worked in favour of Kasya. Much as people emphasised gains for the district more than issues of leadership and gender equality, such a stance could have the potential to enhance political leverage for women in the long run. Government support was also seen as a factor that cushioned Kasya. On the whole however, Kasya made a dent, no matter how small. Sufficient legitimation of women in the post of district chairperson is, however, still a long way off.

The Sub-County (LC3) Chairperson

The sub-county is significant for service delivery and local revenue mobilisation. The centrality of the sub-county is both material and symbolic. In reality, the sub-county is the level at which implementation occurs. District planning is sub-county-based and the ultimate beneficiaries of the development plans are the constituting sub-counties in a particular district. Within the national policy framework of the Poverty Eradication Action Plan (PEAP), the sub-county assumes even more significance in terms of funding activities for poverty alleviation and priority areas of government. Furthermore, the collection of graduated tax is based at this level. Hence, the sub-county chairperson occupies a seat that projects both the generative and the oppressive power of the local state. Here, too, gender discourses regarding who may occupy this seat legitimately are very strong.

In 2002, there was one particularly interesting case in Mukono District. Voters asserted that a particular woman had performed very well as a chairperson in terms of service delivery and implementing sub-county programmes, but they were 'tired of being ruled by a woman'. The sub-county performed very well in terms of district poverty alleviation programmes, including water and sanitation services, feeder roads and schools. The chairperson's self-evaluation in the run-up to the elections was that she had implemented government programmes selflessly and the community was generally happy with her performance. 'There is a time I spent a night at a water source site'- *twasula ku mugga*, she emphasised. On the basis of these achievements she stood for re-election. But during the campaign, the contest turned not on issues of performance and implementation of community needs, but on her status as a woman – on her femininity. Her sexuality specifically came into play in very significant ways. The major reason for her losing related to her gender. *Omukazi atufuga atya* – How can we be ruled by a woman? Other factors contributing to her downfall were traced to the fact that she was a strong supporter of the incumbent government in a constituency dominated by the opposition. The circumstances under which she became a sub-county chairperson were rather different, however, as her case shows:

Case: Namugga (not her real name) and Her Ascendancy as a Sub-county (LC3) Chairperson (1998-2002)

Namugga was persuaded to join the race for parliament (because she was qualified), but was hesitant. As the LC elections approached, the LC1 chairperson asked her if she would stand for LC3 chairperson. Still she was hesitant. 'How could I compete with men who were used to politics?' she said. Another opinion leader approached her, also talked to her husband and pledged support in the campaign. He mobilised a group who visited people and tested the water and found people receptive. Later, they accompanied her in the evenings to introduce her to the constituency. As a teacher, she was not very familiar with the local government, nor had she ever read the Local Governments Act. Hence she talked about ordinary problems such as water, roads and security. Many people wondered why a woman was interested in the post of LC3 chairperson, why she was not going to contest the women's seat as a councillor at LC5. At LC3 she stood against a very powerful and rich male incumbent. Initially people thought she was joking and attended her meetings just to hear what she had to say, but gradually became interested and appreciated what she had to offer. She sponsored a very intensive campaign. There were five candidates, four men and her. For her campaign, she prepared a manifesto in the local language (Luganda). The major opponent did not have a manifesto and was banking on his already acquired political capital. She won the election with a relatively large margin. She represented a promise for change from leadership by self-seekers, to that focused on concrete problems on the ground.

In 1997, Namugga was seen as a person who would focus on the development needs of that particular sub-county. Her gender identity was secondary. Yet, in 2002, gender assumed centre stage. The fact that service delivery had improved during her era was acknowledged, but people claimed they were tired of being represented by a woman. She only won in four of the 26 polling stations (EC records at Mukono District). One official in the district remarked that voters did not know what they wanted and wondered whether giving people power *(obuyinza)* was not antithetical to development *Kale omukyala yakola nyo, naye abalonzi* (This woman achieved a lot for the sub-county, but the voters are unpredictable). This official remarked that the sub-county had, in the past, been plagued by corruption and internal wrangles and Namugga had reversed this to make it one of the best performing in the district.

The meanings embedded in the question of *Omukazi atufuga atya* provide some explanation for the turnaround. First, it suggests the idea of 'too close for comfort'. *Okufuga* does not merely signify leadership, but carries with it elements of domination and vertical rather than lateral power. This case demonstrates and confirms what a number of scholars of gender in situations of transition have observed, namely that in periods of consolidation, politics become more antithetical to women than during periods of crisis (Razavi, 2000; Meintjes et al., 2001). When the sub-county was threatened by corruption, an opportunity arose for a woman to stand. Her femininity was even used to woo voters on the basis that she would bring positive development and minimise intrigue and corruption. As the sub-county stabilised, the notions of womanhood used positively just four years earlier, became the means to attack the female candidate as an intruder in a man's world.

Another woman who contested the sub-county chairperson seat in Kanungu District told her story. Voters campaigned actively against her because as woman, she had no right to occupy a position whose major responsibility was collecting graduated tax and arresting defaulters. The argument used against her was that women did not ordinarily pay tax unless they were in paid employment. Rumours circulated, one of which was that there was once a woman sub-county chief in the same area who summarily arrested men for tax defaulting and when the men needed to relieve themselves she would practically open their trouser zippers herself. In a bid to mobilise women, voters were asked, 'Do you want a woman to go about arresting your husbands for tax?' Interesting to note was the attempt by men to mobilise women using the very constructions that excluded women from decision-making processes. The idea that their husbands would be humiliated if arrested by a woman effectively mobilised women against the female candidate.

The case of Namugga and other women who contested the sub-county chairperson seat demonstrated a backlash. During the first local government elections in 1998 there were indications that women would occupy positions of sub-county chairperson. At that time, the concrete configuration of power was fluid and it seemed to be a mere continuation of the RC system. By the second election in 2001/2 it was clear that gender power took a patriarchal form, such that male power was being redefined as legitimate, whilst women's place in open contests was delegitimated. The actions of voters reflected a concerted attempt to recapture patriarchal definitions of power that were, to some extent, being otherwise undermined by state reforms from above.

The Village (LC1) Chairperson

Francis and James discuss the manner in which the village (LC1) chairperson intervenes in village life, mediating disputes, adjudicating offences and witnessing land transactions. The village chairperson might even assist in graduated tax collection, receive official visitors or write letters to certify residence or ownership of livestock (Francis & James, 2003:335).

The village chairperson assumes critical significance in people's lives. Data at the national level was yet to be compiled, but the districts visited showed that, out of many thousands of villages, at most three women stood and won the post of chairperson. There could be a number of reasons for this trend, the first probably being that localised power is felt directly and hence heavily gendered. The powers and functions of the village (LC1) chairperson, including magisterial adjudication of conflict, bestowes considerable local power on the incumbent. It is very difficult for a woman to wield this power in practical terms, as explained below.

The village chairperson was not a paid post and did not necessarily have an office. The chairperson's home becomes a public place where people could knock at the door any time of the day or night. In the words of one election monitor, 'Men do not want their homes to be turned into a market.' At the level of the household, a woman, especially a wife, found it difficult to turn her home into a public place because of her subordinate position. For a man, such considerations did not arise, because, according to popular perception, the home belonged to him as head of household. This is where the difference lies. Men are able to locate themselves in the local political terrain where they act from a position of strength, as opposed to women who seldom have the same freedom. On the whole, however, the point made earlier about the intricacies of localised power and the meanings that accompany it have a much broader impact on the positions within local government, which will remain male bastions.

What the present investigation revealed was that neither men nor women are opposed to having female ministers and parliamentarians at national level. That the vice-president was a woman, or that, in Mukono, Mbarara and Lira, for instance, women won competitive parliamentary seats, did not have much local significance. This kind of power was not felt directly and was easily ignored. However, matters were different in the sphere of local government, where power was exercised directly in people's daily lives. Power at the local level was likened to a household, where women holding power were seen to rule over men symbolically - as wives ruling over husbands.

This is how the public/private debate maintains powerful validity, not in a liberal sense in terms of the separate existence or boundaries of and between these spheres, but rather relating to their dynamic interaction and its effect on political space. LC elections demonstrated that the local was in many respects highly controlled by normalising and patriarchal discourses about women's and men's spaces. This fact ultimately challenges the view that decentralisation ensures local democracy automatically. This view calls for additional qualifiers of the conditions under which gender hierarchies can be neutralised sufficiently to enable women and men to participate equally. A gender-neutral outcome simply does not exist.

It was discovered that the real issue is how women enter public politics – encumbered in a different way from the men. This can only be understood if the focus is on the totality of people's social lives, and not only on women in public politics. Women cannot, at the individual level, abandon their domestic responsibilities. Nor could women, at an individual level, bear the responsibility of radicalising local politics. As the evidence shows, it is not strategic for an individual woman to challenge voters (men and women) about social issues from the campaign podium. This, indeed, would be seen as social deviance and would be likely to terminate a woman's political career. The nature of electoral politics is such that an individual candidate is at the mercy of voters. The morality requirement had a much larger implication for women's political legitimacy. As Obbo argues, there is a specific agency limitation for individuals or a group that is being 'constantly corrected' (1980:15). The deeply entrenched patriarchal culture requires broader structural change - beyond the personal and more importantly, beyond the local. The local does seem to offer opportunities for marginalised social actors to emerge, but whether this could lead to a broader emancipatory project that transforms the larger gender terrain remains questionable. The local is neither unproblematic nor essentially egalitarian. For local democracy to be achieved, it must be clear how different social groups fit in (Slater, 1989; Schonwalder, 1997). In other words, a process of localising democracy is required.

However, the very existence of 'battles' around gender identity and political space in the local sphere offers scope for change. The existence of such fierce social contesting implies that male hegemony is not immutable and that men too are constantly reasserting and reassuring themselves about their own power and authority. Interestingly, the ideological constructions of women do not necessarily require policing and surveillance in their social roles; women themselves are so embedded in the economy of care that they do not wish to abandon it. Rather, women look for ways to 'reconcile the conflicting desires stimulated by affect and caring on the one hand and by self-fulfilment outside the home on the other' (Molyneux, 1998:238). Hence, women's social embeddedness was somehow self-policing.

The release of such a large number of women into public space, in electoral politics and in councils as a result of affirmative action policies has, on the whole, made inroads into male-dominated political space. Women's active roles in NGOs, CBOs and faith-based organisations has created a degree of leverage, with the potential to make critical inroads into the patriarchal build-up of the political culture. There are spheres where women slowly undermine established rules and norms. The subject of the next chapter is to follow up on these matters and to examine aspects of council politics and women's public presence.

Notes

1. These two elections were organised under the no-party movement system. With the move to a multiparty political dispensation, it remains to be seen whether the gender dynamics will change significantly over the years.

2. The elections studied were conducted under the individual merit system, making the campaign process a critical starting point. With the move to the multiparty dispensation it will be imperative for future research to study the roles of parties and their selection processes as gatekeepers.

3. Nomination fees varied according to levels. District councillors paid Shs. 50,000, sub-county councillors Shs. 20,000, district/ city chairpersons Shs. 200,000, divisions, town and sub-county chairpersons Shs. 50,000 (Republic of Uganda , 1999).

4. In 1996 parliament had passed the Local Governments Bill with provisions that set minimum standards for sub-county chairpersons and district councilors at Ordinary Level (O level) education. Women's organisations opposed the requirement on the grounds that it would disqualify many suitable women because of their generally low education levels. The president also vetoed the minimum standard provisions and these were subsequently eliminated from the published LGA (1997) (Tripp, 2000).

5. This meant that there was no need to ferry supporters from one place to another as in previous elections (local, presidential and parliamentary). This development not only reduced incidences of election violence but also increased the opportunity for the less privileged (in terms of resources) to participate favourably. Ferrying supporters from place to place was expensive and affected women and the poor in particular.

6. This contrasts with official discourse relating to female women councillors, i.e. a councillor who is a woman rather that a women's representative. It therefore means that at the level of political practice, women are taken to represent women.

7. To translate her submission literally, the woman would cook the egg for her children and husband, never herself.

8. Plainly put, *emisomo gya senga* refers to sexual matters in the home, but deeper meanings relate to how a woman should provide all-round care to satisfy her husband.

9. Even at national level, a woman parliamentarian was shown by press 'kneeling in advance' for voters. She was supposedly telling voters that she was going to ask for their vote during the next parliamentary election (see *The New Vision*, 3 October 2000) In another related incident, a wife of a parliamentary candidate went down on her knees and asked voters to vote for her husband 'throwing the rally into frenzy'. 'I have known my husband for 14 years, he is a good man and he does not even go out with other people's wives,' reported *The Monitor* on 19 June 2001.

10. According to a community development officer in Mukono District, a woman appearing at such functions not wearing a gomesi will be considered to be naked *(bukunya)*.

11. The trespass story was a long one. Apparently, this particular woman candidate had accused another woman of trespassing and had had her imprisoned. While she was in prison, her mother died and she could not attend the burial. The woman candidate denied it.

12. One of the candidates for women councillor in Mukono District who had acquired her position unopposed, attributed her success to several factors, the most important of which was that her family was in good standing, her children well cared for, and she had her own garden. She did not depend on the market for food, she said. In other words, she was a diligent woman who worked and grew sufficient food and ensured food security for the family. However, it is doubtful whether such definitions of diligence are adequate for an effective politician.

13. Nicknames such as *mukazi mushaija* (man-like woman), refer to a woman who is proud and trying to be like men.

14. The East Africa Initiatives (EASSI, 1998) which documents a broad picture of council elections and women's achievement, notes that a woman who contested the mayoral seat in Kampala, the capital city, tailed with 0.5% of the votes cast.

15. The feminisation of the deputy took place not only at the local level, but also nationally where, at the time of the research (2002), the vice-president, the deputy speaker, the deputy chief justice and many other prominent deputies were women.

16. A question asked of a number of participants was what they predicted for the next two to three LC elections to the future.

6

Women in Local Councils and the Politics of Presence

Ekitufu obukulembeze bwekikyala tebunyuma (To be sincere, as a woman, leadership is not an enjoyable task) (Interview with Naki (pseudonym), July 2001).

This statement was made by a female district councillor in 2001, in an interview to determine views about the local council elections to be held the following year. She elaborated on her experiences as a councillor and said: 'You do not feel comfortable, you are not yourself...you are not really there, you are neither here nor there'. Significantly, Naki had made her mark in the council. She was known to have made meaningful contributions. Her ideas were respected by both men and women in the council and in the community at large. Other female councillors interviewed showed the same degree of hesitancy and uncertainty. What are the subtexts and the untold stories that lie beneath these sentiments and perspectives? What were the effects, the success and constraints of women's participation in decision-making in local councils?

From total exclusion, women moved into new challenges of inclusion. The purpose of this chapter is to examine women's presence in view of these questions. It sets out to analyse the gendered character and conduct of council politics. It deals with the nature of participation in local leadership and focuses on the different experiences of participation of women and men. In particular, the focus is on women as individuals and as members of a group, and questions women's identity itself. Women's stories point out the ways in which political space is not only imaged but also renegotiated and reconstructed. Definitions and interpretations of participation experienced by men and women – as well as non-participation – are explored.

The issue of women's inclusion in political structures has been approached in many ways, but the dominant one has been to link numbers of women to the articulation of women's and gender interests (Goetz & Hassim 2002, cited in Mbatha, 2003). For example, Mbatha (2003) identifies two challenges with regard to female councillors in South Africa's local government. The first challenge is concerned with the question of institutional transformation, validating women's voices and addressing women's interests routinely in policy-making. Second, is the creation of linkages between elected representatives and constituencies of women who would be able to challenge existing patterns of resource allocation (Mbatha, 2003:207)

This analysis uses Mbatha's (2003) point of departure, but takes a different route with regard to the ultimate questions being asked. The politics of presence of women are analysed with a view to mapping out the broad parameters of the political culture of councils. This approach permits the identification of women's distinctive contribution to politics within the institutional constraints. As shown in Chapter Three, the resources over which local governments have a say are meagre. Hence the main concern is not so much with service delivery outputs, but rather with the interactive and the prospects for the emergence of a democratic culture. This is where the question of voice becomes critical. The issue of women's voices is addressed by investigating deliberative space in LCs and how it is shaping and being shaped by gender discourses. The specific impact of male-defined parameters of public debate is characterised and problematised.

Decentralisation, Deliberation and Decision-making

One of the impacts of the RC system and the subsequent decentralisation process is the tremendous increase in deliberative opportunities. Though the content and value of deliberation can be questioned (Goloba-Mutebi, 1999), the fact is that much more deliberation is taking place than in the past. The councils at each level pass their decisions through council meetings as policy-making spaces. This is especially true at sub-county (LC3) and district (LC5) levels, the two corporate levels in the local government system. The local assemblies function as sources of political legitimacy and contribute to the shaping of political space.

Talking to women, especially councillors at district and sub-county level, the most important impediment expressed was their own inadequacy in deliberation. They felt that women had not had an impact on the councils in as far as deliberations are concerned. In trying to follow up this question, district council meetings were attended to observe their broad culture and orientation.

The District Council, Mukono District

It is approximately 14:30 and councillors are concluding their lunch (what would be seen as 'heavy' in local terms). Everybody is in a jovial mood.

People slowly take their seats and the (white-gloved) sergeant-at-arms breaks the informal after-lunch conversation by announcing the entry of the speaker. It is actually the deputy speaker, a woman. There is some murmuring and laughter in the room, but earnestness quickly takes its place as the deputy speaker walks confidently to take her seat. This is the 11th Mukono District Council Meeting on 11 November 1999. The meeting is conducted in the Luganda language.

The clerk to council (otherwise known as CC) announces the order of the opening rituals. He announces that they will start with the Buganda anthem *(Ekitibwa Kya Buganda)*,[1] a mistake that he rectifies immediately. The politically correct order is then announced, which is, the national anthem, followed by *Ekitibwa Kya Buganda* and a prayer.

The deputy speaker, in an impressively audible voice, announces that the speaker is travelling abroad. She congratulates everyone on the Kabaka's (King of Buganda Kingdom) wedding, which took place in August and makes several announcements, including the death of Mwalimu Julius Nyerere, the former president of Tanzania and a respected African leader, and that of the wife of the speaker, whose last funeral rites were to take place in January. Here she makes a slight mistake and says 1999 instead of 2000. There is loud murmuring and the speaker comments, 'Now I know that you are all attentive.' Then she gains grip of the meeting again.

The meeting proceeds with an address by the district chairperson, which mostly dwells on the issue of headquarters for the district. He gives a very elaborate history of how the current offices occupied by the district were confiscated from Buganda Kingdom during the regimes of Obote and Amin, and how Mukono, despite its fame and glory, does not have district headquarters. He then announces that the construction of the district building is under way (at a total cost of 4.2 billion shillings, equivalent to about USD 4.2 million), although the building process had been wrought with problems in the initial stages. The chairperson also comments on the desire within certain quarters to press for the division of the district and emphatically relays a resolution by the executive that the subdivision of the district was not timely, in view of the impending national referendum on political systems. He also talks about the issue of service delivery, which has proved to be a thorny one, particularly in the era of decentralisation. Other items on the agenda include quarterly reports by the secretary of finance and administration.

> The floor is open and the first member to stand is a female councillor who supports the motion in question and then thanks the executive for services, particularly improved roads in her sub-county. As the meeting progresses into issues of finance and accountability, women are silent, some evidently dozing off.
>
> Though punctuated by the somewhat expected 'slips of the tongue', such as regular referrals to the deputy speaker as 'he', using an unusual but not surprising combination of 'Ssebo[2] Madame Speaker', it is, on the whole, a sober and well-managed meeting (Ahikire, 2003:225).

The above account serves as a basis for analysis of the position of women in councils in as far as deliberation is concerned. The first notable factor is the visual impact of the greater numbers of women in councils. The women's presence therefore changed the male character of this public assembly.

Beyond physical presence, a more significant question ralates to the place and impact of women on political debates. How audible was their presence and participation in deliberations? The overwhelming impression of women's performance in council meetings was their visibility when it came to giving a vote of thanks. According to a community development office in Mukono, this pattern had been coined the 'thanking syndrome'. The other impression was that women generally did well in recalling what was discussed and agreed in previous meetings. According to a number of respondents in Mukono District, the pattern of submissions by women were characterised by *nzijukkira luli...*, meaning, 'I remember we agreed in a certain meeting'.

The most evident pattern was that women councillors were generally mute, contributing little to council debates. This situation pertained in many districts in the country, where only a few women made contributions in councils. A male councillor in Kanungu termed this consistent silence by most women as 'being absent despite being present' (personal interview, February 2003).

Referring to Ghana, Ofei-Aboagye similarly argued:

> Inside the assembly, women have yet to make their presence felt. In spite of the increases in their numbers provided for by the government directive, their performance has been muted. This has been attributed to lack of self-confidence, a limited capacity to

communicate in English and a lack of understanding of assembly procedures. Other problems include being shouted at in assembly proceedings or being ignored by presiding members when they (women) want to make an intervention. The short notices for meetings and transportation costs incurred during the assembly work have also been indicated as constraints (2000:2).

The situation in local councils in Uganda similarly reflects a relatively complex web of realities for women. The underlying causes of women's silence in councils must be understood if this apparent deliberation deficit is to be accounted for. Mapping out the situation in three districts revealed difference (see Table 6.1).

Table 6.1: Mapping out Women's Deliberation in Three District Councils

Deliberation (in numbers)	Mukono	Kabale	Kanungu
High	4	1	1
Low	14	4	4
Very Low (Never Talked in Council)	4	11	4
Total Number of Women in Council	22	16	9
Major Language of Deliberation	Luganda/ English	English	English

To follow the general question of women's deliberation levels, to respondents were questioned about the number of women who were regarded as highly effective regarding participation, who were average in that they sometimes contributed and how many had never having made a verbal contribution at council meetings. In Mukono District 18 women (84 per cent) had contributed to DC debates, four of them substantially. Only four out of the 22 women never spoke. In Kabale, those who talked in council meetings was 25 per cent, leaving 75 per cent never uttering a single word. In Kanungu, five out of nine women were active in the council and four women never spoke. The general perception was that women were timid and reluctant to speak.

Tumutegyereize, a female councillor on Kabale District Council and also the chairperson of the Education Committee (1998-2002) said:

> Even when some women are specifically called upon by the speaker, they just keep quiet and look down. They only grumble outside the meeting (interview, April 2000).

The above observation is similar to one made in relation to a sub-county council in Mukono. In one of the group discussions at Nakisunga sub-county, a male councillor asserted: *Abakyala bateesa olukiiko luwedde* (women tend to deliberate when the meeting is over). He said: 'You will hear them say I wanted to say this or the other.' In his view, this was an intrinsic weakness on the part of the women because they had good ideas but were riddled by what he called 'inferiority complex'.

Several informants argued that women councillors lacked a proactive strategy. Women always supported motions but never sponsored them, even though they were proactive at mobilising for others. The chairperson of the Youth Council in Mukono District elaborated on this point with the following example:

> In the Budget Conference, if a question is asked whether anyone has a comment, women will keep quiet. When the same question is rephrased as: Do you support…? They will all come out to support…and they will stamp their feet and so on…

The secretary of finance Mukono (1998-2002), a woman, also said:

> On budget day, women councillors will stamp their feet, they will send chits to the secretary of finance … they would rather say what they want to say in other ways (interview, July 2001).

The popular view is that women lacked confidence, meaning that the deliberation deficit was located within some innate attributes of women. For instance, the deputy mayor of Njeru Town Council (Mukono) (1998-2002) asserted:

> *Abakyala betya nyo. Ekitufu batya nyo okuswala atte banyooma banaabwe.* (Women lack confidence. The truth is, they are very scared of being humiliated, and they also overlook fellow women).

In his view, women were afraid of being challenged and making mistakes. In Kanungu, a male councillor asserted that if the same correction or point of order was directed at a male and female councillor, the latter would be more affected. He implied that women councillors believed they were challenged because of their gender: phrases such as 'It is because I am a woman' may thus recur. The overall observation hence was that women did not feel at home in councils.

Deliberation *(okuteesa)* is a specific public activity. It is also an aspect of power. Reasons for refraining from participation could lie in individual women and men as social actors. However, underlying causes should be traced to the political culture and the nature of institutions that have evolved historically as principally masculine spaces.

Firstly, council meetings in general and the DC in particular are very formal occasions. The DC is, in fact, locally referred to as a 'mini-parliament', which means that there are specific and exclusive formal rules and regulations of deliberation. One needs to know when and how to move a motion, when to second it, when and how to give a point of information and all other formalities associated with debates in parliament. Tamale's description of the parliamentary procedure holds true for District Council meetings:

> The rules governing the language and manner of debate in the house are extremely formal; any departure from them may lead to a member being called to order… In parliament one says, 'Mr. Speaker Sir, I beg to second a motion' not just 'motion seconded'. Members can only speak after they have risen to their feet and 'have caught the speaker's eye'…Members have to know when and how to stand up and sit down, when and how to bow before the speaker, how to walk in and out… (1999:145).

A challenge some women initially confessed to have confronted was dealing with these formalities, particularly at the beginning of their term. In the meetings attended, it was observed that councillors placed great emphasis on formalities and terminology. This was adhered to strictly, and the slightest mistake would invite hisses, jeers and the like. The emphasis on formality, terminology and point scoring in such public assemblies is described succinctly in a study of the South African parliament, which compared the 'ethos and manner of parliament to the theatre of the absurd with its wasteful and inefficient tradition of a school boys' debating society of endless hot air, rhetoric and point scoring' (CGE, 1999:23; Serote et al., 1996, in Mtintso, 1999:62).

Female councillors in Mukono observed that at the beginning of the term, men who had been in council since the RC system was established used that advantage to undermine new entrants, most of whom were women. New entrants were referred to as *abaana* (children) and they would be told: *Mwe abaana namwe mwogela ki?* (You children, do you also have anything to say?)

The clerk to the Council, Ntungamo District, likened the Council to a court of law:

> The moment you do not give relevant sections of the law, then you are not taken seriously. When challenged, you need to quote another law to support your point (Ahikire & Madanda, 2002:13).

Introduction of such court-like and parliamentary formality into council meetings intimidated all new entrants, especially women. As one woman councillor expressed:

> You want to talk and then you are ruled out of order, or someone raises a point of information. Women would feel ashamed, and they do not like that.... (April 2000).

The point about the impact of formality and legality was validated when DC meetings were compared to committee meetings. Sectoral committee meetings were less intimidating. Here women tended to be more active, audible and visible. For example, in sectoral committee meetings in Mukono District, women talked more frequently and much more confidently. The seating arrangement around the table and the conduct of the meeting, for instance, one did not have to stand to contribute, all combined to distinguish these meetings from the 'mini-parliament', the DC. Committee meetings were less formal and less threatening than meetings of the DC, where deliberation was a contest and where seasoned male politicians dominated.

In the DC, female councillors observed that they were ridiculed and looked down upon. They were also more likely to be interrupted. One councillor put it this way: 'A woman may have a point, but a man may stand up and interrupt and her point immediately disappears.' In Kumi District, women reported even more open aggression from the men. They would be told to 'stand up' or 'speak up', with jeering, murmuring and whistling. This phenomenon was known to be more serious at sub-county level, where the chairperson would, in some cases, interrupt a woman to permit a man to speak. In a DC meeting observed in Mukono (in February 2003), there was a consistent pattern, with the speaker selecting women as the last on the roll of each round of contributors. In addition, women were not expected to be forceful, or to use the same deliberative approaches used by men. If they did they would risk being labelled. For example, *Nalukalala* is a Luganda term for women stepping outside general expectations of womanly behaviour, being 'too forceful to be a woman'. Because men were expected to be strong-willed, there was no equivalent label for men.

Language was another factor that inhibited the women. In a bid to elevate the importance of council meetings, many districts used English as the language of deliberation. There were a few exceptions. In Mukono, as already noted, council meetings, including the DC, were conducted in a very unique way, with English and Luganda (the local language) used interchangeably. A person could make a submission in a mix of the two, depending on what he or she wanted to put across. In some cases, certain Luganda words were employed for more emphasis, respectability and humanism. This blend of languages was agreed upon at the very beginning of the council's term of office in 1998. In the more remote districts of Kabale, Kanungu and Kumi, DC meetings were principally conducted in English. 'These are very important meetings' said the Kumi DC speaker, justifying the use of English in the councils.

In some councils councillors who found it difficult to speak English were permitted to deliberate in the local language, but this did little to encourage non-English speakers. It is unlikely that someone would make a contribution to a debate from which he/she has been excluded because he/she could not follow the language in the first place. Further, since English was regarded as superior, people who made their contribution in the local language were likely to be ridiculed or assigned low status. Even in Mukono, where meetings were conducted in Luganda and there was a sense of general legitimacy, female councillors (1998-2002) observed that submissions made only in Luganda were given a relatively low status. A woman asserted:

> For such a contribution they will just say `noted', only to realise that your contribution does not appear in the record of the council meeting (validation workshop).

There was a concern that, since council meeting deliberations had to be recorded in English (LGA 1997, Third Schedule 10(1)), it made sense to deliberate in the same language, at least for consistency. Problems were envisaged when such deliberations took place in one language while the recording was done in another. In Mukono this was not regarded as an impediment.[3]

Some women councillors demonstrated a clear handicap in resources for public deliberation. Some women did not possess the language for debate and contribution, even in cases where there was no contest at all. In one meeting of the technical committee in Mukono District, there was a discussion on project funds and the issue at stake was that if the district did not spend the money within that financial year the district would be fined. In her contribution, a woman councillor said:

> *Kiri nga omusajja ng'aguze enyama awaka, omukyala nasubira nti era omusajja ajja kugenda atyabe enku, akime amazzi afumbe amale aletere omukyala alye* (It is like when a man brings meat home and the wife expects again the husband to fetch the firewood, the water, cook it and even spoon-feed her).

The derogatory symbolism of marriage is instructive, with the husband being equated to the central government and the wife to local government, capturing yet again the secondary status implied. This illustrates the gendered pattern of the kinds of resources that this particular woman could draw upon. It was highly circumscribed by constructions in the private sphere.

In terms of actual content of deliberation, councillors needed to be well-informed to contribute meaningfully. Information flow was itself gendered. It was not clear to many women councillors how the DC agenda was set. One woman councillor said, *Ebimu tubyekanga bwekanzi* meaning that they were sometimes taken by surprise by the items on the DC agenda. Legally, the agenda was supposed to be circulated for at least seven clear days before the DC meeting, but this seldom happened. In addition, huge volumes of documents, such as budgets and development plans, were distributed just before meetings, or even tabled at the meeting. The technical language in many of these documents tended to conceal more than it revealed, so that councillors without prior knowledge and lacking the skill to scan and cut through the voluminous documents remained marginal to critical debates.

Another aspect related to information flow was that critical information was more easily obtained through personal networks than official communication. Even the process of nominating particular issues for the order paper was not purely formal. To use the term advanced by Beck (2003), there was a 'hidden public' in council activities. For example, it was interesting to note that out of eight women councillors in one of the discussion groups only one was conversant with issues relating to the tendering system and the District Service Commission. This was striking, since tendering was a significant factor in district politics. In defence, the women said:

> So many things are taking place and there is no way you can know. If you try to contribute without sufficient information, that is when you are ruled out of order (December 2001).

Access to this hidden public required constant interaction and presence at district or sub-county offices. But taking the cultural context into account, women could not afford to frequent district offices. A woman who did would court disapproval and her behaviour would be judged as potentially immoral. As asserted in a discussion in Mukono:

> People begin to talk about you: what is she looking for? They even begin to speculate about your moral standing (December 2000).

Men, on the other hand, were free to frequent the offices and were generally well informed about what would transpire in forthcoming council activities. They were able to access both formal and informal networking channels.

Technical staff were also said to disregard women councillors. Even official information was not provided universally. Staff did not support women or take them seriously. They even concealed information when councillors asked for it. In Mukono, apart from the Directorate of Gender and Community Services, all other departments were known to conceal information from councillors, but especially from women. One female councillor felt strongly:

> *Batujerega* (we are often ridiculed). When you enter their offices, you see them 'weighing' you and wondering what you are going to say (December 2000).

On the other hand, some of the technical staff observed that female councillors overstepped their legislative role and assumed the task of implementation. The relationship between technical staff and councillors as the political arm of council was generally problematic, as a number of studies have observed (Lubanga, 1998; Tukaheebwa, 1999; Mabirizi, 2001; Goloba-Mutebi, 1999). This is similar to what Coetzee and Naidoo (2002) report with regard to South Africa, in 'the clash between newly elected councillors and the old guard officials'. However there was an additional dimension when it came to women councillors, namely that technical staff tended to overlook them deliberately (Ahikire & Madanda 2002). One reason could be that there were few women in decision-making positions. As noted in the previous chapter, the powerful positions retained a male character and this impacted on the overall political culture of councils. Until the 2001 Amendment of the LGA, representation of women in District Executive Committees (DWGS, 2002) was poor. Further, women were grossly underrepresented in key technical staff positions. The general image of female councillors as underdogs hence contributed to the kind of response and lack of respect they received from technical staff.

Access to information and the hidden public in council business were also closely related to the functioning of the private sphere. Local councillors, with the exception of the executive, had no offices at the district and were scattered in their sub-counties. In addition to visiting district offices, councillors needed a high level of interaction with each other and with the community at large. Women tended to be constrained in this regard because they had less time to network and because of cultural prescriptions about a woman's role. Analysing responses regarding what female and male councillors did in the evenings and on weekends indicated a critical gender difference. Men were free to visit trading centres, to socialise after DC meetings, to go to bars and exchange ideas or to remain at home. The world of men was not restricted. For women, the care economy and moral expectations made them 'time-poor' (Goetz, 2000). This minimised their capacity for networking. Also, as observed in the discussion on electoral processes, the sieve that women passed through was constructed on the basis of a 'good woman' who would act as a role model to other women. Bars or other socialising spaces were definitely not suitable spaces for 'good' women. In this regard local politics was heavily loaded with normative discourses.

Furthermore LC meetings tended to waste time. Sub-county councils, in particular, experienced problems with time keeping, with meetings often ending late in the evenings. 'Even the very person who called a meeting at 10.00 a.m. turned up at 12.00 or even 2.00 p.m.', complained two women at Nakisunga Sub-county (Mukono). The time factor further compromised women's ability to interact and deliberate effectively. In effect, women councillors could not engage in informal interaction after meetings, yet these interactions provided important strategising moments for influencing the direction of future meetings. In the words of the speaker of Mukono DC:

> When it comes to attending meetings you see women panicking when the meeting is delayed because by 5 p.m. women are already time barred. They have to go home and cook and have to walk miles and miles since they normally have no means of transport (December 2000).

The respondent specifically decried the situation at lower councils, where women were constrained by lack of transport. Whereas men in rural areas, particularly those in the bracket of local leadership, owned bicycles, motorcycles and in some cases motor vehicles, women were less likely to own such means of transport. This further compounded the time constraint. Surprisingly though, absenteeism and lateness (for meetings), often associated with heavy workload, was only reported at lower levels, especially LC1. In all the districts visited, women councillors (at sub-county and district levels) kept time and the problem of absenteeism was almost non-existent.

The limited interaction and availability of information had a great impact on the quality of women's debating. One of the relatively experienced female politicians in the district commented that women often came to the DC meetings unprepared. In this regard, women lacked detailed information - for instance saying: 'In my sub-county, bags of cement meant for a particular school were stolen', when they did not know how many bags of cement or the circumstances under which the cement was stolen. A district officer also commented that 'the bad thing with women councillors is that they tend to present hearsay'. The deputy speaker (a woman) observed that women in the DC sometimes had good ideas but did not lobby sufficiently for support.

One of the generally held views that serves as an explanation for women's lack of participation at meetings is that they are generally less educated than men. The question of whether education could account for women's deliberative deficit in council was investigated.

Table 6.2: Levels of Education and Occupation of District Councillors, Mukono District (1998-2002 Term)

Men					
Education	No.	%	Occupation	No.	%
PLE	1	2.8%	Peasant	1	2.7%
O Level	5	13.9%	Farmer	8	21.6%
A Level	3	8.3%	Secretary	0	0.0
Certificate	4	11.1%	Teacher	4	10.8%
			Business	3	8.1%

Teacher	2	5.6%	Social Worker	2	5.4%
Diploma	13	36.1%	Engineer	2	5.4%
University	6	16.7%	Lecturer	1	2.7%
P/Graduate	2	5.6%	Accountant	1	2.7%
Total	36		Fishmonger	2	5.4%
			Technician	1	2.7%
			Administrator	7	18.9%
			Marketeer	1	2.7%
			Cashier	1	2.7%
			Magistrate	1	2.7%
			Retired	2	5.4%
			Total	37	
Women					
Education	**No.**	**%**	**Occupation**	**No.**	**%**
PLE	2	9.1%	Peasant	4	19.0%
O Level	3	13.6%	Farmer	7	33.33%
A Level	1	4.5%	Secretary	2	9.5%
Certificate	5	22.7%	Teacher	3	14.3%
Midwife	1	4.5%	Business	3	14.3%
Teacher	1	4.5%	Social Worker	1	4.8%
Diploma	8	36.4%	Electrical Engineer	1	4.8%
University	1	4.5%	Total	21	4.8%
Total	22				

Source: District Records, Mukono.

According to the figures above, differences between women and men's education levels (in terms of years of formal schooling) were not as significant as to explain major disparities. In Mukono, for instance, there seemed to be very small variations in the levels of education, also bearing in mind that there were fewer women than men in the council. The same applied to Kanungu District. In the 2002-6 term, Kanungu district council had two male councillors who had barely completed primary schooling, whereas all women had completed ordinary level and above. The major disparity therefore seemed to be in the actual placement in terms of occupation, what Bokemeier and Tait refer to as 'occupational prestige' (1980:247). In the case of Kanungu, men who had barely completed primary schooling had a higher social standing than more educated female councillors and could legitimately participate and deliberate in council.

Occupation and social standing was clear in the case of Mukono. Over 50 per cent of women were placed in the agricultural sector as opposed to 24 per cent of men. Men were also involved in a wide range of socially recognisable activities in the formal sector and lucrative occupations in the informal sector. Even men with less formal education compensated by being involved in occupations such as trading or serving in the army, while women were generally clustered in a few traditional female sectors. One notable exception was the teaching profession. Female councillors who were teachers had an edge over other women in council, since the teaching profession exposed one to public skills of interaction and deliberation.

Another dimension related to the limitations of the law. To qualify to be elected, a person had to be considered a resident of a particular local government (geographically) but not employed by that Local Government Council. The LGA stipulates clearly that a person shall not be elected a Local Government Councillor if that person is employed by that Local Government Council (Art. 117 (2) e). In practice this had a profound gendered implication on the selection process. In the majority of cases women residents with the ability to serve in the position of councillor were health workers, secretaries and teachers, and these particular occupations were also most likely to lie within the confines of a particular Local Government Council. In contrast, few jobs held by men were under the jurisdiction of local government and, in effect, the decentralisation framework indirectly favoured people in business and other market-oriented occupations. It also favoured retired civil servants and former members of the armed forces.

The law had the unintended consequence of narrowing the 'crop' of women who could stand for office - the space was narrower for women than for men. As observed by the director of gender in the Ministry of Gender and Community Development, 'the catchment area' for women leaders in local government was overly restricted. It affected the quality of council because people could not afford to resign their official and secure jobs in favour of becoming a councillor. However, the view of one official from the Ministry of Local Government was that the logic for this provision was to ensure separation of powers. To him, it would be ridiculous for a teacher in a particular local government, for instance, to be involved in registration that affected her/himself. That would 'at once raise a serious problem of conflict of interest, and besides, one should not be allowed to hold two positions. It is against principles of participation and democracy,' he asserted. This is an excellent example of how gender-neutral laws, rules and regulations can have a profound negative impact on women (Kabeer, 1999).

The general picture of deliberation in LCs was therefore that women councillors did not participate effectively. Although this does not imply that all women in the councils were mute and all men participated, but there was a consistent pattern that female councillors as a collective were not principal actors in council debates. The reasons ranged from individual to institutional factors. It will be interesting to examine how the dynamic of multiparty politics plays out in local councils in the future; whether or not women will utilise party spaces for greater legitimacy to a greater extent.

Beyond Deliberation: Gender, Community Politics and the Question of Interest Representation

Decentralisation and women's numerical presence affect local definitions of community leadership. In addition to the issues of deliberation examined above, the ways in which identities are constructed are complex. The following refers to two broad and interrelated questions. One focuses on the success story and what women's presence has contributed to the definition of local leadership. The analysis considers the issue of women's interest representation in local politics and the different ways in which it can be recast to capture adequately the gender dynamics of local politics. The second question relates to the way in which constructions of womanhood constrain female leaders, thus constructing them as less legitimate community leaders.

Women's presence in councils has given communities greater access to feedback. Female leaders were reported to be more inclined to give feedback to the community they had access to, explaining district programmes. A community development officer in Mukono noted that the directorate received more inquiries from citizens on rehabilitation, youth and gender programmes as a result of female councillors' efforts to disseminate information to the community. This could also be due to the fact that female councillors tended to have more linkages with CBOs or NGOs as members or as founders than men.

In addition, female leaders were considered to be more approachable. A male councillor in Kanungu, for instance, observed that the female chairperson had demystified the district chairperson's office because of her openness. The door was always open and she was always eager and willing to listen. *Nomuntu wekizibu kya shillingi bibiri* (Shs. 200) *nawe naza owa chairperson*, (Even a person with such a small problem that can be solved with 200 shillings can also access the chairperson's office) observed a female councillor.

Approachability meant that female leaders received what was seen as 'a stream of visitors':

> You have to be ready to listen to stories on a daily basis. Everyone who has a problem, be it marital, financial or otherwise will come to you for assistance. You are exposed to people's most inner problems. Budgets for weddings, funeral rite functions *(enyimbe)* bachelor parties, name it, will always find their way to your door (FGD, Kanungu District headquarters, February 2002).

A female councillor observed that male councillors did not receive that kind of traffic and, in her own evaluation, this was mainly due to the fact that women tend to be 'feelers' *(Abakyala tusasira mangu)*. But she also hastened to add that the major difference was that, in most cases, women in the community were afraid to approach a male councillor, whereas neither men nor women hesitated to approach a female councillor. Even some men feared male leaders, who seemed either too busy or too impatient to listen. Female councillors found, however, that listening actually cost them much in terms of money and time, let alone the emotional baggage associated with some of the problems brought to them:

> *Omukyara bamubinga ninga yagira ekizibu, yaija kurara owaawe, hakiri nomutekyera aka chai kandi nomwarira. Egyo manya ni shukari yagyeenda. Obundi noraara oshutami orikumu kansolinga* (counselling).
> (When a woman is chased from home or gets any other problem

and she comes to sleep at yours, you at least make her some tea and prepare a place to sleep. Already, sugar is getting used up. Sometimes you stay up late trying to counsel her.) (female councillor, Kanungu)

In a group discussion at Goma Sub-county, one male councillor sought to invert the logic. He argued that sometimes female councillors burdened themselves with other people's problems, which impacted negatively on their effectiveness as leaders and politicians. He gave an example of one otherwise experienced female councillor, previously a delegate in the Constituent Assembly. On her way to officiate at a certain function, she came across a fatal motor accident. She stopped to assist the injured, took them to hospital and even paid condolences to the bereaved. As a consequence, she arrived at the function venue very late. Instead of performing her public task at the function, she started by narrating the story of the accident and why she was late, oblivious of the fact that people were already tired. According to this male councillor, the female councillor did not prioritise her roles. But it could be asked what ordinary people appreciate more, concern over the injured, or rushing away to officiate at formal functions.

The second major aspect identified was that women leaders performed well in non-conflictual contests.' If you want to see us (women) perform, organise a programme for mobilisation or any other activity where there is no opposition,' said one councillor. Specifically, women in leadership positions pointed to the role consensus building, as opposed to blunt competition, in reaching their positions. The chairperson of the Health Committee in Mukono (2001) narrated how she attained the position:

> It was a Council day; it had rained so heavily so the commuter taxis could not move easily as the road was slippery. I hence arrived late. When I got in I had barely taken my seat when one of the fellow councillors told me that things had changed. Committee membership had changed and hence new chairpersons had to be elected. There was strong *kakuyege* (behind the scene politics) and my name was proposed for chair of one of the committees. When we went out for lunch, I approached three councillors (one

> woman and two men). When voting time came I could not believe
> what came out. I was unopposed. It was a big success on my side
> (narrated in a research diary, 2001).

The same woman was elected deputy speaker in 2002 and she talked
about how she attained the position:

> To tell the truth, I don't know. Me I did not lobby but when we
> came to the Council, one councillor proposed my name and
> surprisingly I beat my other four opponents. There were three
> men and two women nominated. I won with 29 votes out of 49
> - more than 50 per cent.

Most life histories of female leaders have one thing in common, and
that is a consensus vote which encouraged them to stand in positions,
whether outside or inside the councils. Many of the female councillors
who demonstrated hesitancy and uncertainty in the run up to the
elections, actually stood. Why they did not want to come out openly in
the initial stages is a question that suggest many possible answers. One
answer might be that they were not career politicians. The emphasis
on consensus as opposed to competition might be seen as an inherent
weakness in women's inclination to seek comfort zones. However, it
can also be argued that, as women gain more legitimacy, a different
political culture of consensus may become normative.

Another emerging phenomenon was that women had become more
visible in posts relating to do with finance. In 1998, the secretaries for
finance in Mukono and Kumi were women. In Kanungu, the secretary
for finance (2002) was also a woman. Discussions with respondents
indicated that these were not isolated cases. Many councils, especially at
lower levels, had women in charge of finance. This is was an intriguing
phenomenon. Finance is normally regarded as a key arena of power,
and therefore a seat one would expect to be jealously guarded by men.
Why finance was becoming feminised, despite its centrality in local
government, was a question posed to different informants. Was this
an indication of women's growing political legitimacy, or had power
shifted elsewhere?

General discussions identified the view that women were appointed in positions in finance because they were seen as less corrupt. *Abakazi tibarakira kucurika karamu* (women do not have a habit of using the pen to do wrong things), was one of the views from Kanungu. The chairperson of Goma Sub-county, a woman (1998-2002), had this to say about embezzlement:

> At least I fear to go to prison. Men are more daring. They can decide
> to steal everything and leave nothing for the intended programme.
> As a woman, I would not be that reckless (June 2001).[4]

Other respondents argued that women were still naive regarding finance, and hence neither able nor clever enough to hide irregularities. Yet others feel that women were placed in such positions because they were easier to manipulate. Views on the appropriateness of appointing women in positions in charge of finance may signify essentialised notions of womanhood, but such views also provide an encouraging sign for building women's effectiveness in local government.

Women, in particular, observed that female leaders were inclined to be more concerned with development than men. More women than men had initiated projects in their areas. The views given above signify subtexts emerging around local notions of womanhood.

Is the Ugandan case one of women representing a new breed of leadership, raising the question of specific women's culture, as Bystyzdienski (1992) argues? Is this experience based on certain innate attributes? Are women more inclined to confront these social issues due to their proximity to the community? Or, is it because of their prior exclusion from mainstream public politics that they bring with them to the councils a different set of experiences? These questions do not have either-or answers, it can be explained by a dynamic blend of several factors which place women in a unique space.

Phillips observes:

> Women's intimate association with childbirth and nurture is said to
> restore the more appropriate dimensions: sharpening awareness of
> the devastations of war, strengthening concern for the young, sick

and old; grounding the abstractions of economic and foreign policy in a more compassionate understanding of daily need (1991:4).

She further argues:

> In form as well as content, women have promised to radicalise the very practices of democracy: to cut through the pomposity of male rhetoric; to subvert unnecessary hierarchies; to open up decision making to those who were once objects of policy; to create the world anew (1991:4).

Do these and other assertions point to an underlying optimism about women in structures of decision-making? Specifically, these assertions also refer to questions of whether or not women are better able to represent women's interests. This intricate and ongoing debate of feminist theorisation is located within the Ugandan context of local politics.

Hassim (2002a) argues that, although it is not self-evident that only women can represent women's interests, their inclusion enables the creation of institutions in which diverse interests can be articulated and acted upon. Coetzee (1996) raises a credible theoretical and practical dilemma for women's inclusion, especially in local government, showing that representation of women's interests is not merely an issue for academic feminist debates. Popular discourse in the media and other arenas construct women as bearers of special interests and this dual mandate tends to set them up for failure, thereby increasing their sense of powerlessness and marginalisation (Coetzee, 2000). While in Uganda, for instance, the legal provision for women councillors does not imply any notion of interest representation, local translations construct women as women's representatives by such terms as *kansara wabakyala* (councillor for women), or *oyo agenda kukikirira abakyala* (the one going to represent women). Similarly, the LC election monitoring report of the NEMGROUP (2002) epitomises this distinctiveness by documenting issues raised by female candidates during the campaigns. These issues include education of children, both boys and girls; provision of clean and safe water; provision of health units with good and accessible maternity centres; provision of improved agricultural skills and seed varieties and child nutrition. The report also documents as a strategic gender need raised by female candidates the formation of women's groups to access credit facilities to reduce poverty, among others. That the report did not seek to document issues raised by male candidates signifies the fact that women were constructed as distinct political actors.

The study pursued this particular issue with a number of councillors. They were asked, 'Do you agree with the statement that women politicians represent the interests of women voters better than men do?' [5] A total of 26 councillors answered the question, with eight men and fifteen women answering in the affirmative and two men and one woman disagreeing. This indicates that there is a general agreement among women and men that women represent women's interests better than men. The most common response was that women understood each other better because of common problems relating to child rearing, home management and marriage. One male respondent indicated that women's participation 'always reminds the menfolk that the women matter, and that the interests which they put forward should be addressed'. Another man said that women needed to be there 'because men would always pay attention to bigger general problems leaving behind women's problems as minor issues'. The other interesting assertion was that while men basically sought to achieve self-esteem, women were more likely to advocate the interests of others. The three respondents who did not agree with the statement said that women were not articulate, they were shy, so could not represent their fellow women adequately. Another view was that petty differences tended to separate female politicians from their electorate and from each other.

Much of the literature on representation relates to the legislative function and how the output of women's inclusion impacts on the policies passed. This is what Lovenduski and Karam, for example, refer to as feminising legislation, by ensuring that it takes into account women's concerns (1998:130). But as noted above, local politics extend beyond deliberation. Consider the case below.

Case: Mutatiina and Busingye (not real names)

Mutatiina (a man) migrated from Kanungu to Bungangaizi in Kibale District. But his wife Busingye did not want to migrate. Without the knowledge of his wife, Mutatiina sold the house in which they lived and left. When the person who had purchased the house appeared, Busingye was appalled but refused to leave because she argued that she had contributed the largest percentage to its construction. Busingye presented the case to the village (LC1) court but it could not be resolved. The majority of the men on the committee were of the view that Busingye should have migrated with her husband. 'She was just being bigheaded', they said. The person who had purchased the house demanded that Mutatiina refund his money, but the latter had no money. Mutatiina was arrested and imprisoned and Busingye consulted the female councillor in her sub-county for advice. 'I had to intervene because the woman was the aggrieved party', said the councillor. However, the councillor later advised Busingye to leave the house because the arrest and imprisonment of her husband had created so much polarisation in the community that it would have been detrimental for her to pursue the case (interview with a female LC5 councillor, 9 February 2003).

What does this example say? The above case exemplifies what female councillors have termed their most 'common business' in their community - dealing with domestic conflict. Women with conflicts in their homes tended to turn to female councillors for advice. It is however important to note that female councillors were more inclined to minimise conflict than to seek justice on the part of aggrieved women. In fact, they advised women to take domestic conflict to LC courts only as a last resort. Even when a battered woman won the case against an abusive husband, the female councillor advised the woman concerned to seek reconciliation. In the example, the councillor advised the aggrieved woman against pursuing the case, because it had polarised the community. Female councillors act within a constraining environment, and they have to employ realistic strategies which may not necessarily be radical. Yet the significant observation is that female councillors are viewed as critical actors in the contest for domestic space; their public presence was hence an important signifier in this arena.

In Kanungu, the female chairperson seemed to have extended the boundaries even further. Many observed that men could no longer freely sell land and other family property as before. Even where a man could win the case, he has inconvenienced by court procedures. A female councillor observed:

> When we found a female chairperson, we were all comfortable. It was easy to access her office and obtain advice. This is especially true with regard to women's domestic problems *(emishango yabakyara)*. We consult her and get clear information on how to proceed.

During a discussion group in Kishenyi, a man remarked: *Omukazi yatumazire hati titukagamba omumaka,* (men's personal power over women (as wives) has been considerably reduced by the presence of a woman district chairperson). One woman in the same group said the female chairperson had potential to 'nurture the women' *(ogu mukazi araza kutworora)*. Women said that even their participation in LC committees had been enhanced because they could afford to come home late in some cases. 'You can go back home in the evening and there is peace', they said. In this way, the presence of more women in public office had increased the possibility of private matters being of public concern – the public had made incursions into the private and vice versa.

Furthermore, in local governments where women held prominent positions, there was greater possibilities for women to benefit from district projects directly. While, in many districts, tendering and construction work were a male preserve, there was a marked difference in Kanungu. A number of women were awarded contracts to maintain feeder and community roads, construct schools and supply foodstuffs to institutions. One councillor asserted:

> Even the one who tendered graduated tickets is a woman. I think the taxpayers do not like it but she has brought better quality than the men who did it previously (group discussion with LC5 councillors, 9 February 2003)

Men did not like the idea of taxpayers' tickets being tendered by a woman in a context where women had a collective identity of not paying tax. But, on the whole, the fact that women were awarded so many tenders was a new phenomenon. The general evaluation was that, where women had tendered, the quality of the services had improved. It was also said that female contractors tended to employ more women labourers.

These examples indicate that it was not 'politics as usual'. Women's presence has reconfigured the local political landscape and stimulated new questions. The examples offer much-needed answers about how to conceive women's interests in the face of diversity. Questions can be posed regarding, which women win tenders, or which women are able to bring their private issues into the public arena.

Womanhood, Leadership and Political Legitimacy

The fieldwork revealed a number of constraints to women's leadership, mainly arising from local constructions of womanhood coupled with the nature of women's inclusion in councils. The gender identity of female councillors seemed to be emphasised in politics in a way that manhood was not. Consequently, it affected women's positionality and undermined their formal political power.

One of the critiques of decentralisation is that it would nurture and eventually give more impetus to local exclusive discourses. Female (local) politicians not only have to work within the framework of rules of the LC but, as female members of the community, they also have to comply with culturally specific demands. Comments about constraints on women councillors illuminated the tendency of men in council to treat female councillors as their wives. For example, women were, in some cases, expected to serve food at functions. One function attended in Mukono was particularly revealing. A woman councillor was presiding over a very formal district function but turned into a server at lunch. There were varied views on this issue. Some people did not see anything wrong with female leaders serving food. The argument was that women served food on a daily basis, so what was wrong with them serving at such a function? Others suspected, or rather speculated, that serving food at important gatherings could help women to build political capital. Others said that political heavyweights at such functions had to be served by somebody they trusted, since there could be people with other motives, for example, to poison the men. One of the highly placed women in Mukono DC asserted:

> We are important people. Fine. But when it comes to food, men still feel that we are women and should serve them. They will always call the nearest women around to serve food. If the district chairperson calls you to serve, you have to do it because you would not like to embarrass him in public.

However, far from being an imposition by men directly, serving seemed to be deeply engrained in women. A former chairperson of Bukinda (LC3) observed that, during council meetings, women promptly went to serve as soon as drinks and snacks were brought to the meeting room. The same observation was made by the vice-chairperson of Njeru Town Council (2001), who argued that, when food appeared, women would forget that they were councillors. 'They want to serve; they want to eat last after they have served the men.' It was further observed that female councillors would castigate fellow women who did not assist with serving and refused to serve them. Whether the motive behind the practice of female politicians taking on domestic service roles was to build political capital or protect visitors, it reflected a deep attachment to service and domesticity.

In the wider community, the large numbers of women in public politics created specific identity issues for men and 'our wives'. There was an overwhelming fear that exposure to public politics undermined men's dominance over their wives. Women's participation in councils changed the rural landscape. Women who were hitherto defined primarily by their private being suddenly became public actors. There is a local saying that women had become Museveni's wives - no longer wives to individual men. *Museveni atumire abakazi batujooga* (Museveni has encouraged women to despise us), was the major concern men expressed in rural areas visited. The symbolism embedded in the above construction says much about wifehood, especially in respect of local politics. That the converse identity of 'our husbands' did not exist, points to the politics of belonging and the social power that men hold over women. There was fear evident about women's relative freedom from the far-reaching confines of wifehood.

One aspect of women's relative freedom related to their sexuality. Because women tended to be constructed as sexual beings in a way that men were not, there was a fear that their increased exposure to formal participation would encourage them to engage in acts of immorality. *Abakyala abamu bayigiddemu obwenzi*, argued an elderly man (some women have become sexually loose in the process). Another sought to make the record even more accurate and said: *gamba nti abasinga obungi bayigiddemu obwenzi* (you could say instead that the majority of women have become loose). Fear about women's sexuality partly explains why the discourse around dress was so strong. As in Buganda, local perceptions were that a man would not 'whisper' to a woman in a gomesi, because he saw her as a mother or wife.

The research did not seek to establish the veracity of these claims relating to sexuality discussions. It became clear that one or two female leaders could have had sexual relations with male colleagues, but in other cases, it was mere speculation. Male leaders with such relationships were not criticised, because men as husbands were not subject to boundaries that wifehood imposed on women. This double standard is instructive about women's otherness in public space. Observations found that the interaction that accompanied leadership did not augur well for definitions and boundaries of womanhood in general and wifehood in particular. In one case a husband prevented his wife from attending a district function with her colleagues from the district. They had come to pick her up for a scheduled district programme. The husband told the wife to choose between him and the LC. *Ebyamwe tebiggwa?* (your business never ends?), he asked. In his view, trips for special occasions were acceptable but not as an everyday affair. The female councillor decided to stay at home to save her marriage. This case demonstrates the struggle that female politicians face on an almost a daily basis. The case also identifies the need for greater structure in local government programmes, so that it appears to be less social functions and more public activities and duties.

This chapter demonstrated that women's activities in councils takes place in a rugged terrain characterised by constraints and multiple sites of action and struggle. Female councillors are seen to be more inclined to support development than men despite the fact that their location in formal processes such as deliberation is encumbered. Young, Edholm and Harris (1997) alert feminist scholarship to the dangers of romanticising women's distinctiveness. They argue that it is not necessary to look behind manifest social forms in order to see women, because such a perspective reinforces the notion of separate spaces for men and women (1977:126). Similarly, Rajan discusses alternative political strategies of persuasion, bargaining and simple suggestion, and questions how far these concepts could be institutionalised in the place of traditional forms of political power (1993:104). Hence claims that women are more inclined to consensual political processes may easily fall into the essentialism trap.

There is a need to understand women's presence in formal politics in a new way. It is imperative to consider women's experiences of presence as new energies brought into the political space by social groups that used to be excluded. Although one cannot argue that female representatives are better placed and can represent women and gender interests better than men, their presence and participation tend to expand possibilities and expectations of community leadership. In essence, women's presence in LCs in Uganda has expanded the range of the 'public', with simultaneous spaces for inclusion and exclusion.

Notes

1. This is the anthem of Buganda, composed in the 1960s. The anthem hails Buganda and its glory, supposedly existing since time immemorial, which the Baganda are asked to commit themselves to preserve. In discussions it was established that in Buganda today the national anthem has to be followed by *Ekitibwa* (at all levels, even in schools).

2. A Luganda word for `Sir'.

3. The issue of language may have another side relating to dangers of localism and politics of exclusion. A nuanced understanding of these concerns must include how language might exclude groups on the basis of ethnicity. Thus the question of language is complex, especially in view of concerns about national integration and ethnic politics. If a local language is the language of local government it

could exclude those who do not belong and create unintended negative consequences for local democracy.

4. A councillor who had been on the previous council said that change was noticeable in the operation of sub-county programmes under a woman chairperson. He observed, for instance, that the budget was always brought to the meeting late in the day, when people were tired, and it would be accompanied by 'fried chicken' as a type of bribe. 'Within one minute the budget would be passed,' he said.

5. Question adopted from Hedlund, G. (1985) *The Political Interests of Gender*, p. 91. The questionnaire was distributed to 30 (of the 64) councillors in Mukono District.

7
Envisioning Gender-Inclusive Local Democracy in Uganda: A Conclusion

The central concern of this book has been the politics of inclusion of women in Uganda's local government. The legally prescribed numerical representation of women in local government decision-making structures led to a change in the terrain at local level. A minimum of 30 per cent women at all LC levels increased women's public presence in community politics significantly. This, together with the decentralisation process, created a new political landscape that calls for a gendered understanding of local-level politics and the inclusive potential for local democracy in Uganda.

The background of the research was the mass struggle against the totalitarianism of post-independence regimes, culminating in the National Resistance Movement ousting Obote's second regime in 1986. In the politics of mobilisation, the struggle provided a foundation for women's ascendance to a specific political constituency. By its nature, the mass struggle had a broader social base than the nationalist struggle for independence. Initially, the most notable change was the introduction of a structure for local administration, the RC system, which redefined local rule and brought into its ambit hitherto excluded groups, namely women, youth and people with disabilities. The dislocation caused by the war lead to post-independence crises and state repression, extreme anarchy and severe economic stagnation, which shaped the nature of politics and the local state. It also had a specific impact on its aftermath. Partly shaped by the fluidity and fragility of the new regime in the initial years, and the openness of the system at a time when the WID discourse was at its height, the term 'woman' became a new political category. Hence the language of representation took on new gendered meanings.

In this regard, positions that lean heavily on the fact of political expediency (Goetz, 2002; Tamale, 1999) and the desire on the part of the regime to be viewed as a 'good international citizen' (Sawer, 1996) cannot be ignored. The analysis sought a broader understanding of wartime gains. This understanding followed closely that of Moghadam, who posited that the outcome of the woman question in revolutionary movements is determined by both structure and agency - the economic, political and ideological factors, the prevailing material conditions of social life, the international environment, the nature of revolutionary leadership and its social programme, the extent of women's participation in the revolution, and the degree to which women are organised and capable of articulating their interests (1993:73). This formed the backbone of Chapter One. The analysis also confirms that transitions tend to provide political openings, with greater general willingness to rethink the bases of social consensus and revise the rules of the game (Jaquette, 1994; Razavi, 2000). A more realistic conception views all these factors as synergistic. The uniqueness of Uganda's reforms with regard to women's political presence, and in the aftermath of the struggle in the context of a weak women's movement at that time, makes a compelling case for the significance of mobilisation politics. One aspect of Uganda's guerrilla war aftermath is the significance of women's roles to the reconstruction project. This book argues that the country was so run down that it required a revitalisation from the foundation up. The uncertainty and fluidity of the transition made it possible for the demands for political representation by a handful of urban women to be heard.

Conversely, the analysis demonstrates the shortcomings of the same mobilisation politics, namely a critical absence of political engagement between women and the state. This general situation at the national level replicates itself at the local government level. Mobilisation politics constructs women's agency as 'the other' and women as 'special' political actors, which impacts negatively on their legitimacy as local leaders.

Mapping out the institutional relations in and possible outcomes of decentralisation, this study established that there has been a relative increase in people's participation at the local level and that local governments have acquired more roles, powers and responsibilities than they had before. However, the value of people's participation is questioned, largely in view of the fact that financial power is still concentrated at the centre, with major development choices being forced onto local governments by the central government. Is it, therefore, that citizens at local level are acting within a merely procedural democracy, as opposed to more substantive citizen participation? To some observers, this raises further challenges for a gender analysis.

The conceptual choice made by this study was to pay more attention to the local configuration of power, even in the context of minimal financial resources. The notion of local democracy was explored, not as an event or a product, but rather as a process within which gender power relations are a constitutive rather than a contingent ingredient. In terms of gender and as in other social inequalities, the local is neither essentialised nor romanticised. Rather, it is problematised, with local politics conceptualised as complex and dynamic. Contrary to the generally held view that decentralisation enables more participation by the unprivileged, including women, this study suggests that this is not always so. Similarly, a complete dismissal of local democracy was avoided. The study followed a path that would unearth some of the gender complexities, its potential as well as dangers.

Considering LC elections and council experiences, there are indications that, in some cases, the local is more defensively patriarchal than the national level. The proximity of the competitive terrain, in particular, plays out the private and public divide in unique ways, with women constructed principally as secondary citizens. In LC elections, the fact that everybody knew everybody else meant a much more intricate process of moral-suasion, a kind of a 'narrow gate', erected to constrain women's legitimacy in public space. Following Kaufman (1997), one begins to realise that existing structures of social prestige and power may reproduce themselves within the local electoral processes, thereby reinforcing masculine supremacy. Men too face constraints of masculinity as demonstrated by the case of vote buying and ethnic identity.

Decentralisation therefore requires additional qualifiers for it to live up to its much popularised promises of participation, accountability and efficiency, taken to constitute a semblance of local democracy. It was demonstrated that, in Uganda, the women's quota for local government worked to break down the masculine face of public affairs in local politics. On its own, decentralisation and the associated transfer of power to people to elect their leaders would not have achieved substantial women's public presence. This is evidenced by the fact that, apart from the reserved seats, women have performed dismally in open and highly competitive elections. Indeed, that the nature of the women's quota in Uganda, which is referred to as directed inclusion in Chapter Four, serves as partial explanation for the ghettoisation of women in local contests. However, election experiences show that the local contest is highly embedded within the social understanding of gender power relations. At the national level, gender identities are more likely to be mediated by factors such as distance, and the space for negotiation is much broader. In local space, women who assume positions of power are ideologically constructed as 'ruling over' men. Because gender identities in this sphere are more likely to be constructed in conjugal terms, this translates directly into a discourse of wives ruling over husbands, hence automatically becoming not only an aberration in terms of the dominant culture, but also engendering highly-charged masculine solidarity. Masculine solidarity does not imply all men against all women, but rather a discourse about 'the order of things' (Fraser, 1989); about gender order, in which women are also mobilised in terms of how they view themselves and each other. This is evidenced by cases of women opposing the idea of a woman 'ruling over' their husbands, affirming the oft-mentioned phrase in Uganda that women are their own 'worst enemy'. The explanation for this phenomenon is, rather, that the gender order has established a form of masculine solidarity and the identification of authority with the male subject, from which the majority of men and women derive their own identities.

The question of quotas in Uganda can thence be rephrased to emphasise other aspects of local politics. The argument is that a greater public presence by women in local politics will, over time, be able to cut deep into people's perceptions of power and politics. Worldwide, the core idea behind quota systems for women is to recruit women into political positions and to ensure that women are not isolated in political life (Dahlerup, 1998:92). Much as opinions vary on the effects and repercussions of quota systems, most views seem to agree that, in the face of deeply entrenched exclusion of women from public politics, some form of quota, a more or less 'undemocratic' (Goetz, 2002) route to achieve inclusiveness is inevitable. More divergent views have therefore centred around the form these quotas should take. The add-on arrangements or special seats, as instituted in Uganda, are least favoured, with quotas in PR electoral systems showing the greatest potential for overcoming voter preference for male candidates while keeping women within mainstream political competition.

Though the main argument of this book is that the quota system for women in Uganda tends to construct women as second-class citizens, the fact that the selection process was not controlled by party mechanisms could have unique benefits. The preserve of considerable numbers of women as a result of quotas imposed from above, without a doubt, politicised gender identities. The quota was beyond the control of local actors. With regard to the resilience of the local space, it can be said that it is at the local level that women's public presence will have the greatest impact – precisely due to the localisation of that presence and its infusion into people's perceptions of power over time. The potential for the politicisation of gender will be even greater once more women move into general seats and contest key leadership positions, such as that of chairpersons at district and sub-county levels.

As evidenced by the analysis of LC elections, the issue of who takes over the domestic roles of wives is very much alive in local politics in Uganda.

And who will make the chapattis? This is a rather fundamental question, one Indian male posed. The man did not have a problem with women (wives) participating in local government (Panchayat raj institutions) as leaders. His problem was, who would perform the caring roles (symbolised by the chapatti) when the wives are busy with leadership business?

What happens to the existing gender division of labour has been glossed over by the overriding objective of entryism - to achieve women's access to public political space without attending to corresponding changes in private power and gender roles. Female local councillors (especially on lower councils) are constantly straddling leadership and wifehood (and motherhood). Contrary to the dominant view that local leadership can be enmeshed easily with the roles that women are already fulfilling (Drage, 1999), this book argues that these roles often pose a critical dilemma for women. Acting in local space means that role expectations, especially in the field of home care, are little changed. Women are not in a different location, as in the case of national politics. The public and the private play out in the same terrain.

Hence the general consciousness about women leaders is not that they are absent, but rather that they are present and yet not able to fulfil their wifely roles as required by community social practice. The study revealed that, the lower down on the LC ladder, the more female councillors' were absent or late, pointing to the practical effects of the dilemma faced by female politicians as a result of proximity to the domestic space. What is required therefore is transformation of the gender order, of gender relations in all spheres, which implies an embrace of a broader emancipatory project to reconstruct gender identities and citizenship in the polity. This argument does not disable the overall thrust about the importance of women's access to public office; rather, it gives it more impetus. The issue is to identify where both small and big victories can be won on the path to that goal.

One of the common issues relating to women's presence refers to inclusion outcomes. This is the point of Jones and Jonasdottir, who state that women's effectiveness in legislative processes should not be judged by how well they emulate the 'formalistic language of power-brokerage' (1988:3). Furthermore, the dual mandate of female local level politicians as individuals or as a group may not only be unrealistic but may also run the risk for setting them up for failure. The discourse of female councillors or politicians, singled out for specific scrutiny, may accentuate their status as 'the other', thereby leaving the male as the normative political subject. As Lovenduski (1997) rightly says it is important to be careful in assessing women's effectiveness, in order not to trivialise their public presence.

At a minimum, it can be argued that the existence of a relatively high proportion of female politicians at local levels seems to promote different strategies of activity and different views about women's interests that contribute to the development of 'a new relation to the political culture influenced by the fact that [women] no longer are tokens in the political system' (Hedlund, 1988:100). It would be naive to believe that women's interests are somehow severed from centres of local domination. Nevertheless, women might represent alternative perspectives on leadership, as evidenced by women's inclination to provide feedback and their close concern with local development problems. In this way, the greatest number of women on LCs could, in the long run, bring about more gender-responsive local governance and politics.

The study has shown that women politicians do, in fact, act in a way that may constitute 'acting for representation'. The majority of women councillors interviewed expressed a desire to do something for women - either to organise groups for credit programmes or income generation, to ensure that local government programmes cater for women or to promote initiatives such as improving child welfare. As examples of domestic conflict have shown, female councillors are seen by constituents as making important contributions to mediating domestic conflict. This is a clear example of how the presence of women in public political space straddles the private in other ways than men do. The examples of domestic mediation emphasise the process of change and the real struggles in a clearly paradoxical manner. At the heart of the paradox is a negotiation about boundaries of the private and public and the difficulties that women politicians face in operating at local level.

The initial conclusion reached by this study was that, in fact, female local leaders were against equality, because they tried to transfer solutions back into the private, by advising women to refer domestic cases to the LC courts only as a last resort, on the basis that these were private matters. Even if a woman won a case, female councillors often actively encouraged her to play down her success in the interest of reconciliation and for the sake of her children. This strategy sometimes worked positively, but not always, like one where a man battered and deformed his wife for reporting him to the LC and making their private matters public.

A greater understanding of the local political landscape requires investigation far below the surface to understand why most female councillors exhibit such a conservative disposition to domestic space. Female candidates did not show any indication of challenging notions of womanhood that, for instance, required them to kneel for voters or dress in a particular manner, as discussed in Chapters Five and Six. Borrowing from Kandiyoti's (1988) much-cited concept, female local leaders were 'bargaining with patriarchy'. They acted within the limits of community culture, yet their very presence tended to challenge the boundaries. At the local level, the cost of open resistance is very high, precisely because of the intimacy of relations in the terrain. Female leaders therefore find that they are more acceptable when they take on a conservative and unthreatening outlook. Their success is achieved by using instrumentalist approaches that tend to discursively play down the issue of what is in it for women - and to conversely emphasise what is in it for men. The question is how far such a strategy can go to realise greater gender equity. Realistically, there are limitations to acting within the bounds of the community. Many female councillors expressed frustration, as evidenced by the phrase, 'Yes, we are interested in substantial gender equality, but how do we do it?' Clearly the question of 'the how' requires a multiplicity of actors, both at the local and national levels, in order to institutionalise gender equality sufficiently in local politics.

Put in perspective, these observations reveal that the decentralisation process in Uganda, together with the space that has been created for women in local government, may have contradictory impacts. On the one hand, there is a relative increase of deliberative energies. Though critics may see this as minimal, on the basis that local governments are mere 'talk shops' without sufficient financial autonomy (Goloba-Mutebi 1999; Olowu 2001), the local political landscape has surely changed. It is not politics as usual. In particular, the kind of relations animated by contestation and interaction at different levels has politicised gender relations. On the other hand, the mode of inclusion of women, together with the general context of presidentialism and patronage politics in Uganda (Crook, 2001; Goetz, 2003b), have constructed subordination in new ways, with women continuing to enjoy limited political legitimacy as local leaders. Sufficient institutionalisation of women's presence and of gender equality in public politics has not yet been achieved. At the local level, thre is a dynamic interplay of local democracy and grassroots tyranny, the outcome of which will depend on the location of a range of political players both at the local and national (as well as international) levels. The discerning moments for future directions will be when the women's movement in Uganda harnesses the points of women's agency and creates broader alliances for gender-inclusive democratic politics. This will be achieved through organisation both at local and national levels, organisation that enables women to articulate social agendas without fear of ostracism and isolation. Indeed, a national woman's agenda is inevitable. This is particularly true after the move to multiparty dispensation where parties take over the role of selecting rulers and determining public policy. The level of organisation of women will determine their engagement in local governance processes in the future.

On the whole, it can be argued that decentralisation and the space created for women's participation, though riddled with inconsistencies, and seemingly rigged to underline women's latecomer and secondary status could, all the same, hold the potential for transforming local politics. The visibility of women has meant that gender power relations have to be confronted in public discourse. Even where gender equality is ridiculed, or seen as a threat to society, there is great potential for change, as women continue their journey from oblivion and silence. It is a step towards localising democracy. 'Whether this is a half full or half empty glass...one notable achievement is that the glass is there at all' (Stetson & Mazur, 1995:12).

Appendix 1: National Resistance Movement

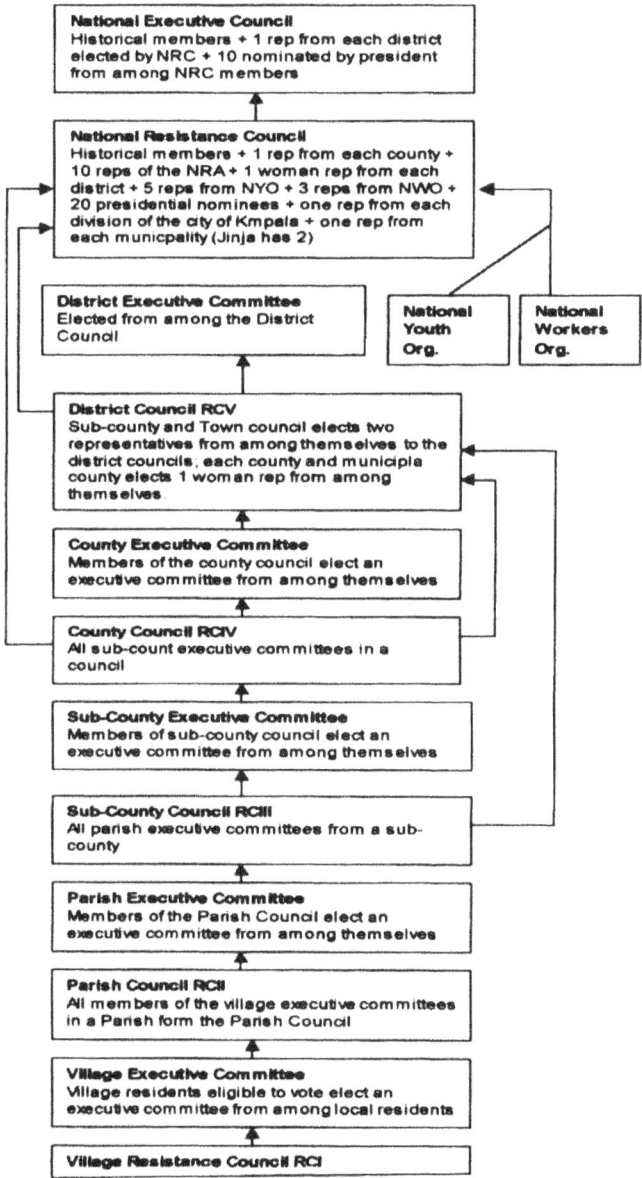

National Executive Council
Historical members + 1 rep from each district elected by NRC + 10 nominated by president from among NRC members

National Resistance Council
Historical members + 1 rep from each county + 10 reps of the NRA + 1 woman rep from each district + 5 reps from NYO + 3 reps from NWO + 20 presidential nominees + one rep from each division of the city of Kmpala + one rep from each municpality (Jinja has 2)

District Executive Committee
Elected from among the District Council

National Youth Org.

National Workers Org.

District Council RCV
Sub-county and Town council elects two representatives from among themselves to the district councils; each county and municipla county elects 1 woman rep from among themselves.

County Executive Committee
Members of the county council elect an executive committee from among themselves

County Council RCIV
All sub-count executive committees in a council

Sub-County Executive Committee
Members of sub-county council elect an executive committee from among themselves

Sub-County Council RCIII
All parish executive committees from a sub-county

Parish Executive Committee
Members of the Parish Council elect an executive committee from among themselves

Parish Council RCII
All members of the village executive committees in a Parish form the Parish Council

Village Executive Committee
Village residents eligible to vote elect an executive committee from among local residents

Village Resistance Council RCI

Appendix 2: Typology of Decentralisation

Type 1
Deconcentration
Which refers to the handing over of some amount administrative authority or responsibility to lower levels... It is a shifting of the workload from centrally located officials to staff or offices outside of the national capital. Deconcentration accords some discretion to field agencies to plan and implement programs and projects within the guidelines set by the central ministry
Type 2
Delegation:
Transfers managerial responsibility for specifically defined functions to organisations that are outside the regular bureaucratic structure and that are only indirectly controlled by the government. It implies that a sovereign authority creates or transfers to an agent specified functions and duties which the agent has broad discretion to carry out. However ultimate responsibility remains with the sovereign authority.
Type 3
Devolution:
Creation or Strengthening – financially or legally of subnational units of government, the activities of which are substantiallyt outside the direct control of the central government. Under devolution, local units of government are autonomous and independent and their legal status makes them separate or distinct from government. They (local units) have corporate or statutory authority to raise revenue and make expenditures. That is local governments are not merely subordinate administrative units, but they have ability to interact reciprocally with other units and government in the political system of which they are part.
Type 4
Privatisation
Where government divests itself of the responsibility for functions and either transfers them to voluntary organisations or allows them to be performed by private enterprises or what is refferrd to as the "market surrogate strategy".
Source: Rondinelli et al. (1984)

Appendix 3: The Structure of Local Councils

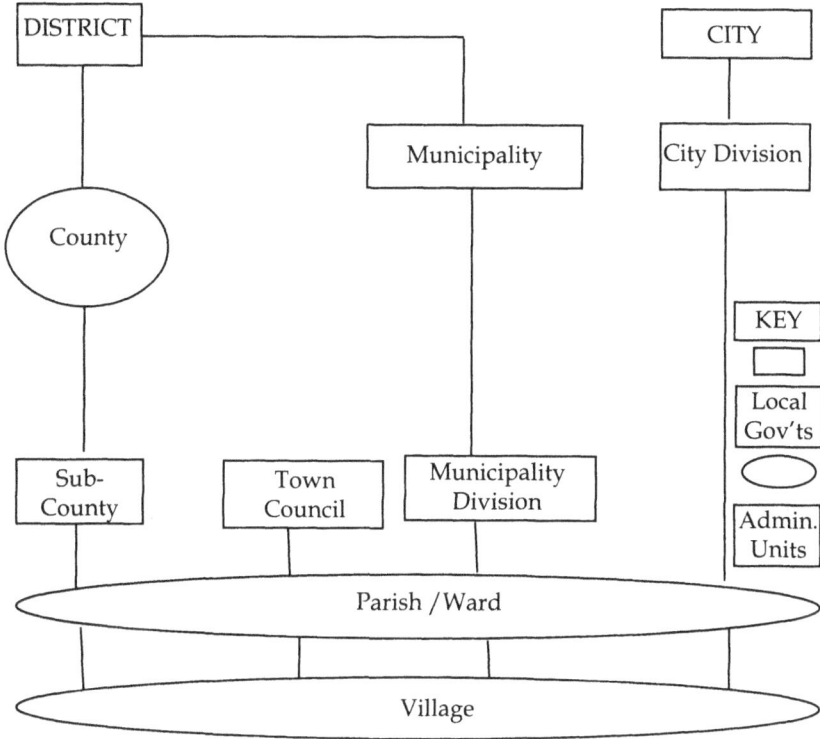

References

Abdullah, H. (1993) 'Transition Politics and the Challenge of Gender in Nigeria', *Review of African Political Economy*, No. 56: 27-37.

Abzug, B. & Kelber, M. eds. (1994) 'Overview. From Ancient to Present Times', in M. Kelber, (ed.) *Women and Government: New Ways to Political Power*, London: Praeger.

(ACFODE) Action for Development (1995) Visible at Last: Non-Governmental Organisations' Contributions to Women's Recognition in Uganda. Kampala: ACFODE.

ACFODE (1996) 'A Woman in Politics', *Arise Magazine*, No. 19: Kampala.

ACFODE (2002) 'Gender Monitoring Reports: 2001/2 Local Council Elections'. Kampala: ACFODE.

Adar, G.K. (1999) 'The Interface Between Elections and Democracy: Kenya's Search for a Sustainable Democratic System, 1960s-1990s, in J. Hyslop (ed.) *African Democracy in the Era of Globalisation*, Johannesburg: Witwatersrand University Press.

Adejumobi, A. (1998) 'Elections in Africa: A Fading Shadow of Democracy?', *Africa Development*, xxiii (1): 41-61.

Agarwal, B. (1997) 'Bargaining and Gender Relations Within and Beyond the Household', *Feminist Economics*, 3 (1): 1-51.

Agarwal, B. (2001) 'Participatory Exclusion, Community Forestry and Gender: An Analysis of South Asia and a Conceptual Model', World Development, 29 (10): 1,623-1,648.

Ahikire, J. (1994a) 'Women, Public Politics and Organisation: Potentialities of Affirmative Action in Uganda', *Economic and Political Weekly*, 29(44): WS77-WS83.

Ahikire, J. (1994b) 'Bringing Women Back in: A Search for Alternative Historiographies', *The Quest*, VIII (2): 3-22.

Ahikire, J. (1998) 'Of Dress and the Mind', *Arise Magazine*, No. 23, Kampala: Action for Development (ACFODE).

Ahikire, J. (2002) 'Decentralisation in Uganda Today: Institutions and Possible Outcomes in the Context of Human Rights', Background Paper, Geneva: The International Council on Human Rights Policy.

Ahikire, J. (2003) 'Gender Equity and Local Democracy in Contemporary Uganda: Addressing the Challenge of Women's Political Effectiveness in Local Government', in A.M. Goetz & S.

Hassim (eds.) *No Shortcuts to Power: African Women in Politics and Policy Making,* London: Zed Books.

Ahikire, J. & Madanda, A. (2002) 'Towards Effective Political Participation and Decision Making for Women Councillors in Decentralised Local Governments and the Role of NGOs in Uganda', Study Report, Kampala: DENIVA (Development Network of Indigenous Voluntary Associations).

Albertyn, C.; Goldblatt, B.; Hassim, S.; Mbatha, L. & Meintjes, S. (1999) 'Engendering the Political Agenda: A South African Study', Centre for Applied Legal Studies (CALS), Johannesburg: University of the Witwatersrand.

Alfonso, D.H. (1997) 'Political Decentralisation and Popular Alternatives: A View from the South', in M. Kaufman & H.D Alfonso (eds.) *Community Power, Grassroots Democracy and the Transformation of Social Life,* London: Zed Books.

Arizpe, E. (1990) 'Democracy for a Small Two-Gender Planet', in E. Jelins *Women and Social Change in Latin America,* London: Zed Books.

Ashaba-Aheebwa, M. (1996) 'Decentralisation in Uganda', Unpublished Paper.

Atienza, M.E. (2000) 'Gender and Local Governance in the Philippines', in J.R. Lee & C. Clark (eds.) *Democracy and the Status of Women in East Asia,* London: Lynne Rienner.

Attahi, K. (1997) 'Decentralisation and Participatory Urban Governance in Francophone Africa', in M. Swilling (ed.) *Governing Africa's Cities,* Johannesburg: Witwatersrand University Press.

Ayenew, M. (2002) 'Decentralisation in Ethiopia: Two Case Studies on Devolution of Power and Responsibilities to Local Government Authorities', in B. Zewde & S. Pausewang (eds.) *Ethiopia: The Challenge of Democracy from Below,* Uppsala: Nordiska Afrikainstitutet.

Ballington, J. (2002) 'Political Parties, Gender Equality and Elections in South Africa', in G. Fick; S. Mentjes & M. Simons (eds.) *One Woman One Vote: The Gender Politics of South African Elections,* Johannesburg: EISA (Electoral Institute of Southern Africa).

Barkan, J. & Chege, M. (1989) 'Decentralising the State: District Focus and the Politics of Relocation in Kenya', *Journal of Modern African Studies,* 27 (3):431-453.

Banerjee, M. (1998) 'Women in Local Governance: Macro Myths, Micro Realities', *Social Change,* 28 (1).

Barret, M. (1992) 'Words and Things: Materialism and Method in Contemporary Feminist Analysis', in M. Barret & A. Phillips (eds.) *Destabilising Theory, Contemporary Feminist Debates*, Cambridge: Polity Press.

Barya, J. J. (2000) 'Political Parties, the Movement and the Referendum on Political Systems: One Step Forward, Two Steps Back?' in J. Mugaju & J. Oloka Onyango (eds.) *No Party Democracy in Uganda: Myths and Realities*, Kampala: Fountain Publishers.

Barya, J.J. (1996) 'Internal and External Pressures in the Struggle for Pluralism in Uganda', in J. Oloka Onyango; K. Kibwama & C. Maina (eds.) *Law and the Struggle for Democracy in East Africa*, Nairobi: Clari Press.

Barya, J. J. (2003) 'Assessing the Legal Framework of Decentralisation in Uganda: Political and Financial Powers', Mimeo, Kampala: Centre for Basic Research (CBR).

Barya, J. J. & Oloka-Onyango, J. (1997) 'Civil Society and the Political Economy of Foreign Aid in Uganda', *Democratisation*, 4 (2).

Baylies, C. & Bujra, J. (1993) 'Challenging Gender Inequalities', *Review of African Political Economy*, 56:3-10.

Bazaara, N. (2001) 'From Despotic to Democratic Decentralisation in Uganda: A History of Accountability and Control over Nature', Unpublished Paper.

Bazaara, N. (2003) 'Legal and Policy Framework for Citizen Participation in East Africa: A Comparative Analysis', Unpublished Paper.

Beck, L. (2003) 'Democratisation and the Hidden Public: The Impact of Patronage Networks on Senegalese Women', *Comparative Politics*, 35 (2):147-170.

Benhabib, S. (1996) 'The Democratic Moment and the Problem of Difference', in S. Benhabib (ed.) *Democracy and Difference: Contesting the Boundaries of the Political*, New Jersey: Princeton University Press.

Bhattacharjee, A. (1997) 'The Public/Private Mirage: Mapping out Homes and Undomesticating Violence Work in the South Asian Immigrant Community', in M.J. Alexander & C.T. Mohanty (eds.) *Feminist Genealogies, Colonial Legacies, Democratic Futures*, London: Routledge.

Bidandi, S. (1998) 'Accounting to Women: Reducing the Gender Gaps in Local Government', Paper Presented at the First National Conference on Ugandan Women and Politics, Kampala: FOWODE (Forum for Women in Democracy), 24 June.

Blair, H. (2000) 'Participation and Accountability at the Periphery: Democratic Local Governance in Six Countries', *World Development*, 28 (1): 21-39.

Blaug, R. (2002) 'Engineering Democracy', *Political Studies*, 50 (1): 102-116.

Blondet, C. (2002) 'The Devil's Deal: Women's Political Participation and Authoritarianism in Peru', in M. Molyneux & S. Razavi (eds.) *Gender Justice, Development and Rights*, Oxford: Oxford University Press.

Bokemeier, J. & Tait, J. (1980) 'Women as Power Actors: A Comparative Study of Rural Communities', *Rural Sociology*, 45 (2): 238-255.

Bolick, C. (1993) *Grassroots Tyranny: The Limits of Federalism*, Washington D.C.: Cato Institute.

Bonnin, D. (2000) Questioning the Boundaries Between the Public and Private: Political Violence, Women's Protests and Reconstruction of Space in Kwa-Zulu Natal, South Africa', Paper Presented at the South African Sociological Association Annual Congress, Cape Town: University of the Western Cape.

Borhaug, K. (1994) 'Local Government and Decentralisation in Sub-Saharan Africa: An Annotated Bibliography', Working Paper No. 5, Bergen: Chr. Michelsen Institute.

Boyd, R. (1989) 'Empowerment of Women in Uganda: Real or Symbolic, *Review of African Political Economy*, 45/46: 106-117.

Bryld, E. (2000) 'The Technocratic Discourse: Technical Means to Political Problems, *Development in Practice*, 10 (5): 700-705.

Buch, N. (2000) `Women's Experience in New Panchayats: The Emerging Leadership of Rural Women', Occasional Paper No. 35, New Delhi: Centre for Women's Development Studies.

Butegwa, F. (2001) Women in Local Government Forum, Workshop Report, Municipal Development Programme (ESA) 12-14 May, Harare.

Button, S. (1984). 'Women's Committees: A Study of Gender and Local Government Policy Formulation', Working Paper No. 45, School of Advanced Urban Studies, University of Bristol.

Byanyima, W. (1992) 'Women in Political Struggle in Uganda', in J.M. Bystydzienski (ed.) Women Transforming Politics: *Worldwide Strategies for Empowerment*, Bloomington: Indiana University Press.

Byaruhanga Rukooko, A. (2000) 'Buganda's Quest for Self-determination: Possibilities and Challenges to Human Rights', Unpublished Paper.

Bystyszienki, J.M. (1992) 'Influence of Women's Culture on Public Politics in Norway', in J.M. Bystydzienski, (ed.) *Women Transforming Politics: Worldwide Strategies for Empowerment*, Bloomington: Indiana University Press.

Bystydzienski, J.M. & Schom, J. (eds.) (1999) 'Introduction'. *Democratisation and Women's Grassroots Movements*, Bloomington: Indiana University Press.

Calhoun, C. (ed.) (1992) 'Introduction'. Habermas and the Public Sphere, Cambridge: The MIT Press.

Carbone, G. (2001) 'No-Party Democracy? Political Organisation Under the *Movement for Democracy* in Uganda: 1994-2000', Ph.D. Thesis, London School of Economics and Political Science.

Chaney, P. & Fevre, R. (2002) 'Is There a Demand for Descriptive Representation? Evidence from the UK's Devolution Programme', *Political Studies*, 50: 897-915.

Chandwong-Okello, L. (1999) 'Civil Society Based Participation in Democratic Local Governance: The Case of Uganda', Paper Presented at a Workshop on 'Strengthening Participation in Governance, 21-22 June, Sussex: Institute of Development Studies (IDS).

Chazan, N. (1989) 'Gender Perspectives on African States', in J. Parpat & K. Staudt (eds.) *Women and the State in Africa*, Boulder: Lynne Rienner.

Cheema, G.S. & Rondinelli, D. (1983) *Decentralisation and Development: Policy Implementation in Developing Countries*, London: Sage Publications.

(CGE) Commission on Gender Equality (1999) 'Redefining Politics: South African Women and Democracy', Johannesburg.

Coetzee, A. (1996) 'The Experience of Women in Local Elections in South Africa', Paper Prepared for the Commonwealth Local Government Forum and Major Urban Areas Association (MUAA), Johannesburg, 7-10 May.

Coetzee, A. & Naidoo, S. (2002) 'Local Government', in G. Fick; S. Meintjes & M. Simons (eds.) *One Woman One Vote: The Gender Politics of the South African Elections*, Johannesburg: EISA (Electoral Institute of Southern Africa).

Colebatch, H.K. (1994) 'Local Councils and Local Services', *IDS Bulletin*, 6 (1).

Conell, D. (1998) 'Strategies for Change: Women and Politics in Eritrea and South Africa', *Review of African Political Economy,* 25 (76): 189-206.

Connell, R. (1987) *Gender and Power,* Oxford: Polity Press.

Conyers, D. (1986) 'Future Directions in Development Studies: The Case of Decentralisation', *World Development,* 14 (5):593-603.

Cornwall, A. (2002) 'Locating Citizen Participation', *IDS Bulletin,* 33 (2):49-58.

Cornwall, A. (2003) Whose Voices? Whose Choices: Reflections on Gender and Participatory Development, World Development, 31 (8) 1325-1342.

Corrin, C. (1999) *Feminist Perspectives on Politics,* London: Longman.

Craig, J. (2001) 'Local Democracy, Democratic Decentralisation and Rural Development: Theories, Challenges and Options for Policy' *Development Policy Review* 19 (4):521-32.

Crehan, K. (1997) *The Fractured Community: Landscapes of Power and Gender in Rural Zambia,* Los Angeles: University of California Press.

Crehan, K. (1999) 'The Rules of the Game: The Political Location of Women in North-Western Zambia', in J. Hyslop (ed.) *African Democracy in the Era of Globalisation,* Johannesburg: Witwatersrand University Press.

Crook, R. (1991) 'Decentralisation and Participation in Ghana and Cote d'Ivoire', in R. Crook and A.M. Jerve (eds.) Government and Participation: Institutional Development, Decentralization and Democracy in the Third World, Report No. 1, Bergen: Chr. Michelsen Institute.

Crook, R. (2001) 'Strengthening Democratic Governance in Conflict-torn Societies: Civic Organisations, Democratic Effectiveness and Political Conflict', Working Paper 129, Sussex: Institute of Development Studies (IDS).

Crook, R. & Manor, J. (1998) Democracy and Decentralisation in South Asia and West Africa: *Participation, Accountability and Performance,* Cambridge: Cambridge University Press.

Dahlerup, D. (1986) *The New Women's Movement: Feminism and Political Power in Europe and USA,* London: Sage Publications.

Dahlerup, D. (1998) 'Using Quotas to Increase Women's Participation', in A. Karam (ed.) *Women in Parliament: Beyond Numbers,* Stockholm: International IDEA.

Ddatta, B. (1998) And 'Who will Make the Chapattis? A Study of All-Women Panchayats in Maharashtra', Calcutta: Street.

De Beauvoir, S. (1949) The Second Sex, London: Pan Books.

Ddungu, E. (1998) 'Decentralisation in Uganda: Process, Prospects and Constraints', Occasional Paper No. 47, University of Iowa.

Ddungu, E. (1994) 'Popular Forms and the Question of Democracy: The Case of Resistance Councils in Uganda', M. Mamdani & J. Oloka-Onyango (eds.) *Uganda: Studies in Living Conditions, Popular Movements and Constitutionalism*, Vienna: JEP Book Series.

Ddungu, E. & Wabwire, E. (1991) 'Electoral Mechanisms and the Democratic Process: The 1989 RC-NRC Elections, Working Paper No. 9, Kampala: Centre for Basic Research (CBR).

Doornbos, M. (1988) 'The Uganda Crisis and the National Question', in H.B. Hansen & M. Twaddle (eds.) Uganda Now: Between Decay and Development, Nairobi: Heinemann.

Doornbos, M. (1999) 'Globalisation, the State and Other Actors: Revisiting State Autonomy' in J. Martinussen (ed.) *External and Internal Constraints on Policy Making: How Autonomous are the States?* Occasional Paper No. 20, Roskilde: Institute of Development Studies (IDS).

Drage, J. (1999) 'Women's Involvement in Local Government: The Ultimate Community Group?' *Political Science,* 50 (2): 195-208.

Department of Women & Gender Studies (DWGS) (2002) 'A Gender Audit of Capacities in Selected Districts in Uganda', Unpublished Report, Kampala: Makerere University.

EASSI (East African Sub-Regional Support Initiative for the Advancement of Women) (1998) *East African Initiatives,* No. 4, Kampala.

Eckert, A. & Jones, A. (2002) 'Historical Writing About Everyday Life', *Journal of African Cultural Studies,* 15 (1).

Edwards, J. & Chapman, C. (2000) 'Women's Political Representation in Wales: Waving or Drowning', *Contemporary Politics,* 6 (4): 367-381.

Eisenstein, Z.N. (1986) The Radical Future of Liberal Feminism, Boston: The Northeastern University Press.

Evertzen, E. (2001) Gender and Local Governance: A Handbook, www.kit.nl/glg/assets/imagesgender-and-local-governance.doc

Fick, G. (2001) 'Gender Equality in the Sphere of Local Government', Local Government Elections 2000: From Transition to Consolidation, Seminar Report No. 4, Johannesburg: EISA (Electoral Institute of Southern Africa).

Fick, G., Meintjes, S. & Simons, M. (2002) *One Woman, One Vote: The Gender Politics of the South African Elections,* Johannesburg: EISA (Electoral Institute of Southern Africa).

Fox-Genovese, E. (1991) *Feminism Without Illusions,* London: The University of Carolina Press.

Francis, P. & James, R. (2003) 'Balancing Rural Poverty Reduction and Citizen Participation: The Contradiction of Uganda's Decentralisation Programme', *World Development,* 31 (2): 325-337.

Fraser, N. (1989) *Unruly Practices: Power Discourse and Gender in Contemporary Social Theory,* Cambridge: Polity Press.

Fraser, N. (1992) 'Rethinking the Public Sphere: A Contribution to the Critique of Actually Existing Democracy', in C. Calhoun (ed.) *Habermas and the Public Sphere,* Cambridge: The MIT Press.

Friedman, S. & Nordlund, P. (1998) 'In Search of Citizenship: Local Democracy and Donor Intervention in South Africa', Report Submitted to SIDA.

Furley, O. & Katarikawe, J. (1999) 'No-party Democracy: Uganda's Election to the Constituent Assembly, 1994', Occasional Paper No. 1, Kampala: Centre for Basic Research.

Galloy, M. (1998) 'Kenyan Women and the Electoral Process: The Vagaries of the Long Road to Leadership', *Southern African Feminist Review,* 3 (1): 3-17.

Gasper, D. (1991) 'Decentralisation of Planning and Administration in Zimbabwe: International Perspectives and 1980s Experiences', in A.H. Helmsing, et al. (eds.) *Limits to Decentralisation in Zimbabwe: Essays on the Decentralisation of Government and Planning in 1980s,* The Hague: Institute of Social Studies (ISS).

Geiger, S. (1997) 'Exploring Feminist Epistemologies and Methodologies Through the Life Histories of Tanzanian Women', Unpublished Paper.

Geisler, S. (1994) 'Troubled Sisterhood: Women and Politics in Southern Africa', Unpublished Paper.

Gibbon, P. (1994) 'Introduction: The New Local Level Politics in East Africa', Research Report No. 95, Uppsala: Nordic Institute for African Studies.

Goetz, A.M. (1992) 'Gender and Administration', *IDS Bulletin,* 23 (4).

Goetz, A.M. (ed.) (1997) 'Introduction' *Getting Institutions Right for Women in Development,* London: Zed Books.

Goetz, A.M. (1998) 'Women in Politics and Gender Equity in Policy: South Africa and Uganda', *Review of African Political Economy,* (76): 241-262.

Goetz, A.M. (2000) 'Accountability to Women in Development Spending - the Local Level', Unpublished Paper.

Goetz, A.M. (2002) `No Shortcuts to Power': Constraints on Women's Effectiveness', *The Journal of Modern African Studies*, 40 (4), 550-74.

Goetz, A.M. (2003a) 'Women's Political Effectiveness: A Conceptual Framework', in A.M. Goetz & S. Hassim (eds.) *No Shortcuts to Power: African Women in Politics and Policy Making*, London: Zed Books.

Goetz, A.M. (2003b) 'The Problem with Patronage: Constraints on Women's Political Effectiveness in Uganda', in A.M. Goetz & S. Hassim (eds.) *No Shortcuts to Power: African Women in Politics and Policy Making*, London: Zed Books.

Goetz A.M. & Hassim, S. (eds.) (2003) 'Introduction: Women in Power in Uganda and South Africa', *No Shortcuts to Power: African Women in Politics and Policy Making*, London: Zed Books.

Goetz, A.M. & Jenkins, R. (1999) 'Creating a Framework for Reducing Poverty: Institutional and Process Issues in National Poverty Policy', Uganda Country Report, Commissioned by the Department for International Development (DFID) & Swedish International Development Agency (SIDA).

Goloba-Mutebi, F. (1999) Decentralisation, Democracy and Development Administration in Uganda 1986-1996: Limits of Popular Participation, Ph.D. Thesis, London School of Economics & Political Science.

Gotz, G. (1996) 'The Process and the Product: The 1995 Local Elections and the Future of Local Government', Johannesburg: Centre for Policy Studies.

Gotz, G. (1997) The Limits of Community: The Dynamics of Rural Water Supply, Johannesburg: Centre for Policy Studies.

Griffin, K. (1981) 'Economic Development in a Changing World', *World Development*, 9 (3): 221-226.

Guidry, J. A. & Sawyer M.Q. (2003) 'Contentious Pluralism: The Public Sphere and Democracy', *Perspectives on Politics*, 1 (2):273-289.

Halfani, M. & Sendero, A.M. (1990) 'Towards the Enhancement of Local Government Management Capacities in Tanzania', Institute of Development Studies, University of Dar es Salaam.

Halfani, M. (1997) 'Governance of Urban Development in East Africa: An Examination of the Institutional Landscape and Poverty Challenge', in M. Swilling (ed.) *Governing Africa's Cities*, Johannesburg: Witwatersrand University Press.

Hansen H.B. & Twaddle, M. (eds.) (1988) 'Introduction', *Uganda Now: Between Decay and Development,* Nairobi: Heinemann.

Hansen, B. (1999) `Policy Making in Central-Local Government Relations: Balancing Local Autonomy, Macroeconomic Control and Sectoral Policy Goals', *Journal of Public Policy,* 19(2).

Harding, S. (ed.) (1987) 'Is There a Feminist Method?', in *Feminism and Methodology,* Bloomington: Indiana University Press

Herzog, H. (1999) *Gendering Politics: Women in Israel,* Ann Arbor: University of Michigan Press.

Harris, J. (2000) 'The Dialectics of Decentralisation', Indian National Magazine, 17 (13) http: www. Frontlineonline.com/ fl1713/17130700.htm.

Hassim, S. (1998) 'Politicising the Subject: Feminist Challenges to Political Science in South Africa', *Politikon,* 25 (2):3-15.

Hassim, S. (1999) 'From Presence to Power: Women's Citizenship in a New Democracy', *Agenda,* 40:6-17.

Hassim, S. (2002a) 'The Dual Politics of Representation: Women and Electoral Politics in South Africa', in G. Fick, Meintjes, S. & Simons, M. (eds.) *One Woman, One Vote: The Gender Politics of South African Elections,* Johannesburg: EISA (Electoral Institute of Southern Africa).

Hassim, S. (2002b) Identities, Interests and Constituencies: The Politics of the Women's Movement in South Africa 1980-1999, Ph.D. Thesis, Toronto: York University.

Hassim, S. & Metelerkamp, J. (1999) 'The Dual Politics of Representation: Women and Electoral Politics in South Africa', *Politikon,* 26 (2): 201-212.

Hassim, S.& Metelerkamp, J. (2003) 'Representation, Participation and Democratic Effectiveness: Feminist Challenges to Representative Democracy in South Africa', in A.M. Goetz & S. Hassim (eds.) *No Shortcuts to Power: African Women in Politics and Policy Making,* London: Zed Books.

Hassim, S.; Metelerkamp, J. & Todes, A. (1987) 'A Bit on the Side: Gender and the Politics of Transformation in South Africa' in *Transformation,* 5.

Hawkesworth, M. (1999) 'Analysing Backlash: Feminist Standpoint Theory as an Analytical Tool', *Women Studies International Forum,* 22 (2): 135-155.

Hedlund, G. (1985) 'Women's Interests in Local Politics', in K.B. Jones & A.G. Jonasdottir (eds.) *The Political Interests of Gender:*

Developing Theory and Research with a Feminist Face, London: Sage Publications.

Hillebrand, E. (1996) 'Ivory Coast: A Formal Decentralisation and a Democratization Yet to Come', *Regional Development Dialogue*, 17 (2):60-93.

Human Rights Watch (1999) 'Hostile to Democracy? The Movement System and Political Repression in Uganda', New York: Human Rights Watch.

Hunt, A. (1996) 'Law, Community and Everyday Life: Yngnesson's Virtous Citizens and Disruptive Subjects', *Law and Social Inquiry*, 21 (1):173-84.

Hyden, G. & Bratton, M. (eds.) (1992) *Governance and Politics in Africa*, Boulder: Lynne Rienner.

IPU (Interparliamentary Union) (2001) Women in National Parliaments, http.www.ipu.org.wmn-e/world htm.

Jacobs, R.N. (1998) 'Women in Local Government: The Namibian Experience', Paper Presented at a Regional Forum on Women in Local Government, Municipal Development Programme, 12-14 May, Harare.

Jayawardena, K. (1986) *Feminism and Nationalism in the Third World*, London: Zed Books.

Jayawardena, P.K. (2000) 'Proportional representation, Political Violence and the Participation of Women in the Political Process in Sri Lanka'. Paper Presented at a Workshop on 'Strengthening Democratic Governance in Conflict-torn Societies',Centre for Basic Research, Jinja Uganda, December 4-7.

Johns, S. & Riley, R. (1975), Local District Councils: Should They be Forgotten?, *Journal of Modern African Studies*, 13 (2): 309-32.

Jonasdottir, A. (1988) On the Concept of Interest, Women's Interests and the Limitation of Interest Theory', in K. Jones & A. Jonasdottir (eds.) *The Political Interests of Gender: Developing Theory and Research with a Feminine Face*, London: Sage.

Jones E. & Gaventa J. (2002) 'Concepts of Citizenship: A Review, *Development Bibliography*, No. 19, Sussex: IDS.

Jordan, J.D. (1984) *Local Government in Zimbabwe*, Harare: Mambo Press.

Jorgensen, J.J. (1981) 'Uganda: A Modern History', London: Croom Helm.

Kaplan, J. (1997) Crazy for Democracy: Women in Grassroots Movements, London, Routledge.

Kabeer, N. (1999) 'From Feminist Insights to an Analytical Framework: An Institutional Perspective on Gender Inequality', in N. Kabeer & R. Subrahmanian (eds.) *Institutions, Relations and Outcomes*, New Delhi: Kali for Women.

Kandiyoti, D. (1988) 'Bargaining with Patriarchy', *Gender and Society*, 2 (3): 274-90.

Kannabiran, L.K. et, al. (1989) *We were Making History: Women and the Telangana Uprising*, New Delhi: Kali for Women.

Kanyeihamba, G. (1988) 'Power that Rode Naked under the Muzzle' in H. Hansen & M. Twaddle (eds.) *Uganda Now: Between Decay and Development*, Nairobi: Heinemann.

Karl, M. (1995) Women and Empowerment: Participation and Decision Making, London: Zed Books.

Karugire, S.R. (1980) A Political History of Uganda, Nairobi: Heinemann.

Kasente, D.; Lookwood, M. & Whitehead (1998) 'Gender Dimensions of Agricultural Policy in Uganda: A C ase Study of Mukono and Masindi Districts', Research Report, Geneva: United Nations Research Institute for Social Development (UNRISD).

Kasente, D. (1994), Women in the Constituent Assembly in Uganda', Mimeo, Kampala.

Kasfir, N. (2000) 'Movement Democracy, Legitimacy and Power in Uganda' in J. Mugaju & J. Oloka Onyago (eds.) *No-Party Democracy in Uganda: Myths and Realities*, Kampala: Fountain Publishers.

Kasumba, G. (1997), Decentralising Aid and its Management in Uganda: Lessons for Capacity Building at the Local Level', Working Paper No. 20, Maastricht: European Centre for Development Policy & Management (ECDPM).

Kaufman, M. (1997) 'Differential Participation: Men, Women and Popular Power', in M. Kaufman & H.D. Alfonso (eds.) *Community Power, Grassroots Democracy and the Transformation of Social Life*, London: Zed Books.

Kayunga, S.K. (2001) 'Decentralisation and the Management of Ethnic Conflict in Uganda', Mimeo, Kampala: Centre for Basic Research (CBR).

Kawamara-Mishambi, S. & Ovonji-Odida, I. (2003) The Lost Clause,: The Campaign to Advance Women's Property Rights in the Uganda Land Act', in A.M. Goetz, S. Hassim (eds.) *No Shortcuts to Power: African Women in Politics and Policy Making*, London: Zed Books.

Kelley, M. (1996) 'Choosing an Electoral System: Structural and Contextual Factors in Women's Political Participation', Mimeo, Centre for Applied Legal Studies, Johannesburg: University of the Witwatersrand.

Khadiagala, L.S. (2000) 'The Failure of Popular Justice in Uganda: Local Councils and Women's Property Rights', *Development and Change*, 32: 55-76.

Kisubi, M. (1996) 'The Process of Decentralisation' in P. Langseth & J. Mugaju (eds.) *Post-Conflict Uganda: Towards an Effective Civil Service*, Kampala: Fountain Publishers.

Kishwar, M. (1996) 'Women and Politics: Beyond Quotas', *Economic and Political Weekly*, Bombay, 26 October: 2867-73

Kwagala, B. (1998) "The Role of NGOs in the Delivery of Health and Water Services", in A. Nsibambi, *Decentralisation and Civil Society in Uganda: The Quest for Good Governance*, Kampala: Fountain Publishers.

Kwesiga, J.C. (1995) 'The Women's Movement in Uganda: An Analysis of Present and Future Prospects', *The Uganda Journal*, 42: 54-73.

Kyomuhendo, J. (1994) 'To Decentralise is to Dig Deep Holes in Districts', *The Monitor Newspaper*, Kampala, October 28.

Lister, R. (2000) 'Gender and Citizenship in Transition' in B. Hobson (ed.) *Dilemmas in Engendering Citizenship*, London: Macmillan.

Lister, R. (1997) *Citizenship: Feminist Perspectives*, Basingstoke: Macmillan.

Larson, A. (2002) 'Natural Resources and Decentralisation in Nicaragua: Are Local Governments up to the Job?' *World Development*, 30(1): 17-31.

Leftwich, A. (1993) 'Governance, Democracy and Development in the Third World', *Third World Quarterly*, 24 (3): 605-625.

Lind J. & Cappon, J. (2001), Realities or Rhetoric: Revisiting the Decentralisation of Natural Resource Management in Uganda and Zambia', Research Report, Nairobi: African Centre for Technology Studies (ACTS).

Lipset, S.M. (1995) *The Encyclopaedia of Democracy*, Vol. III, Washington, D.C: Congressional Quarter.

Livingstone I. & Charlton, R. (2000) "Financing Decentralised Development in a Low-income Country: Raising Revenue for Local Governments in Uganda, *Development and Change*, 32 (1): 77-100.

Londsale, J. (1986), Political Accountability in African History'in P. Chabal (ed.) *Political Domination in Africa: Reflections on the Limitations of Power,* Cambridge: Cambridge University Press.

Longwe, S.H. (2000) 'Towards Realistic Strategies for Women's Political Empowerment in Africa', *Gender and Development in Africa,* 8 (3): 24-30.

Longwe, S. and Clarke R. (1990) 'Woman Know Your Place: The Patriarchal Message in Zambian Popular Songs', Research Report, Lusaka: Zambian Association for Research and Development.

Lovenduski, J. (1997) 'Gender Politics: A Breakthrough for Women Parliamentarians?' *Parliamentary Affairs,* 50 (4): 708-19.

Lovenduski, J. & Karam, A. (1998) 'Women in Parliament: Making a Difference', in A. Karam (ed.) *Women in Parliament: Beyond Numbers,* Stockholm: International IDEA Handbook Series.

Lovenduski J. & Norris, P. (2003) 'Westminister Women: The Politics of Presence', *Political Studies,* 51 (1): 84-102.

Lovett, M. (1989) 'Gender Relations, Class Formation and the Colonial State in Africa' in J. Parpat and K. Staudt (eds.) *Women and the State in Africa,* Boulder: Lynne Rienner.

Low, D.A. (1988) 'The Dislocated Polity', in H. Hansen & M. Twaddle (eds.) *Uganda Now: Between Decay and Development,* Nairobi: Heinemann.

Lubanga, F. & Villadsen, S. (eds.) (1996) *Democratic Decentralisation in Uganda: A New Approach to Local Governance,* Kampala: Fountain Publishers.

Luckham, R.; Goetz, A.M. & Kaldor, M. (2000) 'Democratic Institutions and Politics in the Contexts of Inequality, Poverty and Conflict', Working Paper No. 104, Sussex:IDS.

Mabirizi, F. (2001) 'The Technical Interface Between Decentralised Development Planning and Structural Adjustment in Uganda' *Spring Research Series,* No. 25, University of Dortmund.

Macaulay, F. (1998) 'Localities of Power: Gender, Parties and Democracy in Chile and Brazil', in H. Afsher (ed.) *Women and Empowerment: Illustrations from the Third World,* London: Zed Books.

MacKinnon, C. (1994) 'Towards Feminist Jurisprudence' in M. Evans (ed) *The Woman Question,* London: Sage Publications.

Madanda, A. (2003) 'Affirmative Action in Tanzania', in J. Kwesiga; E. Ward; A. Madanda & N. Tarnzan, *Women's Political Space: The Experience of Affirmative Action in Eritrea, Tanzania and Uganda,* Belfast: Centre for Advancement of Women in Politics (CAWP)

Queens University & Kampala:Department of Women and Gender Studies, Makerere University.

Makara, S. (1998) 'Political and Administrative Relations in Decentralisation', in A. Nsibambi (ed.) *Decentralisation and Civil Society in Uganda: The Quest for Good Governance*, Kampala: Fountain Publishers.

Makara, S. (1997) 'Linking Good Governance, Decentralisation Policy and Civil Society', *Makerere Political Science Review*, Vol. 2: 55-72.

Makara, S. & Tukahebwa, G. (1996) 'Introduction' in S. Makara; G. Tukaheebwa & F. Byarugaba (eds.) *Politics, Constitutionalism and Electioneering in Uganda*, Kampala: Makerere University Press.

Mama, A. (1999) 'Mothers of the Nation, Daughters of the Soil: The Positioning of Women Politicians in a Military State', Paper Presented at the Centre for African Studies Seminar, University of Cape Town, 5 May.

Mamdani, M. (1983) Imperialism and Fascism in Uganda, London: Heinemann.

Mamdani, M. (1996) Citizen and Subject: Contemporary Africa and the Legacy of Colonialism, Kampala: Fountain Publishers.

Manor, J. (1999) The Political Economy of Democratic Decentralisation, Washington D.C.: The World Bank.

Mansbridge, J. (1999), 'Should Blacks Represent Blacks and Women Represent Women? A Contingent "Yes"', *The Journal of Politics*, 61 (3): 628-57.

Mapetla, E. & Rembe, S. (1989) *Decentralisation and Development in Lesotho*, Roma: National University of Lesotho Press.

Marsden, D. (1991) 'What is Community Participation?' in R. Crook and A.M. Jerve (eds.) *Government and Participation: Institutional Development, Decentralization and Democracy in the Third World*, Report No. 1, Bergen: Chr. Michelsen Institute.

Matland, R.E. (1998) 'Enhancing Women's Political Participation: Legislative Recruitment and Electoral Systems', in A. Karram (ed.) *Women in Parliament: Beyond Numbers*, Stockholm: International IDEA Handbook Series.

Matland, R.E. & Studlar, T.D. (1996) 'The Contagion of Women Candidates in Single-member District and Multi-member Districts', *Journal of Politics*, 58 (3): 707-733.

Mawhood, P. (1985) Local Government in the Third World, New York: John Wiley & Son.

Mayaram, S. (2000) 'Towards a Feminisation of the Rural Public Sphere', Unpublished Paper.

Mayaram., S. (1999) 'Backlash Against Women in the Panchayat System', Unpublished Paper.

Mbatha, L. (2003) 'Democratising Local Government: Problems and Opportunities in the Advancement of Gender Equality in South Africa', in A.M. Goetz & S. Hassim (eds.) *No Shortcuts to Power: African Women in Politics and Policy Making*, London: Zed Books.

Meintjes, S. (1996) 'The Woman's Struggle for Equality during South Africa's Transition to Democracy', *Transformation*, 30: 47-64.

Meintjes, S. (1998) 'Gender, Nationalism and Transformation: Difference and Commonality in South Africa's Past and Present', in R. Wilford & R.L. Miller (eds.) *Women, Ethnicity and Nationalism: The Politics of Transition*, London: Routledge.

Meintjes, S. (2001) 'War and Post-war Shifts in Gender Relations,' in Meintjes, S.; Pillay, A. & Turshen, M. (eds.) *The Aftermath: Women in Post-conflict Transformation*, London: Zed Books.

Meintjes, S. (2003) 'The Politics of Engagement: Women Transforming the Policy Process – Domestic Violence Legislation in South Africa' in A.M. Goetz & S. Hassim (eds.) *No Shortcuts to Power: African Women in Politics and Policy Making*, London: Zed Books.

Meintjes, S. Pillay, A. & Turshen, M. (2001) 'There is no Aftermath for Women' in Meintjes et al. (eds.) *The Aftermath: Women in Post-Conflict Transformation*, London: Zed Books.

Meintjes, S. & Simons, M. (2002) 'Women and Democracy, Women in Democracy, Gender and Democracy', in G. Fick; S. Meintjes & M. Simons (eds.) *One Woman One Vote: The Gender Politics of the South African Elections*, Johannesburg: EISA MISR (Makerere Institute of Social Research) (1997) 'Study of the Effects of the Decentralisation Reform in Uganda', Report Prepared for DANIDA, Kampala: Makerere University.

Mohan, G. & Stokke, K. (2000) 'Participatory Development and Empowerment: The Dangers of Localism', Unpublished Paper.

Moghadam, V. (1991) Revolution, Culture and Gender: Notes on the Women Question in Revolutions, Working Paper, World Institute for Development Economics Research, Helsinki: United Nations University.

Moghadam, V. (1993) *Modernising Women: Gender and Social Change in the Middle East*, London: Lynne Rienner.

Molyneux, M. (1985) 'Mobilisation Without Emancipation? Women's Interests, the State and Revolution in Nicaragua', *Feminist Studies,* 11 (2): 227-254.

Molyneux, M. (1998) 'Analysing Women's Movements', *Development & Change,* 29 (2): 219-245.

Montero, A. (2000) 'Devolving Democracy, Political Decentralisation and the New Brazilian Federalism', in P.K. Kingstone & T.J. Power (eds.) *Democratic Brazil: Actors, Institutions and Processes,* Pittsburgh: University of Pittsburgh Press.

Moore. H. (1994) 'Divided We Stand: Sex, Gender and Sexual Difference', *Feminist Review,* 47: 78-95.

Morris, D. (2000) 'Privacy, Privation and Perversity: Toward New Representations of the Personal', *Signs: Journal of Women in Culture and Society* 25 (2): 323-351.

Mtintso, J.E. (1999) 'The Contribution of Women Parliamentarians to Gender Equality', Masters Thesis, Johannesburg: University of the Witwatersrand.

Mugaju, J. (1996) 'The Road to Collapse' in P. Langseth & J. Mugaju (eds.) *Post-Conflict Uganda: Towards an Effective Civil Service,* Kampala: Fountain Publishers.

Mugisha, M. (2000) 'Gender and Decentralisation: Promoting Women's Participation in Local Councils: Case Study, Lira District, Uganda, Accra: Food & Agricultural Organisation (FAO).

Mugisha-Rwabwoogo, O. (1998) *Uganda Districts Information Handbook,* Kampala: Fountain Publishers.

Mugyenyi, M. (1998) 'Towards the Empowerment of Women: A Critique of NRM Policies and Programmes' in H. Hansen, & M. Twaddle (eds.) *Developing Uganda,* London: James Currey.

Muhumuza, W. (2002) The Paradox of Pursuing Anti-poverty Strategies under Structural Adjustment Reforms in Uganda, *Journal of Social Political and Economic Studies,* 27 (3): 271-306.

Mukyala, R. & Tripp, A.M. (1994) 'Gender and Local Politics in Uganda', Unpublished Paper.

Munachonga, M. (1990) 'Women and the State: Zambia's Development Policies and their Impact on Women', in J. Parpart & K. Staudt (eds.) *Women and the State in Africa,* Boulder: Lynne Rienner.

Museveni, K.Y. (1992) 'What is Africa's Problem?' Kampala:NRM Publications.

Museveni, K.Y. (1994) *Sowing the Mustard Seed: The Struggle for Freedom and Democracy in Uganda,* London: Macmillan.

Museveni, K.Y. (1996) Election Manifesto, Kampala.

Mutibwa, P. (1992) *Uganda Since Independence: A Story of Unfulfilled Hopes,* London: Hurst & Co. Publishers.

Mutizwa-Mangiza N.D. & Conyers, D. (1996) 'Decentralisation in Practice, with Special Reference to Tanzania, Zambia and Nigeria, *Regional Development Dialogue,* 17 (2): 77-93.

Muvumba, J. (1997) 'Local Governments Too Weak for Decentralisation', *The New Vision* Newspaper, Kampala: 2 October.

Nabudere, D. (1980) *Imperialism and Revolution in Uganda,* London: Onyx Press.

Nakirunda, M. (2000) 'Women's Organisations and Democratic Governance in Uganda Under the NRM Regime', Working Paper, No. 65, Kampala:CBR.

Namara, A. & Nsabagasani, X. (2001) 'Decentralised Governance and the Wildlife Management Sector: Whose Interests Matter? The Case of Bwindi Impenetrable National Park, Uganda', Unpublished Paper.

Nanduddu, V. (2000) 'Gender and Representational Politics: The Case of Local Councils in Uganda', MA Thesis, Kampala, Makerere University.

Narayan, U. (1989) 'The Project of Feminist Epistemology: Perspectives from a Non-Western Feminist', in A. Jaggar & S. Bordo (eds.) *Gender, Body and Knowledge Feminist Being and Knowing,* Rutgers University Press.

NEMGROUP (2002) Promoting Good Governance Through Election Monitoring: A Report of the 2001/2002 Local Council Elections, Kampala.

New Vision Newspaper, Mukono District Council 2001/2002 Tender Notice, 2 July 2001: Kampala.

Ngabirano, F. (1997) 'Ethnic Nation Building could Kill our Uganda' *The Monitor* Newspaper, Kampala: 8 July.

Nielsen, H. (1996) 'Donor Support to Decentralisation in Uganda: Experiences from Rakai District 1990-5', Working Paper No. 9, Maastricht: European Centre for Development Policy Development & Management (ECDPM).

Nielsen, J.M. (1990) 'Introduction' Feminist Research Methods: Exemplary Reading in the Social Sciences, Boulder: Westview.

Nicholson, L. (ed.) (1990) 'Introduction'. Feminism and Postmodernism, London: Routledge.

Nsibambi, A. (1996) 'The Role and Place of Culture and Decentralisation in Uganda's Struggle for Pluralism', in J. Oloka-Onyango et al. (eds.) *Law and the Struggle for Democracy in East Africa*, Nairobi: Clari Press.

Nsibambi, A. (1997) 'Making Democratic Decentralisation an Instrument of Poverty Eradication: Uganda's Challenge', Paper Presented at the UNDP Development Forum, 4 April, Kampala.

Nsibambi, A (ed.) (1998) 'Introduction Decentralisation and Civil Society in Uganda: The Quest for Good Governance', Kampala: Fountain Publishers.

Nuwagaba, A. (1997) 'Decentralisation and Development Planning in Local Councils in Uganda: The Extent of State Intervention', Unpublished Paper.

Nzomo, M. (1993) `Engendering Democratization in Kenya: A Political Perspective', in M.K. Wanjiku; W. Mukabi Kabira; J. Adhiambo-Oduol & M. Nzomo (eds.) *Democratic Change in Africa: a Women's Perspective*, Nairobi: African Centre for Technology Studies (ACTS).

Nzouankeu, J.M. (1994) 'Decentralisation and Democracy in Africa', *International Review of Administrative Sciences*, 60: 213-227.

O'Barr, J. & Firmin-Sellers, K. African Women in Politics', in M.J. Hay & S. Stichter (eds.) *African Women South of the Sahara*, London: Longman Group.

Obbo, C. (1980) *African Women: Their Struggle for Economic Independence*, London: Zed Press.

Obbo, C. (1986) 'Stratification and the Lives of Women in Uganda', in C. Robertson & I. Berger (eds.) *Women and Class in Africa*, London: African Publishing House.

Obbo, C. (1997) 'What do Women Know? As I was Saying', in K.M. Vaz (ed.) *Oral Narratives Research with Black Women*, London: Sage Publications.

Ofei-Aboagye, (2000) 'Promoting the Participation of Women in Local Governance and Development: The Case of Ghana', Discussion Paper 18, Maastricht: European Centre for Development Policy & Management (ECDPM).

Okumu, W.J. (1992) 'Resistance Council Courts, Democracy and Judicial Change in Uganda', Paper Presented at the Pan-African Law Students' Conference on Democracy, Human Rights and the Environment, Kampala, Makerere University, 3-5 December.

Oloka-Onyango, J. (1989) 'Law, Grassroots Democracy and the National Resistance Movement', *International Journal of the Sociology of Law,* 17 (4): 465-480.

Oloka-Onyango, J. (ed.) (1996) 'Law and the Struggle for Democracy in East Africa', Nairobi: Clari Press.

Oloka-Onyango, J. (1998) 'State Structures and Governance in Contemporary Uganda, Working Paper No. 52, Kampala, CBR.

Oloka-Onyango, J. (2000a) 'New Wine or New Bottles: Movement Politics and One Partyism in Uganda', in J. Mugaju & J. Oloka-Onyango (eds.) *No-Party Democracy in Uganda: Myths and Realities,* Kampala: Fountain Publishers.

Oloka-Onyango, J. (2000b) 'Uganda's Benevolent Dictatorship', http://www.udayton.edu/rwanda/articles/uganda.html.

Oloo, A. (2002) 'Citizen Participation in Local Governance: The Case of Kenya', Unpublished Paper.

Olowu, D. (1999) 'Local Governance, Democracy and Development', in R. Joseph (ed.) *State, Conflict and Democracy in Africa,* Boulder: Lynne Rienner.

Olowu, D. (2001) Decentralisation Policies and Practices Under Structural Adjustment and Democratisation in Africa, Paper No. 4, Geneva: UNRISD (United Nations Research Institute for Social Development).

Olum, Y. (2000) 'The Political Economy of Decentralisation in Africa: The Case of Uganda', Paper Presented at a Conference on 'Challenges to the Social Sciences in Africa in the 21st Century', Kampala, 25-27 October.

Opolot, S. (2001) 'Decentralisation or Balkanisation? A Community's Struggle for Democracy and Control over Forest Resources: The Case of Kilayi Parish, Bufumbo Sub-county, Mbale District, Uganda', Research Bulletin Vol. 3 (2) Kampala, CBR.

Omvedt, G. (2000) 'Women and Political Power, The Hindu' (http://www.the-hindu.com).

Ottoson, A. (1998) 'At Least Our Voices are Now Heard: Changing Meanings of Gender and Power in Rural Uganda', MA dissertation, Stockholm University.

Oyugi, W.O. & Gitonga, A. (eds.) (1987) *Democratic Theory and Practice in Africa,* Nairobi: East African Educational Publishers.

Oyugi, W.O. (1993) 'Local Government in Kenya: A Case of Institutional Decline' in P. Mawood (ed.) *Local Government in the Third World,* New York: John Wiley.

Pankhurst, D. (2002) 'Women and Politics in Africa: The Case of Uganda', *Parliamentary Affairs: Journal of Comparative Politics*, 55 (1): 119-128.

Parpat, J. & Staudt, K. (eds.) 'Introduction: Women and the State in Africa,' Boulder: Lynne Rienner.

Pateman, C. (1988) 'The Sexual Contract', Oxford: Polity Press.

Pateman, C. (1989) 'The Disorder of Women: Democracy, Feminism and Political Theory', Cambridge: Polity Press.

Patterson, A.S. (1998) 'A Reappraisal of Democracy: Evidence in Rural Senegal', *Journal of Modern African Studies*, 36 (3): 423-441.

Perelli, C. (1994) 'Putting Conservatism to Good Use: Women and in Unorthodox Politics in Uruguay, from Breakdown to Transition, J. Jaquette (ed.) *The Women's Movement in Latin America: Feminism and the Transition to Democracy*, London: Unwin Hyman.

Phillips, A. (1991) 'Engendering Democracy', Cambridge: Polity Press.

Phillips, A. (1995) The Politics of Presence, Oxford: Clarendon Press.

Phillips, A. (1996) 'Dealing with Difference? A Politics of Ideas, or a Politics of Presence?' in S. Benhabib (ed.) *Democracy and Difference: Contesting the Boundaries of the Political*, New Jersey: Princeton University Press.

Picard, L. (1979) District Councils in Botswana: A Remnant of Local Autonomy, *Journal of Modern African Studies*, 71 (2): 285-308.

Pieterse, J.N. (1992) *'Emancipation, Modern and Post Modern, Development and Change*, 23 (3): 5-41.

Pinto Jayawardena, K. (2000) 'Proportional Representation, Political Violence and the Participation of Women in the Political Process in Sri Lanka'. Paper presented at a Workshop on 'Strengthening Democratic Governance in Conflict-torn Societies', Centre for Basic Research, Jinja Uganda, 4-7 December.

Pitkin, H.F. (1967) 'The Concept of Representation', Berkeley: University of California Press.

Pottie, D. (2000) 'Women and Local Government: By the Numbers', 'Johannesburg: EISA.

Presely, C. A. (1992), Kikuyu Women, the Mau Mau Rebellion and Social Change in Kenya, Boulder: Westview Press.

Pringle, R. & Watson, S. (1992) `Women's Interests and the Post-Structuralist State' in M. Barret & A. Phillips (eds.) *Destabilising Theory, Contemporary Feminist Debates*, Cambridge: Polity Press.

Rai, S.M. (1994) 'Gender and Democratisation: Or What Does Democracy Mean for Women in the Third World', *Democratisation,* 1 (2).

Rai, S.M. (1996) 'Women and the State in the Third World: Some Issues for Debate' in S. Rai & G. Lievesley (eds.) *Women and the State: International Perspectives,* London: Taylor & Francis.

Rai, S.M. (2000) (ed.) 'Perspectives on Gender and Democratisation' in *International Perspectives on Gender and Democratisation,* London: Macmillan Press.

Rai, S. & Sharma, K. (2000) 'Democratising the Indian Parliament: The "Reservation for Women" Debate', in S. Rai (ed.) *International Perspectives on Gender and Democratisation,* London: Macmillan Press.

Rajan, S.R. (1993) 'Real and Imagined Women: Gender Culture and Post-colonialism', London: Routledge.

Randall, V. 1982. 'Women and Politics: An International Perspective', The University of Chicago Press.

Randall, V. (1987) 'Women and Politics: An International Perspective', London: Macmillan (2nd edition).

Rao, N. (1998) 'Representation in Local Politics: A Reconsideration and Some New Evidence' *Political Studies,* XLVI: 19-35.

Razavi, S. (2000) 'Women in Contemporary Democratisation', Occasional Paper No. 4, Geneva, UNRISD.

Reddy, P.S. (1999) 'Local Government, Democratisation and Decentralisation: Theoretical Consideration and Recent Trends and Developments', in P.S. Reddy (ed.) *Local Government Democratisation and Decentralisation: A Review of the Southern African Region,* Cape Town: Juta.

Reynolds, A. (1999) Women in African Legislatures: The Slow Climb to Power, Johannesburg: EISA.

Ribot, J.C. (1999) Decentralisation, Participation and Accountability in Sahelian Forestry: Legal Instruments of Political-Administrative Control', *Africa,* 69 (1): 23-64.

Rondinelli, D. (1981) 'Government Decentralisation and Comparative Perspective: Theory and Practice in Developing Countries', *International Review of Administrative Sciences,* XLVIII (2): 133-145.

Rondinelli, D.;McColloughJ.S.&Johnson, R.W.(1984)'Decentralisation in Developing Countries: A Review of Recent Experiences', *Staff Working Papers* No. 581, Washington, D.C.: The World Bank.

Rondinelli, D. (1990) 'Decentralisation, Territorial Power and the State: A Critical Response, *'Development and Change*, 21: 491-500.

Rothchild, D. (nd) Strengthening African Local Initiative: Local Self-Governance, 'Decentralisation and Accountability, Hamburg: Institute of African Affairs.

Saito, F. (2000) Decentralisation in Uganda: Challenges for the 21st Century', Unpublished Paper.

Saito, F. (2001) 'Decentralisation Theories Revisited: Lessons from Uganda', *Ryukoku Annual Bulletin of Research Institute for Social Science*, 31: 54-68.

Saito, F. (2002) Decentralisation Measures and Gender Equalities: Experiences in Uganda, *Ryukoku Journal of Economic Studies*, 41 (5): http://www.world.ryukoku.ac.ip/fumisaito/en/publication.html.

Sapiro, V. (1983) 'The Political Integration of Women: Roles, Socialisation and Politics', Urbana: University of Illinois Press.

Sawer, M. (2002) 'The Representation of Women in Australia: Meaning and Make Believe', *Parliamentary Affairs: A Journal of Comparative Politics*, 55(1): 5-18.

Schmitter, P. (1994) 'Dangers and Dilemmas of Democracy', *Journal of Democracy*, 5 (2): 57-74.

Schmitter, P. (1998) 'Contemporary Democratization: The Prospects for Women', in J. Jaquette & S.L. Wolchik (eds.) *Women and Democracy: Latin America, Central and Eastern Europe*, Baltimore: The John Hopkins University Press.

Schonwalder, G. (1997) 'New Democratic Spaces at the Grassroots? Popular Participation in Latin American Local Governments', *Development and Change*, 28 (4): 753-70.

Scott, J.W. (1988) Gender and the Politics of History, Columbia University Press.

Scott, J.W. (1986) 'Gender a Useful Category of Historical Analysis', *American Historical Review*, 91: 1,052-75.

Seeley, I.H. (1978) Local Government Explained, London: Macmillan.

Shaul, S.M. (1982) 'The Status of Women in Local Governments: An International Assessment', *Public Administration Review*, 42 (6): 491-508.

Slater, D. (1989) 'Territorial Power and the Peripheral State: The Issue of Decentralisation', *Development and Change*, 20 (3): 501-31.

Silliman, J. (1999) 'Expanding Civil Society: Shrinking Political Space: The Case of Women's NGOs', *Journal of Social Politics: International Studies in Gender, State and Society*, 6 (1).

Smoke, P. (2000) 'Beyond Normative Models and Development Trends: Strategic Design and Implementation of Decentralisation in Developing Countries', www1.worldbank.org/wbiep/decentralization/library/smoke.decentralization.pdf.

Snyder, M. & Tadesse, M. (1995) 'Nairobi: Women of the World Meet on African Soil', in *African Women and Development,* London: Zed Books.

Sohoni, K.N. (1997) 'Constitutional Remedies are Needed to Carry Women across the Gender Divide', *The Times of India,* January 8.

Sorensen, B.R. (1999) 'State Autonomy and Political Rebuilding after Conflict: Positioning Gender', in J. Martinussen (ed.) *External and Internal Constraints on Policy Making: How Autonomous are the States?* Occasional Paper No. 20, Roskilde: IDS.

Sorenson, G. (1993) 'Democracy and Democratisation: Dilemmas in World Politics', Boulder: Westview Press.

Souza, C. (1997) Constitutional Engineering in Brazil: The Politics of Federalism and Decentralisation, London: Macmillan Press.

Stanley, L. (1994) 'Recovering Women in History from Feminist Deconstruction' in M. Evans (ed.) *The Woman Question,* London: Sage Publications.

Steinberger, P.J. (1999) 'Public and Private', *Political Studies,* XLVII: 292-313.

Stetson, D.M. & Mazur A.G. (eds.) (1995) 'Introduction' Comparative State Feminism, London: Sage Publications.

Stewart, J. (1996) 'Democracy and Local Government', in P. Hirst & S. Khilnani (eds.) *Reinventing Democracy,* Oxford: Backwell Publishers.

Sundar, N. (2001) 'Is Devolution Democratization?' *World Development,* 29 (12): 2,007-2,023.

Swilling, M. (ed.) (1997) 'Introduction' Governing Africa's Cities, Johannesburg: Witwatersrand University Press.

Taaka-Awori (2000) 'Women in Decision Making Positions in National and Local Level Public Office in Uganda', Mimeo, Kampala: FOWODE.

Tadria, H.K. (1985) 'Changing Economic and Gender Patterns Among the Peasants of Ndejje and Sseguku in Uganda', Ph.D. Thesis, University of Minnesota.

Tadria, H.K. (1987) 'Changes and Continuities in the Position of Women in Uganda' in P.D. Wiebe & C.P. Dodge (eds.) *Beyond Crisis: Development Issues in Uganda,* Kampala: Makerere Institute of Social Research.

Tamale, S. (1999) *When Hens begin to Crow: Gender and Parliamentary Politics in Contemporary Uganda*, Kampala: Fountain Publishers.

Tamale, S. (2001) 'Gender and Affirmative Action in Post 1995 Uganda: A New Dispensation, or Business as Usual?' in J. Oloka-Onyango (ed.) *Constitutionalism in Africa: Creating Opportunities, Facing Challenges*, Kampala: Fountain Publishers.

Tamale, S. (2001) 'Bravo Women MPs: From 18% to 24%', Kampala, *The Sunday Monitor*, 1 July.

Tanzarn, N. (2003) 'Affirmative Action in Ugandan Parliamentary Politics' in J. Kwesiga; E. Ward; A. Madanda & N. Tarnzan. Women's Political Space: The Experience of Affirmative Action in Eritrea, Tanzania and Uganda, Belfast: Centre for Advancement of Women in Politics (CAWP) Queens University & Kampala: Department of Women and Gender Studies, Makerere University.

Tetreault, M. (2001) 'A State of Two Minds: State Cultures, Women and Politics in Kuwait', *International Journal of Middle East Studies*, 33 (2): 203-208.

The International Council on Human Rights Policy (2002) 'Local Rule: Decentralisation and Human Rights', Geneva.

Tidemand, P (1994a) 'Resistance Councils in Uganda: A Study of Popular Democracy and Rural Politics', Roskilde: IDS.

Tidemand, P. (1994b) 'New Local State Forms and Popular Participation in Buganda, in P. Gibbon (ed.) The New Local Level Politics in east Africa: Studies on Uganda, Tanzania and Kenya, Research Report No. 93, Uppsala: Nordic African Institute.

Totemeyer, G. (1994) 'Challenges for Democracy, Decentralisation and Empowerment in Africa', *Regional Development Dialogue*, 15 (1): 49-61.

Treacher, A. & Shukrallah, H. (2001) 'The Realm of the Possible: Middle Eastern Women in Political and Social Spaces', *Feminist Review*, 69: 4-14.

Tremblay R. & Kumtakar, P. (1998) 'Governance and Representation: A Study of Women and Local Self-Governance', *The Indian Journal of Public Administration*, XLIV (3): 454-467.

Tripp, A.M. (2000) *Women and Politics in Uganda*, Kampala: Fountain Publishers.

Tripp, A.M. (2001a) 'The Politics of Autonomy and Cooptation in Africa: The Case of the Ugandan Women's Movement, *Journal of Modern African Studies*, 39 (1): 101-128.

Tripp, A.M. (2001b) 'Women's Movements and Challenges to Neopatrimonial Rule: Preliminary Observations from Africa', *Development and Change,* 32 (1): 33-54.

Tripp, A.M. (2002) 'A New Generation of Women's Mobilisation', in A.M. Tripp & J.C. Kwesiga (eds.) *The Women's Movement in Uganda: History, Challenges and Prospects,* Kampala: Fountain Publishers.

Tukaheebwa, G. (1998) 'The Role of District Councils in Decentralisation', in A. Nsibambi (ed.) *Decentralisation and Civil Society in Uganda: The Quest for Good Governance,* Kampala: Fountain Publishers.

Uganda Debt Network (UDN) (2002) *Policy Review Newsletter,* Issue No. 3, Kampala.

Urdang, S. (1995) 'Women in National Liberation Movements' in M.J. Hay & S. Stichter (eds.) *African Women South of the Sahara,* London: Longman Group.

UWONET (1997) 'Vote in the Local Council Elections: Understanding the Local Government Act and Local Council Elections in Uganda', Booklet Developed in Conjunction with the Civic Education Department of the Uganda Electoral Commission, Kampala.

UWONET (1998) Documentation of Women's Experiences in Uganda's Local Government Elections, Kampala.

Van Donk. M. (2000) 'Local Government: A Strategic Site of Struggle for Gender Equity', *Agenda,* No. 45: 4-12.

Vyasulu, P. & Vyasulu, V. (1999) 'Women in Panchayat Raji Grassroots Democracy in India: Experience from Malgudi', Background Paper No. 4, United Nations Development Programmes (UNDP).

Wagaba, F.X. (2002) 'The Decentralisation System: Uganda's Experience', Kampala: Decentralisation Secretariat.

Waghid, Y. (2002) 'Communitarian Deliberative Democracy and its Implications for Political Discourse in South Africa', *Politikon (South African Journal of Political Studies),* 29 (2): 183-207.

Walby, S. (1990) 'Theorising Patriarchy', Oxford, Basil Blackwell.

Walby, S. (1994) 'Is Citizenship Gendered', *Sociology,* 28 (2): 379-395.

Waylen, G, 1994 'Women and Democratisation: Conceptual Issues and Gender Relations in Transition Politcs; *World Politics,* 46 (3): 327-354.

Waylen, G. (1996a) *Gender in Third World Politics,* Buckingham: Open University Press.

Waylen, G. (1996b) 'Democratisation, Feminism and the State in Chile: The Establishment of SERNAM, in S. Rai & G. Lievesley (eds.) *Women and the State: International Perspectives,* London: Taylor & Francis.

Westergaard, K. (1992) 'Local Government in Bengal: Steps Towards Democracy?' in L. Redebeck (ed.) *When Democracy Makes Sense: Studies in the Democratic Potential of Third World Popular Movements*, Uppsala: Akut.

Wells, C. (2001) 'Battle Time: Gender, Modernity and Confederate Hospitals', *Journal of Social History*, 35 (2): 409-428.

Wieringa, S. (1994) 'Women's Interests and Empowerment: Gender Planning Reconsidered', Development and Change, 25 (4): 829-48.

White, G. (1995) 'Towards a Democratic Developmental State', *IDS Bulletin*, Vol. 26 (2).

Whitehead A. (1984) 'Women's Solidarity and Divisions Among Women', *IDS Bulletin*, 15 (1): 6-11.

Wolin, S.S. (1996) 'Fugitive Democracy', in S. Benhabib (ed.) *Democracy and Difference: Contesting the Boundaries of the Political*, New Jersey: Princeton University Press.

Won-Hong, K. (1994) 'Measures to Support Women's Participation in Local Assemblies, with Emphasis on Proportional Representation and Political Party Quota System', *Women Studies Forum*, 10: 24-35.

World Bank (1996) 'Uganda: The Challenge of Growth and Poverty Reduction', Washington, D.C.

World Bank (2000) Entering The 21st Century, *World Development Report* 1999/2000, Washington, D.C.

Wrigley, C. (1988) 'Four Steps Towards Disaster', in H. Hansen & M. Twaddle (eds.) *Uganda Now: Between Decay and Development*, Nairobi: Heinemann.

Wunch J.S & Olowu, D. (eds.) (1990) 'The Failure of the Decentralised State: Institutions and Self-Governance in Africa', San Fransisco: ICS Press.

Young, I.M. (1990) 'Justice and the Politics of Difference', Princeton University Press.

Young, K.; Edholm F. & Harris O. (1977) 'Conceptualising Women', *The Critique of Anthropology*, 3:101-130.

Zouankeu J.M. (1994) 'Decentralisation and Democracy in Africa', *International Review of Administration Sciences*, 60:213-227.

Zulu, L. (2000) 'Institutionalising Change: South African Women's Participation in the Transition to Democracy', in S. Rai (ed.) *International Perspectives on Gender and Democratisation*, London: Macmillan Press.

Official Sources

NRM (1987) The Ten Point Programme of the NRM, Kampala: NRM Publications.

Republic of Uganda (1987) Resistance Councils and Committees Statute.

Republic of Uganda (RoU) (1987) Report of the Commission of Inquiry into the Local Government System.

Republic of Uganda (1993) Local Government Statute.

Republic of Uganda (1993) Decentralisation in Uganda: Popular Version of the Government's Resistance Councils Statute.

Republic of Uganda (1994a) Guidelines to District and Urban Councils for the Management of a Separate Personnel system, Decentralisation Secretariat.

Republic of Uganda (1993) Women and Youth Council Statute.

Republic of Uganda(1994b) Decentralization in Uganda: The Policy and its Implications (2), Decentralisation Secretariat.

Republic of Uganda (1995a) The Constitution of the Republic of Uganda, Entebbe:Government Printer.

Republic of Uganda(1995b) Proceedings of the Constituent Assembly (Official Report), Entebbe: Government Printer.

Republic of Uganda(1995) The Constitution.

Republic of Uganda(1997) The Local Governments Act.

Republic of Uganda(1997) The Movement Act.

Republic of Uganda (1998) Decentralisation Implementation Map, Ministry of Local Government, Entebbe Government Printer.

RoU (1999) A Report on the Local Government Councils' Elections 1997/1998 The Uganda Electoral Commission.

Republic of Uganda (1998) Decentralisation Implementation Roadmap, Ministry of Local Government.

Republic of Uganda (2000) National Programme on Good Governance in the Context of The Poverty Eradication Action Plan (PEAP), Ministry of Finance Planning and Economic Development.

Republic of Uganda (2000) Plan for Modernisation of Agriculture: Eradicating Poverty in Uganda, Ministry of Agriculture, Animal Industry and Fisheries and Ministry of Finance, Planning and Economic Development.

Republic of Uganda (2000a) National Programme on Good Governance in the Context of The Poverty Eradication Action Plan (PEAP), Ministry of Finance Planning and Economic Development.

RoU (2000b) Mukono District Council Budget Framework Paper 2000/2001-2002/2003.

RoU (2001) Uganda Poverty Status Report: Milestones in the Quest for Poverty Eradication, Ministry of Finance, Planning and Economic Development, Entebbe Government Printer.

Republic of Uganda (2002) Report on the 2001/2 Local Government Elections, Uganda Electoral Commission.

RoU (Republic of Uganda) (2002a) Guide to Participatory Planning for Lower Local Councils, Ministry of Local Government.

RoU (2002b) The Poverty Status Report, Ministry of Finance Planning and Economic Development.

RoU (2002c) Kanungu District Local Government, Three-year Development Plan 2002-2005.

RoU (1996) Women and the 1995 Constitution of Uganda, Ministry of Gender and Community Development, WID-DANIDA Constituent Assembly Project, Kampala.

General Newspaper Reports

The New Vision, Kampala

Dates: 9 January 2001, 13 September 2001; 24 August 2001; 3 October 2000; 18 August, 2000; 2 August, 2000; 7 October, 1999;

The Monitor, Kampala

Dates: 19 June, 2001;

The Crusader, Kampala.

Dates: 30 January, 1999.

Group Discussions

LC3 councillors (3 females, 4 males) Ngogwe Sub-county, Mukono, 21 January 2000

LC3 councillors (2 females, 4 males) Nazigo Sub-county, Mukono, 6 January 2000

LC3 Councillors (4 females, 2 males) Goma Sub-county, Mukono, 31 May 2001

Kanjuki LC1 dwellers (8 females, 10 males), 8 January 2000

Group Discussion with ordinary women, (5) Bukinda, Sub-county, Kabale District, 4 April 2004

Group discussion with ordinary men (10) Bukinda Sub-county, Kabale District, 5 May 2001.

Validation workshop with Women Councillors, (12 females, 1 male) Mukono District, 4 December 2000

Workshop discussion Balikyewumya Women's Group, (22 females, 18 males) Misindye, Mukono District 20 July 2001

Kishayo Bee keeping Group (5 females, 6 males) Kanyantorogo, Kanungu District, 8 February 2003

Kishenyi Women's Group (7 females) Kanyantorogo, Kanungu District, 8 February 2003

FGD LC5 Councillors (3 females 4 males), Kanungu District headquarters, 9 February 2003

Focus group discussion, LC3 Councillors, (female, 3 males) Nakisunga Sub-county, 22 June 2001

Meetings Attended

Mukono District Council Meeting, 11 November 1999

Mukono District Council Meeting, 28 May 2001

Mukono District Council, Sectoral Committee meeting, Works and technical Services, 12 May 2001

Mukono District Council, Sectoral Committee meeting, Health and Community Development, 26 May 2001

Mukono District Council, Sectoral Committee meeting, Education and Sports, 5 May 2001

District Leaders meeting at extension of piped water to Mukono Town Council, 27August 2001.

Candidates meeting, LC5 Councillors Elections, Goma Sub-county, Mukono District, 4 February 2002.

Candidates Meeting LC5 Councillors Nenyodde, Nabbale Sub-county, Mukono District, 28 January 2002.

Candidates meeting, LC5 Chairpersons, Mukono District at Njeru Town Council, 30 January 2002.

Candidates meeting, LC5 Councilors Mukono District at Mukono Town Council, 1 February 2002.

Goma Sub-county Budget meeting, 10 July 2001.

Caucus Meeting of LC5 Women Councillors, Mukono District headquarters, 11 November 1999.

Youth Entrepreneurship Scheme (YES) Seminar, Nakisunga Sub-county, 21 May 2001.

Extension seminar on cattle rearing, Balikyewunya Women's Group, Goma Sub-county Mukono, 10 July 2001.

Index

Action for Development, 14
Affirmative Action, 30, 37, 50, 69, 80-84
    Mandatory affirmative action, 109
Africa, 9
Apolo Nsibambi, 80

Citizenship, 44, 45
Conflict, 10
Constitutional change/Uganda, 79-85
Cultural homogeneity/ethnic identity, 70, 74

Decentralisation, 2, 23-30, 49, 75, 146
    critiques of, 170
    institutional relations/outcomes of, 177
    process, 50, 63, 75, 183
Democracy, 29
    democratic justice, 33-34
    local democracy, 23, 25, 30, 44
Donor good-governance agenda, 17, 18

Elections
    adult universal suffrage, 52
    campaigns, 109-119
    education, 158, 159
    electoral system, 88-90, 101, 102
    interest representation, 34-36 161-169, 181
    local government elections, 106-108
    mandates, 109
    reservation/accretion, 90
    women's polls, 91-97
Elite opportunism, 37
Entryism, 180
Extreme separatism, 37

Federalism, 80

Gender,
    audit, 54
    balance, 53, 54
    based disparity, 125
    gendered dual mode, 60
    identity of female councillors, 170
    relations, 46
    victimology, 46

Hope Mwesigye, 80

India, 79, 97-100
Institutions,

    gender capacity of, 82

Josephine Kasya, 132-135

Kanungu, 66, 74
Kumi, 65

Liberal Feminism, 41
Local Councils, 51
    deliberation, 44, 45, 146-153, 161
    gendered character/conduct of, 145-153
    information/communication, 155-158
    parallel structures, 57
    sectoral committee meetings, 152
    structure in Uganda, 52
Local Government, 23, 40, 48-59, 128
    access to positions in, 128-131
    Act (1997), 1, 49, 86, 89
    administrative units, 56, 57, 88
    lower local governments, 54
    structures, 2
    system in Uganda, 106

Marginalised groups, 73-75, 86
Marriage, 154
    belonging, 121-125
Mukono, 54, 65, 74
National Resistance Movement, 3-6, 13-18
Peru, 78
Politics, 40, 43, 65
    formal politics, 173
    local politics, 120-128, 161-181
    mobilisation politics, 18, 19, 78, 176
    Mural suasion/in community politics, 113
    Nationalism, 10, 11
    No-party system, 16, 17
    of leadership, 131-138, 165
    political parties, 16
    political space, 24
    political tools, 45
    public politics, 171, 172
Pragmatic feminist scholars, 35
President of Uganda, 49, 50, 72

Quota system, 39, 40
    Uganda/Committee for, 86

Resistance Council system, 2, 49, 50, 146
    model, 5, 6, 18

South Africa, 11, 12, 37, 39, 79, 97-101
    parliament of, 152
    scholars in, 35
Sri Lanka, 102

Taxation, 55, 56, 61
    central government transfers, 62-64
    local revenue, 61, 62

Tendering process, 66-69
    corruption, 66
    Kanungu, 169

Uganda, 176
    quotas in, 178, 179
    women in local governance, 99

Women
    councils, 71, 72
    empowerment, 31-36
    executive partronage, 15
    in revolutionary politics, 7
    leadership, 170-173
    politics of inclusion, 175-180
    specific patronage mechanisms, 71
    urban women, 8, 15
    voluntarism, 8, 9